Family
Caregiving
in an Aging
Society

FAMILY CAREGIVER APPLICATIONS SERIES

Series Editors

David E. Biegel, *Case Western Reserve University*
Richard Schulz, *University of Pittsburgh*

Advisory Board Members

Volumes in This Series:

Family Caregiver Applications Series
Volume 5

Family Caregiving in an Aging Society

Policy Perspectives

Editors

Rosalie A. Kane
Joan D. Penrod

Published in cooperation with the
Center for Practice Innovations,
Mandel School of Applied Social Sciences,
Case Western Reserve University

SAGE Publications
International Educational and Professional Publisher
Thousand Oaks   London   New Delhi

For information address:

SAGE Publications, Inc.
2455 Teller Road
Thousand Oaks, California 91320

SAGE Publications Ltd.
6 Bonhill Street
London EC2A 4PU
United Kingdom

SAGE Publications India Pvt. Ltd.
M-32 Market
Greater Kailash I
New Delhi 110 048 India

Printed in the United States of America

Library of Congress Cataloging-in-Publication Data

Family caregiving in an aging society: policy perspectives / edited by
　　Rosalie A. Kane and Joan D. Penrod.
　　　　p. cm.　　— （Family caregiver applications series: v. 5)
　　"Published in cooperation with the Center for Practice
Innovations, Mandel School of Applied Social Sciences, Case Western
Reserve University."
　　Includes bibliographical references and index.
　　ISBN 0-8039-5147-7 (alk. paper).　—　ISBN 0-8039-5148-5 (alk.
paper)
　　1. Aged—Home care—United States.　2. Caregivers—Government
policy—United States.　3. Aged—Government policy—United States.
4. Home care services—Government policy—United States.　I. Kane,
Rosalie A.　II. Penrod, Joan D.　III. Series.
HV1465.F36　1995
362.6—dc20　　　　　　　　　　　　　　　　94-49582

95　96　97　98　99　10　9　8　7　6　5　4　3　2　1

Sage Production Editor: Diane S. Foster

Contents

Foreword

It has been 30 years since Ethel Shanas first exploded the myth of family abandonment and 20 years since Elaine Brody conducted her ground-breaking research that first highlighted the significance of the family caregiver as the centerpiece of the long-term care system. It was 10 years ago that I became inspired by the work of these important pioneers in the field of caregiver research and decided to analyze data from the 1982 National Long-Term Care Survey, which provided the first national estimates of family caregivers to the frail elderly.

Over the past decade, the field of caregiver research has burgeoned and the term *family caregiver* is now a part of the American lexicon. This explicit recognition of family caregivers is due in large part to the continued perseverance of researchers who refused to accept the rhetoric that families were abrogating their responsibilities to elders with disabilities. In fact, the research community formalized the caregiver term and helped to create the identity for caregivers themselves. Prior to the flurry of research activity in the 1970s and 1980s, family caregivers were largely invisible; caregiving was seen as help that family members—mostly wives, daughters, and daughters-in-law—were expected to provide without overt acknowledgment or compensation. Today, many family caregivers have become organized and empowered, recognizing that they represent a vital, voting constituency of middle-aged and older adults who stand to benefit as much from long-term care and elder care policies as do their parents and spouses with disabilities. Furthermore, the increasing concern expressed by policymakers about the needs of family caregivers, as well as the attention to these issues in the mass media, is a direct result of the labors of the research community.

We have come a long way over the past 30 years. Today very few people question the important role of families, and women in particular, in providing assistance—physical, emotional, financial—to elderly parents, spouses, and other relatives and friends. The availability of informal caregivers willing and able to provide assistance with personal care, household maintenance, and other daily living tasks is often a decisive factor in determining whether or not the care needs of people with disabilities can be met outside of a nursing home or some other specialized residential care setting. Even when public financing for formal home and community-based alternatives to nursing home care is available, informal care continues to play a pivotal role in making noninstitutional service options feasible. According to data from the 1990 Survey of Program Participation (SIPP), a national survey focusing on noninstitutionalized individuals with chronic disabilities, nearly 83% of such people under age 65 and 73% of such people 65 and older rely exclusively on informal helpers. The 1989 National Long-Term Care Survey documenting patterns of formal and informal care use among community-dwelling elderly with disabilities indicates that over 90% of this population receives care informally from family, friends, and neighbors; about one quarter use a combination of paid and informal help, and only 9% rely exclusively on formal care.

This important volume clearly elucidates the pressing issues in family caregiving policy and critically reviews the wide range of policy directions and initiatives that have been implemented or are currently being explored. Policymakers in both the public and private sectors have begun to translate their concerns about family caregivers into action. The Family and Medical Leave Act, signed by President Clinton during his first month in office, requires employers to allow unpaid leave and to continue health coverage for workers who must leave their jobs temporarily to assume elder care responsibilities. More and more corporations are recognizing that it is good for business, as well as for the employee, to offer elder care benefits. Although some concern remains that families may reduce their caregiving efforts if publicly subsidized long-term care services are provided, many state programs now formally acknowledge the goal of reducing caregiver burden and complementing informal care so that families are able to continue providing assistance. Some even pay families caring for elderly with disabilities through Medicaid waivers and state general revenue funds.

The architects of the long-term care provisions in the Health Security Act of 1994—President Clinton's health care reform proposal—proposed expansion of home- and community-based services to assist informal caregivers as well as the direct beneficiary with disabilities. This plan allowed state flexibility in defining benefits—including the provision of respite care services, the training of informal caregivers, and even payment of family members, friends, and neighbors for care provided. It is interesting to note that although alternative Democratic and Republican legislative proposals reduced the amount of new federal funding, they all included the goal of minimizing caregiver burden and supporting the informal caregiver system.

What about the future of family caregiving? Are we prepared to address the consequences of what Robert Butler has referred to as the "longevity revolution" of the 21st century? Increases in the use of formal helpers to supplement informal caregiving are already under way, and these trends can probably be expected to continue. Such growth would undoubtedly be intensified by a significant expansion of public funding for home- and community-based care. But even if there is no such expansion of public funding, there is likely to be a growing market for paid care. At the same time, there is little evidence to suggest that the supply of informal caregivers is going to "dry up" or that paid caregivers will overwhelmingly displace informal caregivers. Despite changing economics, demographics, and social values, informal caregiving is likely to remain a "normative experience" for Americans for the foreseeable future. As technological advances extend the life expectancy of younger people with disabilities and new diseases such as AIDS continue to ravage this country, the demands placed on family and other informal caregivers are likely to accelerate.

The controversial questions raised by Kane and Penrod in the concluding chapter of this book must be addressed as we usher in the 21st century and begin to experience the dramatic effects of the demographic imperative. These issues include the potential erosion of family care as paid care becomes more available and accessible, the advantages and disadvantages of paying family caregivers, the relative importance of income supports versus services in helping families to cope with the demands of elders with disabilities, the role of women's issues in informing caregiver policy, and most important, the extent to which various caregiver policies and programs actually are successful.

This volume is a tribute to 3 decades of research and policy development in the area of family caregiving. As a consequence of this work, I believe we are moving toward more coherent policies with respect to aging families. I look forward to seeing that movement become a reality.

Robyn Stone
Deputy Assistant Secretary for Planning and Evaluation
Office of Disability, Aging, and Long-Term Care
U.S. Department of Health and Human Services

Preface

This book has had a rather long genesis. We began this project concurrently with a study of the caregiving experience of families whose relatives were discharged from hospitals after treatment for a stroke or a hip fracture. With funding from the Vira I. Heinz Endowment, we followed a group of families for a year to explore their responses to the immediate aftermath of a medical event that inevitably required some care. We were interested in learning something about the range of activities undertaken by families, which family members were involved, and how—if at all— they worked with paid caregivers. We wanted to know in family members' own words how they thought caregiving affected them—their relationships with the relative they were assisting, their relationships with other relatives, their social lives, their emotional lives, their work lives (if applicable), and their financial status.

Like others who ventured into the study of family care before us, we found variable terrain. People caring for their spouses were different than those caring for their parents or some other relative, and they described their experiences differently. Family members who first faced the need to care for their relative as a result of the hospitalization that brought them into our study differed from those with a long history of caregiving before that hospitalization. Caregivers who were already caring for *other* relatives, or who needed care themselves had particular challenges. Taken together, our respondents reported problems and anxieties associated with giving care, but they also reported positive features. Many of them told us they were doing what comes naturally, but, nonetheless, their lives were often shaped by their caregiving activities. Many put in enough hours to equal a half-time job, and more than a few reported more than a full-time job's worth of family caregiving time. Often family care, measured in jobs and tasks, continued at a substantial clip even while relatives were in a nursing home. Formal home care—that is, care from agencies and paid personnel—was modest in volume and tended to taper off after the period immediately following discharge from the hospital.

We realized we were seeing a somewhat different face of family care than is usually presented in the literature. We began in the middle of the motion picture with a hospitalization and a group of people who inevitably would need some help after discharge. This put us in a position to observe how much of that help came from one or more family members and how family care ebbed and flowed with individual need. Our glimpse was different than the one afforded at the end of the motion picture, when family members are heavily involved in caring for people with severe need and a "primary family caregiver" has been formally identified (e.g., in the family care of people with advanced Alzheimer's disease).

Policies for family care of the elderly need to embrace all situations—those with acute care needs and ongoing needs, those who are dying and those who will live a long time, those with only one family member available to help and those with a small cadre of willing assistants. Policies need to be applicable to older people who are married and unmarried; who live with their families and who live alone, who are cognitively intact and who are incapable of decision making because of brain-altering diseases. The policies also need to serve families of different kinds, employed and retired family members, family members with loving emotional ties to the person needing help and those with troubled histories, families who live nearby and far away. Despite voluminous research on family caregivers, widespread awareness of the volume of family care, and the general agreement that family care is necessary to balance the long-term care budget, no coherent set of family policies has emerged. Families are alternatively exalted as the unsung heroes and heroines of long-term care or vilified as deserters. They are goaded to do more and protected from doing too much, all by beneficent health and social service professionals and planners. Yet the goals of family caregiving policy remain unexpressed.

The purpose of this book is to explore family caregiving policy for the elderly. We sought to examine what it is, by default if not by planning, and to explore the ramifications of various policy departures from the status quo. We hope that this effort will spawn targeted, policy-relevant research and discussion about how policies toward family caregivers could help us move toward an ideal vision of the aging society in the next century.

Rosalie A. Kane
Joan D. Penrod

Acknowledgments

Many people helped us and encouraged us with this project. We are especially grateful to the Vira I. Heinz Endowment and our project officer, Dana Phillips, who funded our research and gave us unfailing moral support, as well. We also thank the Health Care Financing Administration and the Office of the Assistant Secretary for Planning and Evaluation at the U.S. Department of Health and Human Services for funding the original study of post-acute care to which our family caregiving work was appended, as well as to the U.S. Administration on Aging for its support of Rosalie Kane's conceptual work in long-term care during the entire period. The ideas in this book are, of course, our own and not necessarily those of any of our research sponsors.

In December 1990, the Vira I. Heinz Endowment sponsored a working conference on family caregiving policy in Morgantown, West Virginia, where the first versions of the six contributed chapters in this book were presented. We thank all the authors of those chapters for their participation at the conference and thereafter and for their patience while this book took shape. We also thank the researchers and policymakers who attended the conference, led discussions, and shared their insights with us.

Appreciation is owed to our collaborators in family caregiving research, including Colleen King and Lana Herskovitz, who headed our data collection group; and Robert Kane, Michael Finch, and Jon Christianson, who worked on aspects of the analysis. Our former colleague, Cheryl King Thomas, was extraordinarily helpful in pulling together the West Virginia conference and doing other background work. Secretarial help over the course of this long project has been ably provided by Ann Mulally, Robin Fordham, and Kristen Olsen.

Most of all we are grateful to all those who shared with us their own family stories of family caregiving.

1

In Search of
Family Caregiving Policy

General Considerations

ROSALIE A. KANE
JOAN D. PENROD

Family is a central fact and metaphor of human life. The public appetite for family sagas seems insatiable. Novelists ranging from literary giants such as Tolstoy and Thomas Mann to popular fiction writers can readily captivate attention with multigenerational stories of how families nurture, protect, influence, and occasionally injure their members over the decades. These stories are fascinating precisely because they deal with the familiar human predicament in all its infinite variation.

In contemporary political life, the American family is also evoked regularly as the central unit of social and political life. The ambiguous catchphrase "family values" has become a watchword for people with vastly differing philosophical orientations to the role of government and the nature of public and private responsibility. In particular, the discourse has dealt with who has family values, who does not, and what the government should or should not do about it.

Buried beneath the rhetoric are some important messages. The family has tremendous enduring power. It is a structure of human life as old as the species. Whatever one's view of family values, families are clearly of value. Few disagree that public policies must permit families to thrive and that individual well-being is linked to family preservation and well-being.

Beyond the rhetoric, however, the family is hard to define. It includes people with kinship ties who may live in households that are far apart and people unrelated to each other who have voluntarily combined resources and residence. Families exist within families, as offspring of a set of parents create their own households. Increased life expectancy, combined with multiple marriages and diverse patterns for age of childbearing, has created many variants of intergenerational families. The modal family is no longer an employed man with his homemaker spouse, two children, and assorted pets (if this ever was a valid description of the way most Americans live).

The often-heated political discourse about families reflects an aware-ness that much of what happens to and in families is not a purely private matter. It matters to society. This book examines one place where family life and public policy meet: long-term care for older people.

FAMILIES AND LONG-TERM CARE

Long-term care refers to the wide range of assistance that elderly people with disabilities need to survive and live meaningful lives. The majority of such people get that help from their families, not from nursing homes, from home health agencies, or any other paid helpers. In a shorthand that would undoubtedly confuse family caregivers, policymakers and re-searchers have come to call help given by families *informal care,* which they contrast with help from professionals, dubbed *formal care.* The policy debate thus far has largely been cast as a question of the relationship between formal and informal care. Should informal care continue to be the norm? When is formal care so obviously necessary that it should be subsidized for poor people or (depending on one's philosophy) insured for all people? If formal care is made available and affordable, will informal care disappear? What would be the economic and social consequences of a reduction of informal care? Such questions have been endlessly dis-cussed and studied, but the debate has not been informed by consistent or clear definitions of either formal or informal care.

What do families do when they provide so-called informal care? The answer is, it varies. They worry; they gather at times of crisis to wait, watch, and plan together; they help older people make decisions; they may provide money; they may arrange "formal" services. Family members telephone and consult with professionals, they transport their relatives to treatment, they help with the complexities of bill paying, they figure out how to obtain the public and private benefits to which the older person is entitled. They also provide physical help. Family members cook meals, launder clothes and linens, clean houses, give baths, and even help their relatives use the toilet or eat. Family members are heavily involved in supervising the safety of those who cannot protect themselves.

Family members also do nursing and medically oriented care such as giving pills, injections, and intravenous medication; helping with range of motion exercises; repositioning the bed bound; and sometimes manipulating elaborate equipment, such as dialysis machines and ventilators. And when relatives are temporarily or permanently living in nursing homes or other group residential settings, family members often continue to perform many of these functions, including the most concrete types of help.

The care just described can be labor-intensive. It is hard to imagine a funding source that would compensate anyone for all the hours expended by family members who help and care for older people in their homes. At certain thresholds of disability, in-home services are more expensive than services in group settings, where a paid staff can achieve economies of scale and scope. Obviously staff members can do a variety of activities for a person simultaneously, and they can serve several people simultaneously at less cost than serving a single person.

Family members also combine their activities, of course—every mother or homemaker knows how to do more than one thing at a time. An older person receiving care may eat food prepared for the whole family. The soiled linens of an incontinent person may be done with the family wash. A visit to a relative that would occur anyway because of love or duty may be the occasion for oversight or tangible assistance. For precisely this reason, determining when family life ends and informal care begins is exquisitely difficult. This distinction becomes important if and when one tries to count the time and cost of family caregiving.

FAMILY CARE AND AGING

This book is not about all policy for family care; it is more narrowly about family care for older people. The family is obviously a vehicle for care of people of all ages. It nurtures minor children, sick or well. Husbands and wives pledge devotion in sickness and in health. But when we turn the spotlight on older people needing care (for convenience, using the conventional age 65 cutoff level), certain features merit noting.

Typically, more than one family household is interested and involved in the well-being of the older person. As Elaine M. Brody points out in Chapter 2 of this volume, many older couples and individuals live independently of their offspring by mutual choice, but family ties usually remain vital.

Second, the family caregivers most often and most intensively involved with an older person, especially the people over 80 who most often need long-term care, are themselves well over middle age. The stereotype of the working woman, torn between the demands of job, young children, and aging parents, does exist in the real world, but it is less common than another stereotype, an elderly wife caring for her husband while her own retirement age offspring look on or help out from the sidelines. Another common scenario involves a widower or, more likely, a widow who maintains an independent household and receives help from adult children at times of acute health crisis or for chronic disabilities.

A third feature of family care for older people is that the nature of the moral and legal obligation to older relatives differs from the responsibilities of parent to young child and husband to wife. Family members may be linked to their older relative by common history and experience and by ties of affection and gratitude. Older people often have strong feelings of obligation toward the younger generations. More assistance flows down the generations to children, grandchildren, nephews, and nieces than in the opposite direction. The well-being of older people is adversely affected if they believe they are a burden to their children.

The way the duties of the young to the old are articulated will undoubtedly be influenced by cultural and religious values and overall societal resources. Some of these duties may best be expressed communally, so as to spread resources evenly and reduce a perception of being a burden. That decision has already been made by income guarantees to the elderly. Should the same logic apply to long-term care? Some compelling arguments can be made for such societal solutions, although some moralists pose countervailing views. For instance, they argue that intimate care should be given by people who are likely to care about, as well as care for, the individual—an argument that is rejected by some advocacy organizations speaking on behalf of young adults with disabilities. Of course, emotional and social support of old people could well be provided voluntarily by extended family members while tangible help is purchased from strangers. Some policymakers fear that family members would withdraw their presence if it were not necessary for daily survival, and others are concerned about the cost of paying for care when family members are on the scene and, for the most part, have done the job without compensation.

The fourth issue is that partly because of increased life expectancy at birth and in childhood and partly because of the ability of medicine to bring about what has been called "the survival of the unfittest," the sheer number of older people expected to need care has induced a sort of policy panic. The likelihood of the whole country having an age distribution similar to that of Florida in the 1990s is viewed more as a problem than an accomplishment.

Five, we must acknowledge that some older people have no family, or no family members who can help. In the latter situation, family may be too far away, too ill, or too estranged to take on caregiving roles. Long-term care policy for the elderly must address all older people. One strategy is to make eligibility for public long-term care benefits contingent on having no family to help; the other extreme is to peg benefits firmly to the measurable needs of the older person, regardless of the availability of family. As a society, we are unlikely to adopt either strategy but rather to seek some complex middle ground. In any event, solutions will require juggling ethical, practical, and economic considerations.

Finally, elderly people have preferences about who they want to help them with care. Analogies to the care of children are particularly unhelpful here. Although parents learn to their chagrin that children also have opinions, the decision-making role of parents toward a developing child who happens to need extra care for health reasons is vastly different from the proper decision-making role of adults toward their parents or grandparents. Long-term care policies for children can be advanced within a generally accepted model of parental duties and rights. Lacking such a model for the family relationships of older people, one either needs to develop a model philosophically or hold as a given that preferences of both the old person and the younger person will vary widely. One also has to decide how much weight to give to the older person's views. The current tendency to treat elderly people with disabilities like children who need cajoling and protecting will be hard to counteract.

CURRENT POLICY AMBIGUITY

In many spheres, the United States is accused of lacking a family policy. If we are looking for a coherent, systematic set of deliberate, interlocking policies, then family care of the frail elderly follows this rule. Although public long-term care programs depend on and are built around high expectations for family care, one would be hard put to identify a consistent set of goals and related policies for the family.

Family support programs of various kinds do, of course, exist, and some are discussed in this book by Rhonda J. V. Montgomery (Chapter 3) and Vernon L. Greene and Patricia D. Coleman (Chapter 4). These include individual-level programs designed to help family members who are giving care, such as educational programs, support groups, and respite care services. They also include long-term care services, usually for low-income people, that provide benefits directly to the older person and thus relieve family members to some extent. (The benefit structures for these programs are typically designed parsimoniously, so that a person with substantial disabilities would still depend on family help to remain in the community.) Also, many jurisdictions support the family financially through tax incentives or direct payment: The latter often is part of a Medicaid personal attendant program. Taken together, these activities represent substantial efforts in support of family caregivers. However, they do not represent a coherent philosophy, which is hard to find, even within a single state.

Instead, we have ambiguous, often unstated, and sometimes conflicting policies for specific programs. As Pamela Doty points out in this volume (Chapter 6), many programs make an implicit assumption that family members are the first-line troops of long-term care. Some case management programs that allocate limited public dollars also have explicit injunctions not to replace the family, although the force of this directive is blunted by another injunction, that their role is to minimize family burden through judicious ordering of formal services. Thus two pieces of conventional wisdom coexist and both inform practice: One should not use formal care to substitute for family care, and one should consider that the whole family is the client receiving service.

Similarly, specific programs require family members to be on the scene or, conversely, to be absent before the benefit kicks in. Commonly, those offering hospice or high-tech home care decline to serve clients without an involved family member willing to give care. Other programs allocate meager resources by limiting care to those without family help. Should priority for formal home care be given to those who have fewest resources, those living alone, or those without families at all? Should priority be given to those who may need help at the margin to maintain the family's effectiveness? Which stance is fairest to the older person? To families? To society? These quandaries are not resolved by current policies, which include various, often conflicting, options.

Why do we need an overall public policy on these issues? Two reasons why family caregiving policy should be articulated more clearly come to mind. First, such policy may be needed to respond to an idealized vision of individual and family life. If we had a notion of how we would like to see the generations interact, our policies could be designed to encourage those goals. In some ways, the aging society that has been so nervously anticipated may have caught us unawares. As Robert Butler (1975), Thomas Cole (Cole & Gadow, 1986), and others have suggested, we have failed to articulate a view of how we expect people to behave in the face of the new demographics. What are people to do with 30 years of retirement, 40 years of empty nests, and marriages that are expected to endure for 60 years or more? What meaningful roles can be forged for people who are needed neither for procreation or labor force productivity? Leaving aside disability and disease, how are family members expected to engage each other across four or five generations? Without these scripts, policy will be reactive rather than based on positive images.

But there is a second reason, albeit reactive, for family policies. That is, we may develop policies to correct what appear to be problems in family and community life. For example, if we believe that the public cost of long-term care is too great, we want to encourage family members to do more. If we believe that family care is less productive than labor force participation, we develop policies that allow families to opt out. If we believe that families are doing a poor job of family care, we might design ways to improve their performance. If we believe that caregiving imposes excessive burden or distress on some family members, we might develop policies to alleviate that problem. If we believe that some people are forced into the labor market to care for other people's family members when all concerned would be best served by their taking care of their own, we might even consider paying some family caregivers.

Some of the people believe all of these things some of the time, which poses a problem. The professional and popular literature is full of conflicting statements. Family members are deserting their relatives. Family members are wearing themselves out in the service of their relatives. Family members try to do too much. Family members don't do enough. Family members need teaching and supervision from professionals to give adequate care to their relatives. Family members need to purchase low-cost help without the obstruction of professionals.

Unfortunately, all of these statements can sometimes be true for some people. It is surely a myth that older people have been abandoned wholesale by their relatives, yet some families of some old people are out of the picture. (Whether one would want to conscript the unwilling family member into this role is another question, which we take up in the last chapter.) The main point here is that so many different variants of family structure and family behavior exist that one is hard put to generalize about the good and bad news of family care. It is hard to articulate whether public policy should be designed to maintain current levels of family care, to encourage more family care for longer periods of time, to help people do family care well, or to relieve people when the effects of family care are mostly negative. Outside of the movies, one cannot shoot multiple targets with a single bullet. The challenge is achieving multiple goals from the same set of policies.

PUBLIC POLICY APPROACHES

A range of policy directions are possible, and many are discussed in the following chapters.

Benign Neglect

No policy is a de facto policy. If subsidized services are extremely limited or made available only in unattractive forms, the prospective beneficiaries and their families are less likely to take up the benefits. For example, nursing home care is widely regarded as intrinsically unappealing because of the nature of the nursing home and the requirements for divestment of financial resources. Thus policies that make publicly subsidized long-term care available largely in nursing homes will deter potential consumers from taking up benefits and relegate their care to unpaid family members by default. The message is that long-term care is largely a private matter to be financed or managed as best the individual can. If the individuals in question are poor, frail, very old, or cognitively impaired, their family members will inevitably be involved in providing financial help and care.

Short of doing nothing, what other responses can public policy take? Based on one's vision for the future or one's view of the current problems, a range of coercive or encouraging policies could be developed. If we were to draw inferences from the potpourri of programs that are currently found around the country, elements of these policy approaches exist (and indeed coexist) already in many jurisdictions.

Mandated Family Responsibility

If we believe families are skirting their moral responsibilities, public policy could require in-kind or monetary payment from adult children and grandchildren of the elderly to fund both home care and nursing home care. The Internal Revenue Service could be enlisted to ensure that the payments are deducted from wages. Such a policy strikes us as both mean-spirited and doomed to failure at a time when child care payments are difficult to collect and when the family is so difficult to define. But in the current fiscal climate, increasing calls are made for requiring family members to take care of their own.

A variant of mandated family responsibility is mandated individual responsibility. This becomes family policy in the sense that some older people may be forced to spend on their own care money that younger relatives expect to inherit and, indeed, that old people would prefer to leave to their heirs. In the absence of compelling evidence, an unshakable belief exists that the public costs of nursing homes would be much lower if only families were not colluding to divert or shelter the resources of old people. Unfortunately, research is lacking on the incentives that prompt family care and devotion and on the practical effects that being able to bequeath or inherit wealth has on the activities and well-being of all family members across the life span.

Direct Services to Family Caregivers

By public policy, it would be possible to direct services to family caregivers themselves, to help them in their tasks or to help them cope with any untoward consequences of the role. Such strategies, if they stand alone, have the advantage of being relatively inexpensive. They reinforce rather than attenuate ideas of family responsibility.

If we think families need help in learning how to perform caregiving roles, we could allocate public money for classes or support groups to assist them. Such interventions have the virtue of being simple and inexpensive, but in this volume Vernon L. Greene and Patricia D. Coleman (Chapter 4) point out that the efficacy of such measures is far from established. From our own research, we believe that education of family caregivers needs to be carefully targeted and timed. Feedback from caregivers suggests that classes on how to bathe one's spouse are superfluous, especially for one who has been doing it for years.

Suppose we observe, as has Steven Zarit (1989), that people who give heavy levels of care to family members are more likely to be clinically depressed than their age counterparts. A direct response would be to provide mental health services for those suffering these consequences. Again one would need to target the effort (perhaps to those caring for people with Alzheimer's disease or other caregivers at high risk of mental illnesses), and again one should not assume the efforts will be efficacious.

More Formal Care

A more direct approach to a view that family caregiving sometimes causes problems for family caregivers is to increase the availability of formal services. This, in turn, would allow family members to reduce or stop their care.

In this regard, respite services is a popular concept. Simply stated, respite services are long-term care services offered on a temporary or intermittent basis to relieve family members who have primary caregiving responsibility. These may be home care services provided on a regular schedule; live-in care in the old person's home to permit the family member to leave for an extended period of time (perhaps for a holiday, perhaps for their own health reasons); day care to remove the older person from the home and allow the caregiver to have space as well as time; and short admissions to nursing homes, board and care homes, and other group residential settings.

The actual content of respite services is identical to the services that might be developed for the person with a functional impairment. Whether providing home care or so-called respite care, the formal caregiver performs the same tasks. In both cases, the type and intensity of care depends on the needs (and, one hopes, wishes) of the older person. The difference is one of stated purpose. Respite care is offered to relieve family members who are deemed to have the primary responsibility. Home care, day care, and residential care benefits grow out of a societal responsibility and are meant to benefit the functionally impaired person directly. In the last chapter, we return to this subject to describe the widely different premises and incentives in these two formulations and to discuss the advantages and disadvantages of continuing to construe respite care as something separate from ordinary formal care.

Regardless of how respite care is viewed, all formal care serves families, at least indirectly. To the extent that benefits are available in a desirable form, family members are not constrained to provide them. Thus eligibility policies for formal care may also be family policies because of their explicit or implicit rules about the circumstances of coverage. If families are the first line of care, which family members count? Must they live with or near the older person? Do only those family members who identify themselves count, or are family members pursued? What constitutes an acceptable exemption of a family member? Should public programs make judgments about who is in a realistic position to help his or her mother? Does the mother's opinion or preference matter?

Views about the merits of both respite care and increased formal care entitlements should rationally flow from information about the extent to which family caregivers do a good job with particular situations and about the consequences to family members of being caregivers. The latter, often summarized as "caregiver burden," is one of the most-studied subjects in gerontology. The cumulative research has certainly proved that family caregiving can be perceived as burdensome and stressful, with *burden* viewed as a multidimensional concept, including physical, social, emotional, and financial stress. Research has also shown that burden has both a subjective and objective component. However, researchers have found that the subjective feeling of stress is weakly correlated with the objective facts of the case—that is, how disabled the person is and how much help is being given. At present, we cannot predict—with sufficient precision for policy design—who will experience high levels of burden. Nor are we sure that those who experience burden and stress will experience relief if they are absolved of caregiving responsibilities.

Factoring in family burden poses another problem. We lack normative information about family well-being in the absence of giving care. The highs and lows of family life that render it interesting, joyful, demanding, and, at times, anguishing occur independent of whether an elderly relative is receiving help. We need to consider when and in what ways family care of the elderly introduces an ingredient that needs special attention.

Much of our understanding of family care of the elderly is derived from clinical situations. That is, we learn from aggregating the experience of people who seek help with their roles or who are observed by formal caregivers (such as home health agencies, hospital discharge planners, or physicians) to be heavily involved with the care of people who have come to their attention. We have also learned a great deal about family caregiving from spouses and adult children who care for a relative with Alzheimer's disease. Indeed, the Alzheimer's Association has espoused the language of family caregiving and, through its supportive activities, helped socialize neophytes to the difficulties and challenges of the role.

Given a disease that robs its victims of their pasts and personalities and that makes heavy and increasing demands on a family member's time, self-identification as a family caregiver seems a natural development. But it also seems likely that most husbands, wives, parents, and adult children who help each other do it almost as a matter of course, without elaborate forethought or self-consciousness. We know relatively little about family caregivers who may be on automatic pilot. How much are they giving? How is it divided among family members? When does it become too much? When, if ever, do people begin to define themselves as family caregivers?

Financial Incentives and Compensation

If we view some kinds of family care as burdens that fall unpredictably and unfairly on some members of society, we may advocate policies to redress the balance. For example, tax exemptions—or, more generously, tax credits—could be used to effectively add to the income of family caregivers. If we believe that low-income people are often forced into the labor market when they and their elderly family members would be better off if they could act as family caregivers, we might endorse policies to pay at least some family members directly. Indeed, some people argue that as long as strangers are being paid to care for the elderly, family members should also be eligible to receive the funds because they are likely to do a more conscientious and loving job. Others would hold that the delicate fabric of family could be destroyed by introducing mercenary motives or setting a dollar value on family care. On a more coldly calculating basis, moreover, budgeters are concerned about induced demand for compensated family care: Few older people would be adverse to augmenting the income of their relatives.

ORGANIZATION OF THE BOOK

In the rest of the book, some of the issues raised here are explored in greater depth. In Chapter 2, Elaine M. Brody describes the reality of family care, a reality that she brought to the attention of the American public over decades of research and writing. She eloquently documents how the family has provided the continuous thread of long-term care, an activity she describes as "invented" by the family. She also points out the enormous diversity in family structures, challenges, and responses to challenges that constitute family care today. Brody anchors the subsequent discussion with facts about family care. She also leaves a message that counseling is a crucial and underdeveloped service that is needed to help family caregivers define and live with their roles.

Chapters 3, 4, and 5 describe the state of the art of three types of family caregiver programs, helping us consider the adequacy of current policies of that type and the needs for the future. Rhonda J. V. Montgomery (Chapter 3) reviews respite care, a subject to which she herself has contributed research data. She points to the equivocal or disappointing results of many controlled studies of the effects of respite care: Often such benefits are barely used by the demonstration group, and when used, they typically fail to influence the well-being of family caregivers or the likelihood that the older person will remain out of a nursing home. Montgomery emphasizes the possibility that we have looked for the wrong effects with the wrong measurements. The knowledge that respite care is available in emergencies may provide important security for families to carry on. When these emergencies include their own hospitalization or family funerals, they may not return with an improved overall well-being. More importantly, she calls attention to the careless specification of the features of respite care that may be helpful for particular kinds of families under particular circumstances. In other contexts, Montgomery has likened this deficiency of information to prescribing medications with no discussion of the dose, the duration, the indications, and the contraindications.

In Chapter 4, Vernon L. Greene and Patricia D. Coleman examine the panoply of programs designed directly for family caregivers—for example, therapy programs, support groups, and educational interventions. Such programs have their proponents, but the research evidence on their behalf is plagued by small, self-selected samples. Moreover, Greene and Coleman suggest a need to tap new information technology to provide family caregivers with information and support in ways that can be timely, cost-effective, and conducive to the caregiving situation.

In Chapter 5, Nathan Linsk and his colleagues summarize information about family compensation that they gathered for a recent book on the same subject (Linsk, Keigher, Simon-Rusinowitz, & England, 1992). Their review indicates that family compensation is already part of public policy through a welter of inconsistent and piecemeal programs that vary both across and within states. Some confusion exists as to the main goal of compensating families: enabling families to continue care; providing income and benefits to caregivers who leave or fail to enter the labor force, so that they do not fall behind their working counterparts; or providing income to low-income families.

We then turn in Chapter 6 to a discussion of how families are taken into account in planning and allocating formal care. In part using original data from her own observational studies, Pamela Doty describes how the presence or availability of family help is implicitly and explicitly treated in the decisions hospital discharge planners make about home care versus nursing home care, and in the decisions case managers make about allocating home care.

In Chapter 7, Marshall B. Kapp examines legal and ethical issues related to family care. The chapter ranges widely, covering liability concerns held (perhaps unnecessarily) by formal caregivers when they rely on informal care, possible legal limits on the role of family in regard to nursing functions, conflicting roles in financial planning, and family rights and duties in medical planning.

Based on all the information and insights in these chapters, we return again to family policy in the last chapter. There, we draw some tentative conclusions about how to proceed in developing family caregiving policies that will serve our aging society well into the next century.

2

Prospects for Family Caregiving

Response to Change, Continuity, and Diversity

ELAINE M. BRODY

RAPID RISE OF FAMILY CAREGIVING RESEARCH

A major and early watershed conference on older people and the family was the 1963 symposium on the three-generation family sponsored by the Gerontological Society and Duke University (Shanas & Streib, 1965). Although the conference was about the *three*-generation family, the *four*-generation family had already become a common phenomenon. At that symposium the participating scientists laid to rest (at least from a scientific standpoint) the assumption that modern families, adult children in particular, do not take care of the elderly as they did in the past. The evidence presented was so definitive that Irving Rosow called the conference "a benchmark of the final respects paid to the isolated nuclear family before its interment" (Shanas & Streib, 1965, p. 341). However, the conferees acknowledged that the effects of caregiving on the caregivers were hardly touched upon. In the 1960s, a trickle of clinical studies about those effects (e.g., Brody & Spark, 1966; Posner, 1961) began, and the forerunner of large-scale studies was carried out in the United Kingdom (Grad & Sainsbury, 1966; Sainsbury & Grad, 1966). Research on this subject swelled in the late 1970s, becoming a major stream of research in the 1980s.

Meanwhile, pressed by life extension and the consequent rise of chronic disease, the family was inventing long-term care. Attempts to define the phrase *long-term care,* now such a familiar part of our vocabulary, were

15

not made until the late 1970s (Brody, 1977; U.S. National Committee on Vital and Health Statistics, 1978). Recognition that professionals and government must play a major role in providing such care and in shifting from an emphasis on episodic, short-term, acute care was even more recent. But the role of the formal system has not been translated into comprehensive legislation.

We have come a long way in a short time. Virtually all that is known about long-term care and family care has been developed in the last 15 years. We know that families have been loyal and steadfast, and that they, not the formal system, provide 80% to 90% of personal and instrumental help to older people. Families link old people to the formal system, respond in emergencies, provide intermittent and acute care, share their homes with older people who live in the community despite severe disabilities, and provide the essential emotional support. Families make strenuous efforts to avoid institutionalization of elderly family members, and when such a plan becomes necessary, they take that step with the utmost reluctance.

We now understand that the "substitution theory" has no foundation. That is, formal services do not encourage families to reduce or withdraw the amount of care they provide, nor does home care substitute for nursing home care. The famous General Accounting Office study (U.S. General Accounting Office, 1977) showed that nursing home care actually is less costly than community care for older people with severe disabilities. We have learned that women, primarily wives, daughters, and daughters-in-law, provide the bulk of long-term care for such people. Not to deprecate the roles men play, the socialization of females to the caregiving role happens very early and is a profound and compelling influence throughout their lives.

We now understand that the adverse emotional effects of caregiving can be severe, affecting a substantial proportion of family caregivers. (That statement tends to be based on cross-sectional data, of course.) The other half, who do not show significant stress effects at any given time, may do so as time goes on, as their elders become more disabled and as the caregivers themselves grow older. Only longitudinal studies can inform us about those processes.

Substantial progress has been made in documenting the physical health effects that caregivers experience. However, we know virtually nothing at this time about the dollar costs of health and mental health care for caregivers themselves. We are beginning to learn about the previously hidden financial costs that are incurred when caregivers give up their jobs, reduce their work hours, refuse promotions, and so on—the opportunity costs.

Recently, our tunnel-vision focus on the "principal" caregiver has yielded to a view through a wide-angle lens that includes other family members: the roles of the caregivers' husbands, siblings, and children and the effects *they* experience as a result of the caregiving situations.

We have developed a technology for functional assessment of the old in order to determine the nature and number of helping services they need. But we do not have a methodology for determining the capacities of their family caregivers to provide those services.

We are aware that even when services are readily available to caregivers at high risk, they are not greedy about using them. In a large study of caregivers to Alzheimer's patients in Philadelphia, for example, only about half of those high-risk caregivers used respite services, even though they were offered at no cost. Moreover, those who did avail themselves of the offered respite were extraordinarily modest in their requests (Lawton, Brody, & Saperstein, 1991).

We are aware of the unevenness and scarcity of services, lack of adequate funding, lack of a sufficient cadre of workers with adequate education and training, poor quality of some services, and other problems. Access problems have recently been documented thoroughly by the U.S. Office of Technology Assessment (1990) in reference to Alzheimer's patients and their families.

On balance, we know that the needs of the old for care have far exceeded the capacity of the family to fulfill. Moreover, the definitive study by the Brookings Institution has shown that most people could not afford private long-term care insurance (Rivlin & Wiener, 1988; Wiener, Illston, & Hanley, 1974).).

CHANGE, CONTINUITY, AND DIVERSITY

Today we know that the balance between family care and formal care must shift. The challenge is to figure out how social policy can effect that shift. Certainly we know enough to take meaningful steps toward translating available knowledge into policy and practice. But we have much to do in pushing the frontiers of knowledge further, because there is a good deal of unfinished business on the family care agenda.

There will always be unfinished business. We cannot assume that a neat list of agenda items can be drawn up and checked off in turn as each is accomplished. Change is the only constant in addressing the relevant issues. Social and economic trends are not always predictable and require constant monitoring by research. The number and proportion of older people in the population inevitably continues to change. Their characteristics and needs change in unpredictable ways as each new cohort enters the aging phases of life and as new scientific and social developments occur. The health status, values, lifestyles, preferences, socioeconomic status, personal resources, and even the ethnic backgrounds of the elderly are changing. Some disabling diseases may be ameliorated in the future—if we can solve the problem of Alzheimer's disease, for example; however, some new ones emerge, such as HIV. Changes also occur in the environment in which caregiving takes place—in the social and economic climate and in social policies that create, eliminate, or reduce services, entitlements, and facilities. Nor are values immutable, although they change slowly and unevenly.

The field is now engaged in three additional and interrelated stages of research. First, we are beginning to address *diversity,* to fill in the broad outlines that have been delineated to describe caregivers and caregiving. Beyond recognizing that caregivers are males and females, spouses and children, we now perceive that different individuals and different groups have different capacities, styles, and tolerances to give different kinds of care at different times in their lives to older people whose needs and wishes reflect similar diversity.

Second, there is now general awareness of the need for longitudinal studies that address *change* and *continuity.* Some things change and some do not; there often is tension between change and continuity.

Third, respect for the value of *qualitative study* has reemerged. Amid the outpouring of quantitative data, clinical and ethnographic studies are coming into their own to help us understand the processes that are at work within people. The changes that occur in the broad socioeconomic environment interact not only with each other, but also with other sets of changes. Those other sets of changes occur across the life course of individuals and families in response to developmental tasks, to shifts in dependency due to the processes of aging and decline and the trajectory of disability, and to changing role requirements and opportunities. These kinds of changes speak to the inner processes or subjective experiences of caregivers.

Values, too, evidence change and continuity, values such as those pertaining to family care of the aged, the acceptability of formal services, gender-appropriate roles, and so on.

Thus, as we assess where we have been in order to translate the accumulated knowledge into social policy, as we attend to that unfinished business, key concepts are change, continuity, and diversity. A long-term care system must be flexible and sensitive in responding to those processes.

EXAMPLES FROM RESEARCH
AT PHILADELPHIA GERIATRIC CENTER

Let me illustrate change, continuity, and diversity and the need for longitudinal and qualitative studies with fragments of my own research at the Philadelphia Geriatric Center.

In the late 1970s, the goal of a pair of studies of three generations of women was to detect whether the women's changing roles had resulted in changing attitudes and behaviors about family care of the elderly. We saw both change and continuity. Large majorities of all three generations of women continued to be firmly in favor of family care of the elderly. That value had not changed; it was constant despite women's changing roles.

However, we also saw change across the generations in women's attitudes toward gender-appropriate roles. Majorities of all three generations of women thought that sons should do the same things as daughters to help dependent elderly parents, but each progressively younger generation was more in favor of egalitarian behavior. When we looked at the actual behavior of the women, we again found continuity, because it was the women-in-the-middle, the middle generation of women, who were providing the bulk of care for those of their elderly mothers who needed it. Also, the older members of the middle generation were doing much more caregiving than those at the younger end of that generation, and they were much more likely to share their households with elderly parents with disabilities. That is, as women grew older, their responsibilities were peaking rather than beginning to diminish, as popular notions would have us believe.

A third study contrasted women who were working and those who were not working, all of them meanwhile taking care of their parents. The goal was to examine their behavior in more detail in the context of the influx of women into the workforce. Again we found change, continuity, and diversity. About 28% of the women we had classified as nonworking were actually working women who had quit their jobs to take care of elderly parents. Similarly, 26% of the working women were conflicted: They were either considering quitting, had already reduced the number of hours they were working, or had made other kinds of adjustments in their vocational lives. The 1982 long-term care survey data found almost identical proportions of women who had taken just those actions (Stone, Cafferata, & Sangl, 1987).

The tension between change (the new values) and continuity (the old values) was evidenced by the diversity of the women's characteristics.

Those who had quit their jobs were older, had been helping longest, had parents with the most severe disabilities, were more likely to share their households with their parents (always a strong predictor of stress), and had less education, lower family incomes, the least paid help, and the lowest status jobs. The women who were considering quitting were more likely to be their parents' sole family helper and had problems similar to those of their peers who had already left the workforce. However, they also had the highest-level jobs, were the most career-oriented, were most likely to hold the new views about women's roles, and had the most paid help. Of course, the study also included women who had not worked (and held the least egalitarian attitudes) and those who were working but were not thinking of quitting (and were in the best health, had parents with the least severe disabilities, and felt the most in control of their lives). In short, the women evidenced change and continuity in their values and behaviors in a great diversity of ways.

We do not know what actions those particular women will take in the future. Longitudinal studies are needed to follow women as they move in and out of the workforce. What came through clearly was that the old values were holding very firm indeed. Women were not neglecting their elderly parents; the parents of the women who were in the workforce were getting just as much care as the parents of the women who were not working. There was a slight reduction in the amount of care the women themselves were providing, but that was offset by the care being purchased for the parent during the hours in which the women were working.

A theme that emerged as we talked with women in qualitative studies was the importance of work to them. Although some were "career" women, most were not professionals. Most women across the nation work because they and their families need the money, but they also enjoy the stimulation and the sense of doing a job well. One woman who had left her job commented, "Women like me are dinosaurs," implying that the women of the future will not leave the workforce to care for parents. Another said, "I was so good at what I did, and the children were proud of me for working."

Another of our findings was that these women were not simply taking care of one older person; they had multiple caring responsibilities. About 22% of them were simultaneously taking care of another older person, and half of them had helped another older person in the past. They were having "caregiving careers" that went on for many years.

A fourth study, still in progress, recognizes the fact that many women today are not married during their parent care years. This is accounted for by high rates of divorce, the increase in the number of women remaining unmarried, and the fact that rates of widowhood soar beginning in middle age whereas elderly parents live longer into advanced old age and disability. In fact, 44% of parent-caring daughters in the 1982 long-term care survey were not married, being never-marrieds (13.4%), widowed (14.2%), or divorced-separated (16.2%) (Stone et al., 1987). The goal of our study, therefore, is to compare the parent care experiences of women in different marital statuses: married women, widowed women, divorced women, and women who had never married.

In our initial analysis of the data (Brody, Litvin, Kleben, & Hoffman, 1990), the married women proved to be best off of all the groups. They knew it, and they said so. They had much more in the way of financial support, with family incomes double those of the other groups. They also had more socioemotional support, often referring to their husbands as their "stabilizers" or as a "rock of Gibraltar" with whom to talk over parent care difficulties. The men also were helpful with instrumental tasks. The women who did not have husbands were lonely and concerned about what would happen to the elderly parent if something should happen to them. They missed having someone to talk things over with, and they felt that they had no one on whom to depend.

One of the fallouts of women's changing roles, then, has been the large number of parent-caring women who do not have the support of a husband or, in many cases, of children. Young adult children and children in their late teens often provide a backup system of help that usually does not appear in data about caregiving. Those children may not give the day-to-day care, but they are there when Grandma is sick or Mom must do something important and needs somebody to stay with the older person, or when emergencies occur.

TRENDS IN FAMILY CARE

Let us examine some of the trends that illustrate the interplay of continuity and change in the evolution of family care.

Multiple Caregiving

Continuing demographic changes are further reducing the supply of filial caregivers and increasing the pressures to care for several older people.

Having fewer children means having fewer daughters. Because many daughters are also daughters-in-law, the potential for multiple caregiving is increasing. Fewer children, combined with increasing mobility, means that more older people will not have children close by when help is needed. The problems of such older people and their geographically distant children have been receiving considerable attention.

Multiple caregiving may also increase because older people who have no children on whom to depend will be more numerous. At present about one fifth of older persons have no children on whom to depend. Although they probably do not do as much as children, nieces and nephews often rise to the occasion to help childless older people, even when they are caring for their own parents.

Grandfilial Caregiving

The number of grandchildren who are responsible for helping one or even two generations undoubtedly is increasing. The early data from the Kane studies (Kane & Penrod, 1993; Kane, Penrod, Finch, Thuras, & Kane, 1993) show that only 3% of the caregivers in the study are grandchildren. This may happen more frequently in the future, as the population ages and the very old are more likely to lose their aging children through death.

Parenthetically, caution is suggested about saying *only* 3% have this problem, or *only* 20% experience financial stress in caring for an older person, or—as one researcher reported—*only* 40% of caregiving daughters suffer from severe emotional stress effects. The people who are experiencing a particular problem may find little solace in being part of what someone else considers *only* a small group. Moreover, the proportion of individuals affected does not accurately reflect the impact on the many additional individuals in the caregivers' families who, in a ripple effect, also feel the repercussions. We must look at all of the subgroups, the mosaic of caregiving, the diversity, as well as the main, broad trends.

Women in the Workforce

Despite temporary plateaus for various reasons, the proportion of women in the workforce has steadily increased in the past several decades. Writing in 1989, Otten predicted that women will account for almost two thirds of the labor force growth by the end of the 20th century.

Changing Ethnicity

A major changing scenario concerns the ethnic composition of our population (for detailed data and discussion, see Valle, 1989). Right now ethnic minorities—African Americans, Hispanics, Native Americans, and Asian Americans—constitute about one fifth of the U.S. population. However, 34% of all children who are under the age of 10 are African American or Hispanic. Although minority people 65 and older are fewer proportionately now, those ethnic groups are growing very rapidly indeed. Between 1970 and 1980, the minority population 65 and over increased 40% for African Americans, 91% for Hispanics, 31% for Asian Americans, and 71% for Native Americans. Thus we can anticipate not only increasing ethnic diversity among older people but parallel diversity among their caregivers. Their patterns of care, needs, and preferences will inevitably affect delivery styles of various entitlements and services that they find acceptable. By the middle of the next century, these groups will constitute the majority of Americans.

High Rates of Divorce

High rates of divorce are continuing. Uhlenberg, Cooney, and Boyd (1990) point out that divorce has been increasing not only among young women but also among older women. As a result, more women are entering old age without husbands. Uhlenberg et al. project that by the year 2025, about half of all women who enter old age will be without husbands. These elderly women will be depending on middle-aged women, more of whom will also be without husbands. That is, there are two generations of women without husbands, who are in poor economic circumstances and have other related problems—one generation depending on another. Because women with the fewest competing responsibilities tend to become caregivers to an elderly parent, many of those middle-generation daughters will experience the loneliness, lack of support, and lack of instrumental help that the not-married women in our study evidenced.

One of the consequences of high divorce rates is that the proportion of families with children under 18 that are single-parent families has risen from 13% in 1970 to 27% in 1988. The average family income, including child support, for single mothers was half that of single fathers ($12,000 versus $24,000); two-parent families fared the best (about $40,000) (U.S. Bureau of the Census, 1989). Of all single-parent families, 80% are headed by the mother. How will this play out when those single mothers—

who so often need to work while they're taking care of their children—are also responsible for an elderly parent?

Double Dependency

More young women are having a first child at later ages. Therefore, they may have an old parent to care for and young children at the same time—a situation characterized as *double dependency*.

Another form of double dependency occurs because more young adults are living with their parents for longer periods of time. The proportion of 18-to-24 year olds living with their parents rose from 47% in 1970 to 54% in 1988 (U.S. Bureau of the Census, 1989). Thus, more nests are remaining filled for longer periods of time or are being refilled with young adults who return to the parental home, sometimes with their own children, because of the high divorce rate and the economy.

Still another form of double dependency relates to people with developmental disabilities. The number of older people in this group is increasing rapidly. In the 1940s, life expectancy for those with developmental disabilities was 12 years; now most people in this group live into their 50s (Lewin, 1990). More caregivers, then, are taking care of adult children with developmental disabilities at the same time that they're taking care of elderly parents. Their caregiving careers last virtually a lifetime. Parents of adult children with developmental disabilities have a unique, especially poignant fear about what is going to happen to that "child" when they are no longer around.

Subjective Experiences

Other sets of changes and other kinds of continuity occur within individuals and within families, and these too must be considered in assessments of the family's capacity to provide care. These inner changes or subjective experiences are important because they explain why women are primarily the ones to become caregivers and why some go on for many long years despite severe disadvantage to their own health, to their families, and to their vocational lives. Some women spend more time taking care of older people than they do in raising their own children. These inner processes also explain why so many people refuse the services that they need. The subjective processes clearly indicate the need for sensitive counseling as part of any good long-term care system.

Some of the inner themes caregiving women experience were identified in a qualitative study by the Philadelphia Geriatric Center (for detailed case material and discussion, see Brody, 1990; for ethnographic analysis, see Albert, 1990). Based on other research reports, these themes seem universal.

Caregiving as a Woman's Role. A major and fundamental theme women experience is that caregiving is a woman's role—that is, there is a profound acceptance of the proposition that caregiving is their job. Beginning almost at birth, women are subject to a deep and early socialization into the caregiving role. One woman illustrated this well when she said,

> When my mother was pregnant with me, she was expecting to have a son. When I was born, she said to the nurse, "How can that be? I thought I was going to have a boy." She was very upset, but her friends and the nurses reassured and consoled her. They said to her, "That baby, she'll be a comfort to you in your old age."

Thus, the newborn baby was assigned the role of caregiver to her mother.

Another daughter was asked if her brothers participated in the care of their mother, who was extremely disabled. The woman looked surprised, and said, "A daughter-in-law is not the same as a daughter," spontaneously identifying the daughter-in-law as the one who would have to provide care if the son participated in caregiving. Although not all daughters-in-law accept the role of caregivers, many do when no daughter lives nearby. They have the same profound socialization to caregiving as the woman's role.

An example from the Philadelphia case studies is that of a daughter-in-law who was taking care of her mother-in-law and was grateful to her husband (the elderly woman's son) for his help. When the research interviewer arrived to talk with the caregiver, the son greeted her and said sadly, "My wife will be down in a minute. My poor wife has been carrying trays up to the third floor three times a day for 35 years." She had taken care first of her grandfather-in-law, then of her grandmother-in-law, and now it was her mother-in-law who was on the third floor receiving those trays. When the interviewer talked with the daughter-in-law herself, she asked, "What about your husband? Does he help you with caregiving?" The daughter-in-law replied,

> Oh, my husband is just wonderful. He is so creative. Do you know what he did? He rigged up a buzzer system all over the house, so when my mother-in-law wants me all she has to do is press a button, and I can hear her wherever I am.

Making Everyone Happy. Women often feel, "I must do it all, I must do it well, I must make the old people happy, I must make *everybody* happy." One woman added, "Only I am miserable." Because women see it as their job to make their family happy, they experience any conflict in the family as their fault.

Caring and Caregiving. Many women confuse caring and caregiving. They feel that if they don't *do* it all themselves then they don't *care* enough, that they're simply not fulfilling their responsibility. "No matter what I do, it's not enough," they say. And no matter how much they do, they often feel guilty.

It's My Turn. A fourth, often-heard theme is, "I do it because it's *my turn.* My mother took care of me, and now it's my turn to take care of her." The expectation that the daughter must do everything for the parent that the parent did for her when she was a small child is obviously unrealistic. It's one thing to lift a rosy, 12-month-old baby and another to lift and turn a person of 87. It's one thing to change the diaper of a young baby, another to do so for an incontinent older person. The trajectory of change and expectations are different when caring for a child and an older person. When a child is growing and developing, each new step along the way is greeted with pleasure, as an accomplishment. The child is moving toward more independence. With the older person, most often one can expect a steady decline, and emotional reactions are quite different.

Control and Power. Emotional strain is often involved in the rebalancing of control and power, when the dependency/independency relationship between adult child and elderly parent shifts due to the increasing disability of the older person. At times the parent retains control and the psychological balance of power, with caregiving daughters being unable to extricate themselves from long-standing, problematic relationship patterns. Common refrains are:

> My mother still intimidates me.
> My mother won't let anybody other than me take care of her.
> My mother doesn't let us leave her alone in the evening.

Most professionals identify with the problems of older people, and we emphasize the importance of protecting their rights and control over their own lives. However, sometimes it is the caregivers who need protection and help in redressing the balance of power and control. Some who cannot do it themselves refuse help, even at the cost of severe suffering not only to themselves but to other family members. We talk of empowering older people, but we also should think of empowering their caregivers.

Ages and Stages. Different caregivers are at very different ages and stages. Some are in their 30s, some in their 70s, and most are in between. Caregiving is not "developmental" in the sense of the traditional developmental stages of growth and change in human beings. Neugarten and Hagestad (1976) have pointed out that "off time" events are more stressful than "on time" events. That is, an event is "off time" when it occurs at an unexpected time of life. Caregiving women in their 30s who have young children and are also taking care of the elderly say, "I'm too young for this to be happening to me." Women in middle age say, "I thought I'd be free at this time of my life. My husband is looking toward retirement, and we planned to do a little traveling. Instead, my empty nest is being refilled." And older women, those in their 60s and 70s, even in their 80s, say, "I'm too old for this. I'm old myself."

Pressures From Professionals and Religious Leaders. A recurrent theme concerns the powerful pressures caregivers receive from religious leaders and professionals. Again and again, overburdened caregivers say, "My priest (or my pastor or my rabbi) says to me, 'Do it. God will reward you. It's your job.' " The biases and judgmental attitudes of some professionals are illustrated very clearly in Pamela Doty's contribution (Chapter 6) in this volume. In one of the cases she describes, for example, a daughter did not want to take her disturbed father into her home because he had already set a boarding house on fire. The landlady had called an ambulance and sent him to a hospital emergency room. In the view of the discharge planner, the solution to the problem was for hospital staff "to work on the family by cajoling or browbeating and shaming them into doing their duty."

Such themes illustrate that change, continuity, and diversity occur within individuals and families as well as in broad socioeconomic trends. The changes, continuities, and diversities have ethical implications. There are no "norms" nor is there a single or simple answer to the question, "What *should* adult children do?" Professionals face the ethical dilemma of determining whose needs are paramount and the balancing of older person's and caregiver's needs.

Ironically, women today seem to be taking on more and more responsibilities as they grow older. They give more care and heavier care to elderly parents, and they often have husbands as well as parents who need help. More women are working longer. And there has been much publicity about grandmothers who are now raising grandchildren because their young adult children have dropped out into the drug culture.

A number of good recommendations come to mind: continuity of care, a range of services and facilities, reduction in the chaos of hospital discharge process and the process of admission to nursing homes, recruitment and training of workers, advocacy, education of families in caregiving techniques, a system with linkages, and so on. If a long-term care system is to be flexible in responding to the change, continuity, and diversity that occur in both broad socioeconomic processes and in people's inner processes, it must incorporate the pivotal, central service of counseling. Case management should not be construed as a mechanistic job of simply arranging services, steering people to the sources of those services, and monitoring them over time. Case managers must also understand how people function, understand what the psychological barriers are to using offered services, and know how to help them overcome those barriers. To underline, case managers must be sensitive to and respond flexibly to the effects of change, continuity, and diversity in each family as they interact with the unique constellations of people's inner feelings and experiences. That is the real challenge.

As professionals, we often emphasize the negative emotional effects of caregiving, which have been documented so well, and the negative physical effects, about which data are emerging. We know about the contributors to those stresses, but we do not ask what social policy can do about these emotional issues. We concentrate on the services that are tangible and easy to describe. Conflict, guilt, anxiety, depression, relationship problems, and the like seem too slippery for social policy. But they are not, if skilled case management that includes counseling is available and sensitive to the issues described.

Finally, we all know there's no simple or single solution. There will always be some strains and some pain. Benevolently intended programs have limitations, and societal provisions cannot solve all problems. But as a society, we are not doing our best right now. True, we do not know all we need to know. But surely we know enough to make a start.

3

Examining Respite Care

Promises and Limitations

RHONDA J. V. MONTGOMERY

INTRODUCTION

Respite services are among the most widely advocated forms of support for families assisting impaired members in their homes. Both practitioners and researchers have suggested that respite care can relieve the burden of the caregiving situation and, perhaps, even allow families to continue care for elders who would otherwise have been placed in a nursing home (Brody, 1985; Doty, 1986; Pratt, Schmall, Wright, & Cleland, 1985; Scharlach & Frenzel, 1986; Zarit, Todd, & Zarit, 1986). Despite this belief in the benefits of respite care, information, particularly about the impact of these services on families, is limited, widely scattered, and often difficult to obtain.

The term *respite care* has been used to refer to a wide range of services intended to give temporary relief to families caring for members with disabilities. This concept of care developed in the United States as a corollary of the de-institutionalization movement in the early 1970s for children and adults with developmental disabilities. As families assumed the primary responsibility for relatives with developmental disability, the need for temporary relief from their caregiving responsibilities created a demand for respite services. Recognition of the parallel need for relief of family members caring for frail elderly with disabilities has been very recent in the United States, and formal respite services are not widely available.

Despite a general consensus that respite means "an interval of temporary relief," there is almost no agreement as to the composition of the services

29

that are to provide this relief. Respite programs have ranged from volunteers providing short periods of companionship to short stays in institutions. This ambiguity has been a major barrier to increasing knowledge about respite and its impact on families and public services. The only common element of these services appears to be the purpose, which is to provide a rest for caregivers.

RESPITE MODELS

In an earlier publication, I used the three dimensions of *time, place,* and *level of care* or *tasks* to develop a topology of respite models (Montgomery, 1988b). The location or setting in which services are provided serves as the most basic dimension to distinguish three general types of respite programs. Services can be provided in a client's home (in-home services), in a group or institutional setting (out-of-home services), or in multiple settings (combination program). Out-of-home services include foster homes, adult day-care centers, respite facilities, nursing homes, and hospitals.

Within the three general types, there are a number of possible variations depending on the level of care and the duration and frequency of respite episodes. Programs may vary along a continuum from low to high levels of care, and respite episodes may be for short periods of a few hours to long stays of up to 6 weeks. Clients may be able to use services as frequently as once or twice a week or as infrequently as once or twice a year.

Institutional Models

The earliest respite programs for the elderly population were established in hospitals in Great Britain (Delargy & Belf, 1957; Packwood, 1980). This institutional model has been replicated in the United States and Canada in acute hospitals, nursing homes, and specialized facilities (Crossman, London, & Barry, 1981; Dunn, MacBeath, & Robertson, 1983; Ellis & Wilson, 1983; Hasselkus & Brown, 1983; Huey, 1983; MacCourt & Southam, 1983; McFarland, Howells, & Dill, 1985). Institutional respite usually takes the form of holiday admissions or intermittent readmissions. Holiday admissions allow the caregiver to vacation while the elder is placed in the institution for a 1- or 2-week period. Some programs limit respite care to a single 2-week admission, whereas others allow repeated admissions. Intermittent readmissions or floating-bed programs provide for scheduled repeated admissions. Intermittent readmission programs may be for short periods of 2 or 3 nights repeated as frequently as every 2 to 3 weeks, or for longer periods of 1 or 2 weeks repeated less frequently. Both nursing homes and hospitals can offer personal care, skilled nursing care, and intermediate care.

Out-of-Home Community Care

The most common form of out-of-home respite is provided through adult day-care centers (Montgomery, 1984; Stone, 1985; WSDSHS, 1986). Usually such care is offered on a regularly scheduled basis for about 5 to 6 hours each visit (Sands & Suzuki, 1983). Adult day-care centers are best able to serve clients who need minimal assistance and, often, will not enroll clients who are incontinent or who wander (Danaher, Dixon-Bemis, & Pederson, 1986). However, there has been a recent trend to develop day-care programs specifically for persons with Alzheimer's disease or other related disorders (Mace, 1986). Other forms of out-of-home respite discussed in the literature include foster care and family cooperatives. These models of respite have been primarily available for those with developmental disabilities (Hildebrandt, 1983). Experiments with family cooperatives for the frail elderly have not been successful (Lawton, 1981).

In-Home Care

In-home respite care can be provided by a sitter/companion, homemaker, home health aide, or a nurse (Isett, Krauss, & Malone, 1984; McFarland et al., 1985; WDHSS, 1982). Some programs provide all of these levels of service whereas others offer only companion or sitter services. Several public and private initiatives have encouraged the development of volunteer respite programs. These volunteer programs are usually confined to the companion level of care (Lidoff, 1983; Montgomery & Borgatta, 1985). The duration of respite varies among in-home programs. Some programs limit their services to short periods of 2 to 4 hours whereas others only provide in-home respite for periods of 24 hours or more (Nyilis, 1985). Overnight respite for extended periods of several days or a week is far less common.

Comprehensive Care Models

Comprehensive respite programs consist of combinations of the different respite models. Such programs offer multiple levels of care in multiple settings for a variety of time periods. These combined programs are often able to meet the needs of a wide range of clients (CDHS, 1985; Dixon-Bemis, 1986; WDHSS, 1981; WSDSHS, 1986) and to adapt to changing needs of clients.

Comparisons Across Models

Despite the wide advocacy for respite services and the increasing number of programs offered throughout the country, little information is available about the relative merits and problems associated with the different models. In the absence of any published studies that evaluate and compare different models of respite, our knowledge of their relative merits largely stems from program descriptions and anecdotal observations. Out-of-home respite care is seen as having the advantage of allowing caregivers to remain in their homes and enjoy privacy and time alone with other family members, which are so often craved (Crossman et al., 1981). The care receiver in turn has the opportunity to meet new people and to be stimulated by new activities. This is an advantage emphasized by respite programs operating in adult day-care centers (Danaher et al., 1986; Ellis, 1986; Sands & Suzuki, 1983). Advocates of out-of-home programs also note the potential benefits from the health screening process that accompanies placement in an institution or participation in a day-care program and from suggestions that staff members can make to families for improved care and changes in medical routines (Ellis, 1986).

Institutional respite tends to be less flexible than in-home care. Most programs offering institutional respite find it extremely difficult to offer emergency respite because of the cost of setting aside a bed for emergency cases (FLTC, 1983; Scharlach & Frenzel, 1986). Placement in an institution for short periods can also be very disruptive for some patients who suffer from dementia or confusion. Some institutions are not able to care for very confused clients who are inclined to wander (Ellis, 1986). Even clients who are not prone to confusion need time to become oriented to the new environment (FLTC, 1983). Sometimes elders are resistant to institutional respite, fearing that the respite is the first step toward permanent placement. There is some indication in the literature that this is not an unrealistic fear (FLTC, 1983; Scharlach & Frenzel, 1986). Although the daily cost of institutional care is usually less than that of in-home services for the same amount of time, the overall costs are higher because stays are usually much longer (Montgomery, 1988a). Clients with minimal impairments sometimes find placement in an institution too confining

(Packwood, 1980). At the same time, Huey (1983) notes that staff frequently complain that respite clients tend to be demanding and want room and maid services.

The most frequently requested and used service is in-home respite care provided for short periods, usually by a home health aide (CDHS, 1985; Montgomery & Borgatta, 1987; NYSDSS, 1985; WSDSHS, 1986). Programs that offered both in-home and out-of-home services have discovered that in-home services were most often preferred (CDHS, 1985; WSDSHS, 1986). Families tend to find such services most convenient and relatively economical when respite is offered for short periods. The one program that reported a preference for institutional services also indicated that these services were covered by Medicare whereas the in-home respite services were not (Nyilis, 1985). In-home programs also have the advantage that caregivers do not have to arrange for transportation and the routine of the elder is not disturbed. When an in-home program offers multiple levels of service, this model can be very flexible. Programs that are limited to companion-level care, which is the case for most volunteer services, are unable to serve a large proportion of the target population (Montgomery & Berkeley-Caines, 1989; Montgomery & Hatch, 1987; NYSDSS, 1985). Also, some families have been uncomfortable with strangers coming into their homes (Danaher et al., 1986; Hildebrandt, 1983).

DELIVERY OF RESPITE CARE

In addition to the dimensions of setting, level of care, and time that have been used to delimit a topology of respite services, several other critical characteristics vary among programs and should be considered in the development and study of respite. These characteristics include financing, eligibility criteria, and staffing.

Financing

Respite care has been financed through a broad range of public and private mechanisms (Stone, 1985). In Great Britain and other countries, respite care has been fully funded as a part of the national health care system. In the United States, respite care has been unevenly funded and, for the most part, offered as a pilot or demonstration program or as part of another ongoing program. The funds for these services have come from Medicare waivers, Medicaid waivers, state funds, private agencies, and fees.

Eligibility

Often the eligibility criteria of respite programs are dictated by the financing mechanism. When respite is offered on a fee-for-service basis, few criteria have been established. When services have been offered through publicly funded programs, eligibility is often restricted to low-income persons and/or persons vulnerable to nursing home placement (Meltzer, 1982; Stone, 1985). As in the case of financing, no clear patterns of eligibility have emerged. However, restrictive targeting practices do appear to have implications for the impact of respite, implications that will be addressed later in this chapter.

Staffing

The staffing of programs is also related to financing mechanisms and eligibility criteria. When programs are restricted to elders with high levels of disability, the staff must have higher levels of skill. When funding sources are limited, an effort is made to employ volunteers. However, this practice can influence eligibility criteria because volunteer programs cannot offer skilled care. In short, although it is clear that the issues of financing, eligibility, and staffing are interrelated and critical, the literature provides little consistent information about these aspects of respite services.

Outcomes of Respite

The widespread advocacy for respite services primarily stems from the belief that respite care will temporarily relieve the burden of caregivers and result in long-term benefits for the caregiver's well-being, which in turn will enhance the capacity of caregivers to continue with their tasks. Hence the critical outcomes of respite that have been studied include satisfaction with services, the caregiver's well-being, and patterns of institutionalization.

Satisfaction

The most pervasive finding in the literature regarding the impact of respite services is that caregivers like the service and generally find programs to be valuable (Burdz & Bond, 1988; FLTC, 1983; Howells, 1980; Kosloski & Montgomery, 1990; Lawton, Brody, & Saperstein, 1989; Montgomery & Berkeley-Caines, 1989; Montgomery & Borgatta, 1985,

1987; NYSDSS, 1985; Packwood, 1980; Scharlach & Frenzel, 1986; WDHSS, 1982). Although it is not unusual for families to be apprehensive at first, most caregivers have felt that the respite programs in which they participated satisfactorily met their needs. Among the benefits identified by caregivers have been relief from tasks, psychological support, stimulation for the elder, and health assessments of the dependent that led to changes in medical routines. Concerns of the caregivers or dissatisfaction with respite care tended to center on increased confusion and dependency of the elder and disruption of home routines, all of which were sometimes created by the respite service, especially in hospital settings (FLTC, 1983; Packwood, 1980; Robertson, Griffiths, & Cosin, 1977). Scharlach and Frenzel (1986) noted that some care recipients did not like the nursing home setting because they did not like being around persons with more severe disabilities than their own. Studies that queried caregivers about future use of respite indicated the majority would use respite again (Lawton et al., 1989; Montgomery & Borgatta, 1985, 1987; Packwood, 1980).

Caregiver Burden/Well-Being

From the perspective of many providers and some researchers, satisfaction and felt relief are sufficient criteria to advocate for expanded, affordable respite programs, (e.g., Lawton et al., 1989). Others concerned with public policy and the goal of conserving public dollars argue that the benefits of respite must be demonstrated in more substantial ways (Callahan, 1989). Specifically, there has been a general expectation that respite care will (or should) result in net savings to the public purse by reducing or delaying the use of more costly forms of care, especially institutional care. Therefore, public policymakers and researchers have been most interested in the impact of respite care on caregiver burden and/or well-being and the impact on nursing home placement.

To date, a limited number of controlled studies have looked at these critical variables, and the evidence regarding burden and well-being is uneven. Burdz and Bond (1988) assessed the impact of a 2-week respite stay in a nursing home for 55 caregivers. Based on interviews conducted with caregivers 3 weeks after the stay, these researchers found that people receiving respite care reported significantly fewer memory and behavioral problems for the elders regardless of the diagnosis. However, they did not find significant differences between the treatment and comparison groups in the burden scores. Similarly, Lawton and his colleagues (1989) reported no differences in caregiver well-being between the experimental and control groups in their study of 642 caregivers.

Findings from a study by Montgomery and Borgatta (1985) that investigated a volunteer respite program revealed a reduction in objective burden for spouse-caregivers (see also Montgomery & Hatch, 1987). A more recent study by Montgomery and Borgatta (1989) of 541 caregivers participating in a paid-respite demonstration program did not replicate this finding. However, it did reveal a significant difference between the control groups and the treatment groups in subjective burden when the sample was restricted to those caregivers assisting elders who continued to reside in the community 1 year after services were initiated. This pattern has also been observed in a more recent evaluation of a six-site respite program sponsored by the Michigan Department of Mental Health (Kosloski & Montgomery, 1990).

Institutionalization

Findings related to nursing home placement have been even more limited than those related to caregiver burden or well-being. The study of volunteer respite by Montgomery and Borgatta (1985) reported no impact of the respite on nursing home placement. Lawton and his colleagues (1989) found no differences between the experimental and control groups on the elder's risk of death or risk of institutionalization. However, they did report a 22-day difference between the two groups in the number of days spent in the community. This finding is difficult to interpret because movement from the community could be due to institutionalization or death.

Finally, Montgomery and Borgatta (1987, 1989) found no differences between the control group and the respite treatment groups in nursing home placement. For the subsample of elders who did move to the nursing home, there was a difference between the treatment and control groups in the number of days elders resided in the nursing home. The effect of the treatment differed by the relationship of the caregiver to the elder. In the group of elders cared for by adult children, there appeared to be a delay in nursing home placement. In contrast, among the elders cared for by a spouse, the number of days the elder spent in a nursing home was greater for the treatment group than for the control group (Montgomery, 1988a). Taken together, these findings suggest differential effects of respite care on caregivers in different situations.

A recent reanalysis of the data that capitalizes on its longitudinal nature further supports the notion that effects of respite care may depend on characteristics of the individuals of the caregivers' situations. This multivariate analysis using event history techniques revealed a significant relationship between nursing home placement and eligibility for program respite services when caregivers were followed over time (Montgomery & Kosloski, 1990). Controlling for key demographic, attitudinal, and situational characteristics, receiving respite care was found to have a positive relationship with nursing home placement.

Although this finding may be alarming to individuals interested in reducing costs of long-term care, it is consistent with earlier findings from the New York respite demonstration project (FLTC, 1983). That report suggested that respite care in an institution was associated with nursing home placement. One plausible explanation to account for this pattern is that the positive experience of respite and the corresponding relief from caregiving tasks encouraged caregivers to share their difficult load with other qualified formal providers. That is, respite provided a testing ground for placement and, when experienced positively, led to permanent placement.

A second but not necessarily mutually exclusive explanation for this pattern is that the use of respite services, when available, may be a stepping stone along the caregiving career that immediately precedes institutionalization. From this perspective, respite may be seen as appropriate and beneficial in the critical period before placement, but it may not be a deterrent. In fact, it is possible that the relief of respite care in this critical period may actually accelerate institutionalization.

In any case, the evidence regarding outcomes of respite care is disappointing, if the criteria of monetary savings are used to measure success of respite services. However, several factors deserve consideration before respite is dismissed as a nice but low priority service for public funding, likened by one expert to "free haircuts" (Callahan, 1989, p. 5). A negative response is premature given the limited number of studies completed to date and the myriad of research, service delivery, and ethical issues that remain unaddressed. It is important to remember that the limitations in knowledge affect our ability to draw both negative and positive conclusions about the efficacy of respite care.

Research Issues

Given the widespread belief of service providers and policymakers that respite care does assist caregivers of functionally impaired older people developing adequate data about its efficacy as a support service is imperative. The small number of controlled design studies completed to date should not be considered an adequate base for drawing definitive conclu-sions about the relative merits of respite care. Rather, these studies should be viewed as sources of guidance for future research, which is necessary to advance our knowledge.

Clarity and Intensity of Respite Services

One barrier to an adequate test of the impact of respite services rests in the sheer diversity of services that have been considered respite services. The impact of an institutional respite program is quite likely to be substan-tially different than that of an in-home service or that of respite care provided through the informal network. To date, insufficient attention has been given to accurately describing the service intervention and/or describing differences in impact between services (Lawton et al., 1989; Montgomery & Borgatta, 1989). Future studies need to carefully describe the type of services delivered, as well as the intensity of the service, so that accurate conclusions can be drawn. The impact of respite care may not be uniform for all types of respite services. Furthermore, the impact of services may depend on elder and family characteristics and the quality of services (Applebaum & Phillips, 1990; Lawton et al., 1989; Montgomery, Kosloski, & Borgatta, 1989; Wallace, 1990). Attention also needs to be given to other services that families might use as alternate forms of respite care. Because alternate forms can include informal as well as formal services, this description can become very complicated.

Representativeness of Samples

A second consideration for future research must be sampling proce-dures and sample composition. Previous studies have relied on clinical and self-selected convenience samples, which are not likely to be repre-sentative of the families that could potentially benefit from respite care. Indeed, past studies have tended to include families with higher income and educational levels than do national samples of caregivers (Lawton et al., 1989). Also, minority groups have been underrepresented among all studies of caregivers, a fact that appears to hold true for studies of respite care as well.

An equally serious problem for the assessment of respite is the tendency of families to wait until a crisis point to seek and use any type of support service (George, 1988; Montgomery & Borgatta, 1987). This fact can have implications for the accurate assessment of respite services. If families do not use services until a crisis point, the preventive goal of respite may never be realized. The lack of observed impact on families in previous studies may be due in part to their long delay in seeking help. There may be little potential for delaying or preventing nursing home placement if support services are sought too late in the caregiving career (Montgomery & Borgatta, 1987).

In contrast, if studies include families with very limited needs (e.g., the elder has a low imparment level or caregiver stress is very low), then the impact of respite care may not be easily documented. Lawton et al. (1989) suggest that some threshold level of high need may be required for respite intervention to affect subjective well-being. These two opposing possibilities point to a major issue for future research: factors affecting utilization.

Utilization

Apart from the obvious dearth of controlled design studies to test the impact of any service intervention, the biggest barrier to the assessment of respite's impact has been the patterns of utilization. In both the Phila-delphia-based study (Lawton et al., 1989) and the Seattle-based study (Montgomery & Borgatta, 1987), the investigators reported substantial lack of use of intervention services by persons in the treatment groups.

Lawton et al. (1989) reported that only half of persons eligible for the experimental program used these additional resources. Montgomery (1986) reported that 36% of eligible caregivers used no project services, and on the average, those who did use services used only 63% of the resources available to them. This pattern has also been reported by George (1988). This lack of utilization by eligible caregivers is an important research issue for future studies to address.

First, the low-use pattern substantially decreases the likelihood of observing statistically significant differences between treatment groups and control groups in the respite studies because it substantially decreases the strength of the intervention. This is especially true when large portions of the control group are receiving some service that functions as respite outside the program under study, as was the case in the study conducted by Lawton and his colleagues. In truth, the studies to date have been weak tests of the possible impact of respite.

Also, the clinical or volunteer nature of the samples used in previous studies has precluded consideration of persons who do not even seek respite services. The factors affecting their decision are likely to be different from the factors affecting the decisions of persons who seek but then do not use the services. Together these considerations underscore that studying service use is crucial to investigating service effectiveness. As Wallace (1990) reminds us, availability of services is only one factor affecting use. Several other factors, including convenience, accessibility, quality, and acceptability, must be considered.

FUTURE DIRECTIONS

Conceptual Issues in the Study of Utilization

The patterns of respite care use are important to study, not only because lack of utilization can prevent accurate assessment of impact but also because patterns of use may provide valuable knowledge and insight concerning the needs of caregiving families, the appropriate design and delivery of respite services, and issues of who should be targeted.

Although little is known about the correlates of respite use, a few recent studies have focused specifically on the use of services by caregivers (Caserta, Lund, Wright, & Redburn, 1987; Gwyther, 1990). Additionally, a much larger literature has developed on service use among the elderly in general (Krout, 1983a; McCaslin, 1988; Wallace, 1990; Wolinsky, Moseley, & Coe, 1986). Home care use has been a particular focus (see Benjamin, 1990). For the most part, the work in this area has been guided by the Anderson and Newman model (1973), which advances three classes of variables as predictors of service use: predisposing, enabling, and need. Future investigations of respite care would do well to build on this literature to learn more about the predictors of respite use.

Defining Need

Of special interest are variables that define need. In the past, numerous need indicators have been advanced, including functional status, diagnosis, and perceived health status. Yet, these more objective measures of need have not accounted for as much variance in service use as measures of perceived or self-reported need. In the study conducted by Caserta et al. (1987) that focused on caregivers' participation in Alzheimer support groups, the most common reason given for not using respite was a perceived lack of immediate need.

Perceived need or the perception that a service is a source of assistance for one's own situation entails two judgments. First is the judgment that assistance or support of some sort is required in one's current situation or status. Second is the judgment that a particular service, either a specific program or a generic service such as respite, will provide that assistance or support. That is, the second element of perceived need is really a judgment as to whether a service will be "useful" to one's situation. Hence, need as most frequently defined by providers—in terms of impairment levels, health status, or stress—is not necessarily need as perceived by caregivers. McCaslin (1988) notes that self-reported need for a service appears to express a view that a given program is personally useful rather than indicating actual or intended use. This latter dimension of "perceived need" is closely related to knowledge or awareness of services.

To judge a program useful or not useful, needed or unneeded, a caregiver would have to have some awareness of the services provided and the way in which they are provided. For example: Where is the service delivered? How much will it cost? How well trained are the workers? Is it difficult to arrange for? Are workers dependable? Are workers trustworthy? This knowledge of services does not necessarily have to be accurate for a caregiver to arrive at a judgment of need, but it would seem that accuracy would improve the caregiver's ability to make a judgment.

In the past, although knowledge has consistently been one of the best predictors of service use of all types, measurements of knowledge have been vague or ambiguous (McCaslin, 1988; Wallace, 1990). Among the elderly, knowledge of a service or a program name, such as Meals on Wheels, is seldom accompanied by an awareness of which services are actually provided or where such programs can be found (Krout, 1983a, 1983b). Because *knowledge* of a service (or lack of it) is likely to influence an individual's *perception of need* for that service, the two concepts, as most frequently measured in previous research, are not distinct concepts. McCaslin (1988) suggests that need and knowledge are "best understood as representing a general positive orientation to the formal service system which is perceived as a known resource with relevance to the individual's current or future situation" (p. 597).

Hence, although self-perception of need and service knowledge have consistently accounted for a large amount of explained variance in use, operational measures of these concepts have been too vague to predict usage rates or to guide the development of programs that will actually be used by their intended clientele. Information is needed about the relationship between service delivery characteristics and caregivers' perceptions of perceived need and, ultimately, their use or nonuse of services (Krout,

1983a; McCaslin, 1988; Wallace 1990). In this way, findings can be used
to identify or modify and target specific service delivery characteristics.

Factors Influencing Use

The general literature on home care services, as well as the more limited
literature on respite care, suggests a large number of factors that could
potentially affect respite use and require simultaneous investigation.
These variables can be grouped under three general headings: (a) demographic and background characteristics, (b) factors that determine the
timing of respite use or the point in a caregiving career that the caregiver
"perceives need," and (c) aspects of service delivery that are likely to affect
respite use.

Demographic and Background Variables. The profile of respite users
presented earlier does not address the more important question of how
representative such samples are of potential users. Indeed, there is evidence that users of respite services are a select subpopulation that tends
to have a higher income and education level than the larger population of
potential users and tends to include high proportions of whites and low
proportions of minority groups (Lawton et al., 1989). Any effort to evaluate the efficacy of a respite program must focus on the total population of
caregivers who could benefit from respite care rather than the subpopulation from which most samples have been drawn. This total population
should include users of services, seekers of services (e.g., persons who
seek help but do not use it), and nonusers (e.g., persons who do not even
inquire about help).

Factors Affecting When Respite Is Sought and Used. As previously noted,
the perception of need for a service and, ultimately, the decision to seek
the service involves a judgment as to whether one's condition or situation
requires some form of assistance. The literature suggests several factors
that would create a condition of need, including measures of health, levels
of assistance, measures of burden, and the availability of alternative
sources of help from the formal system and informal support network.
These measures might all be conceived of as factors that determine the
"time" that need is recognized in a caregiving situation.

Aspects of Service Delivery. The least studied variables hypothesized
to affect service use are aspects of service delivery and clients' percep-

tions of the utility of the service. It is not unreasonable to expect that, like any product on the market, services that do not appear useful will not be used. Experience with respite programs and general marketing knowledge suggest that two factors are most likely to affect a client's perception of service utility: the *quality* and *convenience* of available services. In turn, these two factors are likely to be influenced by a number of other aspects: whether the caregiver is a professional or a volunteer, the amount of training of workers, the extent of advertising and outreach attempts, the cost of respite to the family, the type of setting, the availability of transportation, the flexibility of scheduling, and the reliability and consistency of workers (Applebaum & Phillips, 1990; Gwyther, 1990; Wallace, 1990).

Including these variables in any future investigation will make it possible to assess the program design (as experienced by the lay public) and its influence on respite use. This direction in research will be very important because program characteristics are much more amenable to change than are individual attitudes. Characteristics could conceivably be designed to minimize resistance to using respite services.

As the discussion above illustrates, the investigation of utilization patterns and factors affecting use will not only enhance our ability to judge the merits of respite programs, but should have implications for the design and delivery of services.

Rethinking Targeting

Closely tied to the investigation of use patterns is the issue of targeting. Because respite has been put forth as one of a constellation of home- and community-based services intended to reduce institutionalization, it has usually been targeted to families most vulnerable to nursing home placement, in which vulnerability is usually determined by the functional level of the elder. Yet few data support the assumption that the most impaired are the most vulnerable. More important, the practice of making respite available only to those close to or at a crisis point may actually work against the viability of respite services as the preventive force they are intended to be. The appropriate targeting of services remains a question worthy of serious investigation and will likely rest on greater investigation of use patterns.

Similarly, the ideal or desired forms of respite services will remain unknown until greater knowledge of use patterns is obtained. The flexibility that families need to meet their changing needs is likely to require a continuum of services. Unfortunately, because respite services have been limited in most communities and states and offered through demonstration programs, respite has usually been offered in a single form with little flexibility. Greater knowledge about the relationships between individual and family characteristics and the characteristics of services they use is required to design services that will meet the needs of a wide range of caregiving families as their circumstances change.

Facing Ethical Issues and Pragmatic Dilemmas

In addition to focusing on issues of research design, factors affecting use, and targeting practices, attention must also be given to important ethical and value questions surrounding respite. In particular, scholars, practitioners, and policymakers must directly confront underlying assumptions about the purpose of respite and expectations for outcomes of respite use. Like other forms of home care, respite care has been subjected to the "cost-effectiveness trap" described by Weissert (1985). Rather than being promoted as a service necessary for the well-being of family caregivers, respite has been developed and advanced as a vehicle for saving public dollars while at the same time benefiting family members. Such an argument is pragmatic in times of limited resources, and it is nonproblematic as long as evidence can be produced that attests to the respite's success in meeting both monetary and human needs. However, when evidence questions that success, there is likely to be much debate, as evidenced in the exchange published in *The Gerontologist* in 1989 (see Callahan, 1989; Lawton et al. 1989; Letters to the Editor, 1989).

This exchange highlighted several related and critical questions associated with most forms of nonmedical long-term care services. Is it appropriate to expect that a single service offered in isolation from other support services can make a major impact on caregiving attitudes and behaviors? Given the extended time over which many families care for an elder, respite may only be beneficial for a short period and incapable of altering patterns of caregiving or institutionalization.

If this is the case, is satisfaction with a service or enhanced well-being for a short, but critical, period a sufficient or appropriate reason to make such services available? This question is indeed a values question embedded in individual and societal beliefs about family, individual, and societal responsibilities. There is no doubt that current public policy would affirm the necessity and moral obligation to provide food or medicine for the well-being of older people despite potential public costs.

However, no such consensus exists about the necessity of supports to assure or enhance the probability that family members are nonburdened as they attend to the care of their older, frail relatives. Before respite care is dismissed as a nonbeneficial, expensive service, attention should be given to the assumptions underlying such a dismissal. Should cost savings be the criterion for judgment? Should long-term effects be expected? Are short-term human benefits affordable? What are the relative costs and benefits for family members versus the costs and benefits for the public? How do we distribute the burdens of care for the chronically ill? These are difficult and complex questions that require serious attention as respite care is considered within the context of long-term care policy.

CONCLUSION

In summary, like other forms of home care for the chronically ill, respite care has been subjected to the cost-effectiveness trap. It has been developed primarily as small pilot programs and demonstration projects, with the expectation that it will reduce costs of long-term care. Due to lack of consistent financing, respite has not, in reality, been widely available, and its merits have not been adequately assessed. As researchers and policymakers have studied respite, the primary outcomes of interest have been caregiver burden, caregiver well-being, and the reduction of institutionalization.

To date, the evidence of positive outcomes is gloomy. Yet the number of studies completed is extremely small, and all have suffered from some serious limitations, including lack of clear definitions, lack of controlled design studies, and low utilization. The low use of available services is especially problematic, and it is tied to issues of adequacy, quality, convenience, and acceptability. Without more substantial knowledge about the factors that influence respite use, it is impossible to assess its true merits. At this point, there is insufficient evidence to argue for or against respite services, but there is ample evidence to argue for more carefully designed studies of respite use and impact. It is anticipated that such studies will help guide the development and targeting of respite services in the future.

4

Direct Services for Family Caregivers

Next Steps for Public Policy

VERNON L. GREENE
PATRICIA D. COLEMAN

INTRODUCTION

About 4.2 million Americans provide care to an impaired spouse or parent, and 2.6 million of them are the primary caregiver (Stone & Kemper, 1989). As the U.S. population ages, the incidence and prevalence of older people with impairments will increase dramatically over the next several decades. The number and proportion of people involved in family caregiving will increase commensurately. This population appears to be at a substantial degree of elevated risk for symptoms of psychological stress, disruption of social functioning (including employment), and decrements in physical health, some of which very likely arise from the caregiving role.

Many caregivers live lives of great pathos and self-sacrifice, often exhibiting a quiet but genuine heroism. They thus seem both vulnerable and particularly deserving of help and support from the broader society. This situation has led to a growing interest in clarifying the needs of these caregivers and developing intervention strategies designed to meet them. A more calculated policy interest in the plight of family caregivers arises from the recognition that the budgetary costs of replacing their voluntary efforts, should they flag under increasing demographic and social pressures, will be enormous.

In this chapter, we begin by reviewing findings of the negative consequences for caregivers in the areas of mental and physical health, as well as employment, and income security. We follow this with brief reviews of services developed to respond to these needs, concentrating primarily on therapeutic, supportive, and educational services. We conclude with an assessment of where we stand, in a practical sense, with these intervention models and suggest some future directions for development that seem promising.

NEGATIVE CONSEQUENCES OF CAREGIVING

Providing long-term care to elderly relatives is associated with a variety of negative consequences for caregivers (Horowitz, 1985). The physical, emotional, and work-related burdens associated with the caregiving role have received considerable attention in the recent gerontological literature, and most of the direct services to caregivers appear to be directed at these concerns.

Physical Health and Caregiving

The relationship of health outcomes to caregiving is important both in itself and inasmuch as it affects the caregiver's capacity to provide ongoing care to the older person with functional impairments. Providing care to frail elderly persons can involve a considerable amount of physical labor, supervision, and vigilance. Heavy lifting and turning, frequent bedding changes, dressing, toileting, bathing, and an increased amount of cleaning and laundry can put physical strain on caregivers. Most caregivers to the frail elderly are middle aged or young-old. The average age of the informal caregiver is 57; however, more than one third are over 65 and 10% are over age 75 (Special Committee on Aging, 1988). Thus the physical stresses of caregiving may make these older individuals an especially vulnerable group, exacerbating already existing chronic illnesses such as arthritis and osteoporosis (Sommers & Shields, 1987) and hypertension (Crossman et al., 1981). Furthermore, the well-established link between chronic stress and the development of physical illnesses such as hypertension and cardio- vascular and respiratory disease suggests that caregivers may have higher rates of physical illness because they are chronically subjected to the stresses of caregiving.

Several studies have investigated health-related outcomes associated with providing care to the functionally impaired elderly. Illness effects are assessed using measures of self-reported health, presence of particular illnesses, use of health and medical services, and objective physiological measures (Schulz, Visintainer, & Williamson, 1990). In general, caregivers report poorer physical health relative to their age-matched peers from random community samples (Haley, Levine, Brown, Berry, & Hughes, 1987; Stone et al., 1987). In several studies, caregivers report a variety of chronic illnesses, such as hypertension, arthritis, back pain, cardiac disease, cataracts, circulatory and gastrointestinal disturbances, and hypochondriasis (Archbold, 1983; Baillie, Norbeck, & Barnes, 1988; Busse, 1976; Crossman et al., 1981; Dellasega, 1989; Fengler & Goodrich, 1979). Caregivers also report chronic illnesses more frequently than noncaregiver comparison groups (Haley et al., 1987; Pruchno & Potashnik, 1989).

Stone et al. (1987) found that caregivers perceived themselves to be in poorer health than their age-matched peers in the U.S. population in 1982. Haley et al. (1987) found that people caring for a demented relative reported poorer self-rated health, more chronic illnesses, and more use of prescription medications than control subjects matched on selected attributes such as age, sex, race, and marital status. These observed differences persisted with statistical controls for education and income.

Pruchno and Potashnik (1989) found that women caregivers 65 years of age or older who were providing assistance to spouses with Alzheimer's disease were more likely to report their health as fair or poor compared to general population norms for existing databases, controlling for age and gender. In contrast, George and Gwyther (1986) found no evidence that their sample of 510 caregivers rated their health as worse than random community samples.

Although these studies suggest that caregivers perceive their general health as worse relative to the general population, one cannot draw firm conclusions because the effect of income may be confounded with the perception of health across the studies (Schulz et al., 1990). For example, the caregivers in the study by Stone et al. (1987) may report poorer health because they have lower incomes than their age peers in the U.S. population. Similarly, the somewhat higher socioeconomic status (as measured by household income and perceived economic status) of the caregiver sample studied by George and Gwyther (1986) may account for the finding of no differences in self-rated health between the caregiver group and community sample.

A number of studies point out that caregivers link their perceived deteriorating health to providing care (Barusch, 1988; Chenoweth & Spencer, 1986; Dellasega, 1989; Koopman-Boyden & Wells, 1979; Pratt et al., 1985). Snyder and Keefe (1985) reported that about 70% of the caregivers they studied cited a decline in physical health because of their caregiving role. Frankfather, Smith, and Caro (1981) found that some family members attributed specific physical ailments that they had developed (e.g., hypertension) to their caregiving responsibilities for community-dwelling elderly with disabilities. Noelker and Wallace (1985) and Young and Kahana (1989) have noted that caregivers, especially wives, daughters, and daughters-in-law, experience physical declines due to the care they provide.

Gaynor (1989) described the changes in health over time among wives caring for husbands with disabilities. After 24 to 32 months of providing in-home care, caregivers reported health problems that were caused by or related to their caring tasks. Furthermore, physicians verified the wives' assessment that their poor health was due to the stress of providing care. They described themselves as "unhealthy" and "never really feeling well." They were chronically fatigued from sleep interruptions and frequently took tranquilizers and aspirin preparations; some had developed stress-related disorders, such as hypertension and colitis, requiring medical surveillance.

A recent study by Kiecolt-Glaser et al. (1987) showed that the chronic stress of providing care to Alzheimer's patients appeared related to poorer immune responses in caregivers relative to matched controls. These findings could not be ascribed to the effects of nutrition, sleep, or other variables.

As noted, caregivers report a variety of chronic health problems, and a few studies have documented that these illnesses are more prevalent in caregiving samples than in matched controls. For example, 44 primary caregivers having daily responsibility for an elderly relative reported more chronic illnesses than a similar comparison group in the study by Haley and colleagues (1987). Pruchno and Potashnik (1989) found that caregiving spouses had higher rates of diabetes, arthritis, ulcers, and anemia relative to those sampled in large random community databases.

Studies examining patterns of using health and medical care services among caregivers have reported conflicting findings. In general, caregivers do not appear to use more services than the general population (George & Gwyther, 1986; Kiecolt-Glaser et al., 1987; Pruchno & Potashnik, 1989), although they report higher rates of chronic illness and psychotropic medication use (Haley et al., 1987; Pruchno & Potashnik, 1989). On the other hand, at least one study (Haley et al., 1987) found that caregivers to Alzheimer's patients reported a greater number of recent physician visits than matched controls.

Employment and Caregiving

Substantial numbers of informal caregivers combine employment with elder care responsibilities (Stone et al., 1987), and this trend is expected to grow considerably in the coming years as a result of increases in the labor force participation of women, an aging workforce, and longer life expectancies (Scharlach, 1989). Recent research has focused on the impact that caregiving has on employment and the adjustments made in the personal and work lives of caregivers with dependent care responsibilities (Anastas, Gibeau, & Larson, 1990; Brody & Schoonover, 1986; Neal, Chapman, Ingersoll-Dayton, Emlen, & Boise, 1990; Scharlach & Boyd, 1989). The conflicts and pressures experienced by employed caregivers and their potential impact on the caregiver's work performance have made elder care an emerging corporate concern (Creedon, 1988), leading some to speculate that elder care may be the employee benefit of the 1990s (Creedon, 1988; Friedman, 1986).

Estimates vary on the extent to which caregivers combine employment with elder care responsibilities. Most investigators report that an estimated 20% to 30% of workers have elder care responsibilities (Anastas et al., 1990; Creedon, 1988; Neal et al., 1990; Scharlach, 1989; Scharlach & Boyd, 1989). Most employees who also provide elder care are women (Friedman, 1986). These studies survey specific employers (Scharlach & Boyd, 1989) and often have low response rates (Anastas et al., 1990; Neal et al., 1990).

Only two recently published studies provide more representative estimates of the extent to which caregivers combine work and elder care. The first national estimates were reported by Stone et al. (1987), using data from the 1982 National Long Term Care Survey and Informal Caregivers Survey. They found that 31% of informal caregivers for noninstitutionalized older people with disabilities held full- or part-time jobs. A more recent study by Stone and Kemper (1989), using data from the 1984 National Long Term Care Survey, reports much lower estimates of the prevalence of combining employment and elder care responsibilities. They estimated that just under 2% of those who are employed full-time have caregiving responsibilities, much lower than the earlier estimates. However, they note that their definition of help is much more restrictive than the one used in other studies and that their estimate only applies to full-time workers. If the definition of care is restricted to help with only Activities of Daily Living (ADL) or Instrumental Activities of Daily

Living (IADL), then the numbers of children and spouses providing elder care while employed may be much smaller.

The type and amount of services provided by working caregivers to elderly relatives suggest a considerable commitment to their role. Studies by corporations and researchers indicate that caregivers spend, on average, between 6 and 16 hours per week providing care to functionally-impaired relatives and friends (Anastas et al., 1990; Creedon, 1988; Gibeau & Anastas, 1989; Scharlach, 1989). Furthermore, the amount of time spent on caregiving tasks varies with the type and level of cognitive impairment, living arrangements, and functional impairment of the care recipient (Anastas et al., 1990; Brody & Schoonover, 1986; Scharlach, 1989). Some employed caregivers report spending as much as 35 hours per week in caregiving tasks (Creedon, 1988). Employed caregivers also provide the same type of services as their nonemployed counterparts, such as personal care, instrumental, and financial support (Creedon, 1988). The types of assistance most frequently provided include emotional reassurance and companionship, transportation, home repairs, and financial support (Anastas et al., 1990; Brody & Schoonover, 1986; Creedon, 1988; Scharlach, 1989; Scharlach & Boyd, 1989).

Several studies have noted the conflicts experienced by working caregivers and have documented the adjustments workers make in their personal and professional lives to accommodate their roles as caregivers. Employment status has been linked to the likelihood of placing an elderly relative in a nursing home (Scharlach, 1989), and some caregivers, predominantly women, are more likely to leave the labor force because of the demands of caregiving (Brocklehurst, Morris, Andrews, Richards, & Laycock, 1981; Muurinen, 1986; Special Committee on Aging, 1988; Stephens & Christianson, 1986; Stone et al., 1987). The tendency for females to leave the labor force to take on caregiving obligations for children and elders is linked to women's lower wages, retirement benefits, asset income, loss of social networks, and their poor economic position in older age (Stone & Kemper, 1989).

Furthermore, work performance can be negatively affected. In a recent employee survey of 1,898 employed caregivers, 40% of employees reported that caregiving interfered with work activities, and more than 40% had taken vacation time to assist with an elderly relative (Scharlach & Boyd, 1989). One third of caregiving employees had left work early at least once, and approximately 15% had arrived late to work or had to extend a break or lunch.

Friedman (1986) reported that employed women with elder care responsibilities experienced stress, depression, and financial strain, and they
used benefits such as sick leave, personal time off, and vacation time to
provide care to others rather than to maintain their own mental health and
well-being. Other problems that have been reported include increased
rates of tardiness and absenteeism, time off during the workday, work
interruptions, excessive personal phone calls, anticipated job turnover, time
off without pay, adjusting work schedules, reducing work hours, using
vacation time and personal leave to care for an elder, increased turnover,
morale problems, and missed career opportunities (Anastas et al., 1990;
Azarnoff & Scharlach, 1988; Brody, 1985; Magnus, 1988; Older Women's
League, 1989; Scharlach & Boyd, 1989; Winfield, 1987).

The documentation of these problems and the potential effect on work
performance has established the corporate rationale for involvement in
elder care. These efforts range from the provision of information to actual
changes in company policy and employment practices. Information and
referral services appear to be the most common corporate response to the
needs of employed caregivers. These services include worksite-sponsored
lunchtime seminars, caregiver fairs, telephone referrals, availability of
video- and audiocassettes, and information handbooks on a variety of elder
care topics, such as normal physical aging, financial and legal concerns,
caregiver wellness, and community services (Azarnoff & Scharlach, 1988;
Dusell & Roman, 1989; Friedman, 1986; Ingersoll-Dayton, Chapman, &
Neal, 1990). These services are often part of the employer's Employee
Assistance Program (Creedon, 1988). In January 1988, IBM instituted a
nationwide network of counselors (Eldercare Consultation and Referral
Service, ECRS) to provide personalized consultation to its employees
regarding elder care options and referrals to local service providers
(Halcrow, 1988).

On-site support programs have been initiated by several major corporations (Creedon, 1988). For example, Con Edison, Ciba-Geigy, and Mobil
have contracted with case management and counseling organizations to
provide seminars on aging and service delivery for their caregiver employees (Friedman, 1986). Efforts to provide on-site, employer-sponsored,
adult day-care centers are in the planning stages at several corporate sites
(Dusell & Roman, 1989), although they are still not commonly available.
At least two major corporations, Wang and Stride-Rite, have opened
on-site elder day-care facilities (Azarnoff & Scharlach, 1988; Dusell &
Roman, 1989; Shapiro, 1990). Some companies offer on-site, professionally led support groups (Dusell & Roman, 1989; Ingersoll-Dayton et al.,

1990), whereas others hold off-site groups at the end of the workday (Dusell & Roman, 1989).

Employer-sponsored financial assistance to caregivers is available, but limited. Some employers allow employees to purchase long-term care insurance at group rates (Dusell & Roman, 1989), including nursing home fees (Azarnoff & Scharlach, 1988), and one supermarket chain provides cash benefits to reimburse employees with elder care expenses (Dusell & Roman, 1989). A few companies contract for respite services and provide financial support for the use of the service on a cost-matching basis with their employees (Friedman, 1986). Finally, some larger companies (e.g., Travelers) have set up flexible spending accounts through employer-sponsored dependent-care assistance programs. These allow workers to set aside a certain amount of pretax dollars for elder care expenses (Shapiro, 1990). In some instances, the employer makes matching contributions. However, the elderly person receiving care must meet the tax-law definition of a dependent, and this restriction limits use of the service (Friedman, 1986).

A frequent corporate response offers employees work scheduling options, such as flextime and unpaid leaves of absence (Azarnoff & Scharlach, 1988; Creedon, 1988). For example, AT&T and its major unions allow workers to take up to 1 year of unpaid leave for a sick relative, and Remington Products, Inc., reimburses employees for half the amount of hiring someone to come into the home for a few hours so they can go out (Shapiro, 1990). Statutory provisions for family leave, whether initiated at the state or federal level, have not been successful. An analysis of 28 states that had either passed or initiated family leave bills in 1987 showed that only four had passed bills and only one of those included elder care in its provision (Wisensale & Allison, 1988).

In summary, it appears that major corporations with substantial resources are the ones taking the lead in addressing elder care issues in the workplace. Indeed, Magnus (1988) has noted that despite considerable corporate awareness of the elder care issue, most employers are reluctant to provide benefits; historically, providing any new employee benefits is usually resisted (Creedon, 1988). Yet, as the literature shows, family issues have relevance to job performance. When elder care or child care problems arise at home, time, energy, and resources must be found to manage them. Often, time and energy, are taken from the job and directed to family and home, which can be translated into corporate costs (Creedon, 1988).

However, many employers are responding. Findings of absenteeism, tardiness, lost productivity, misuse of company time, excessive personal phone calls, and so on among working caregivers are being addressed in some fashion by new company initiatives such as case management services, information and referral programs, support groups, and flexible scheduling. Furthermore, these services are reported to be most helpful to employed caregivers (Anastas et al., 1990; Azarnoff & Scharlach, 1988; Creedon, 1988; Gibeau & Anastas, 1989; Scharlach, 1989; Scharlach & Boyd, 1989). Adult day care and respite care have also been cited as being very helpful (Anastas et al., 1990; Gibeau & Anastas, 1989), but these services are not widely available and tend to be expensive (Friedman, 1986).

Mental Health Consequences of Caregiving

Emotional strain is generally felt to be the most prevalent and difficult aspect of caregiving to deal with (Cantor, 1983; Horowitz, 1985). The literature suggests that caregivers of the elderly experience considerable psychiatric morbidity, such as depression, demoralization, anger, and anxiety (Baillie et al., 1988; Barusch, 1988; Fengler & Goodrich, 1979; Gallagher, Rose, Rivera, Lovett, & Thompson, 1989; Haley et al., 1987; Jones & Vetter, 1984). One study (Ekberg, 1986) has found that caregiving spouses manifest the symptoms of burnout in its first two stages (emotional and physical exhaustion; resentment, negativism, and cynicism). Caregiver stress and mental illness are risk factors associated with elder abuse (Kosberg, 1988). Females are more likely than male caregivers to report depressive symptoms (Anthony-Bergstone, Zarit, & Gatz, 1988; Fitting, Rabins, Lucas, & Eastham, 1986), and elevated rates of psychotropic drug use by caregivers have also been reported (Clipp & George, 1990; George & Gwyther, 1986; Pruchno & Potashnik, 1989).

A recent review of the empirical literature (Schulz et al., 1990) finds good evidence that caregivers, on average, exhibit greater levels of psychiatric symptoms (for example, depression and demoralization) on self-report measures than appropriate comparison groups. There is also some support for increased clinical psychiatric illness requiring professional intervention among some caregivers (Cohen & Eisdorfer, 1988; Gallagher et al., 1989). In addition, depression in caregivers has been found to predict declines in their physical health over a 6-month period, suggesting a "wearing out" over time as caregivers neglect to care properly for themselves (Pruchno, Kleban, Michaels, & Dempsey, 1990).

Despite much evidence suggesting increased adverse mental health effects as a consequence of caregiving, caution is advised in interpreting the significance of these findings for at least two reasons (Schulz et al.,

1990). First, the samples on which these studies are based are likely to be nonrepresentative of the general caregiving population. Because many respondents are recruited from support groups and local media solicitations, strong selection biases may be operating to favor the more distressed end of the caregiving spectrum. Second, there is no distinction between normal caregiving stress and clinical psychiatric episodes. Because most of the caregiving literature is cross-sectional in nature, we do not know the extent to which stress may precipitate major depressive disorders.

EDUCATIONAL PROGRAMS/ SUPPORT GROUPS/OUTREACH

Most of the tasks associated with caregiving, such as providing direct assistance, helping with intrapersonal and interpersonal tasks and conflicts, and interacting with the broader health and social services networks (Clark & Rakowski, 1983; Horowitz, 1985), are amenable to education and support group efforts. This may explain, in part, why most services to caregivers seem to involve interventions with an education or social support component. A few of these services have concentrated on outreach strategies, such as training clergy and volunteers to locate and provide information to caregivers (Halpert, 1988; Sheehan, 1989). Others include the development of telephone networks between caregivers to encourage informal support systems (Goodman & Pynoos, 1988, 1990). However, most interventions emphasize coping and adaptive strategies to help caregivers gain social support (the effect of which is to moderate stress effects), help ameliorate the morbid reactions described above as a consequence of unmet emotional needs, and help caregivers remain in their roles longer to reduce use of more expensive formal services (Doty, 1986).

Most of the education/support groups are time limited, and they usually focus on practical issues (e.g., information about the care receiver's condition, processes of aging, self-care, home care skills, financial/legal issues), feelings (e.g., encouragement of various emotional reactions to caregiving and how to cope constructively with them), and developing both formal and informal support systems (Toseland & Rossiter, 1989). Most participants are caring for an elder with Alzheimer's disease or other cognitive or neurological impairment (Aronson, Levin, & Lipkowitz, 1984; Barnes, Raskind, Scott, & Murphy, 1981; Chiverton & Caine, 1989; Friss, 1990; Haley, 1989; Haley et al., 1987; Heagerty, Dunn, & Watson, 1988;

La Vorgna, 1979; Lazarus, Stafford, Cooper, Cohler, & Dysken, 1981; Lipkin & Faude, 1987; Pratt, Nay, Ladd, & Heagerty, 1989; Steuer & Clark, 1982; Toseland & Rossiter, 1989). The remaining groups are usually caring for elders with nonspecified illnesses but chronic impairments (Cohen, 1983; Crossman et al., 1981; Greene & Monahan, 1987, 1989; Johnson & Maguire, 1989; Montgomery & Borgatta, 1989; Rodway, Elliot, & Sawa, 1987; Safford, 1980).

Education and support group interventions tend to be enthusiastically endorsed by the participants (Chappell, 1990). Caregivers have reported reductions in burden, anxiety, and depression, positive personal changes in coping with the caregiving role, increase in informal support networks, improved intrafamilial and staff communication, and greater understanding of the elder's problems and the caregiver's own needs (Barnes et al., 1981; Chiverton & Caine, 1989; Glosser & Wexler, 1985; Greene & Monahan, 1989; Johnson & Maguire, 1989; Montgomery & Borgatta, 1989; Rodway et al., 1987; Toseland, Rossiter, & Labrecque, 1989). Some studies have suggested that services can delay nursing home placement (Greene & Monahan, 1987; Montgomery & Borgatta, 1989), although services may encourage institutional placement among spouse caregivers (Montgomery & Borgatta, 1989).

Although most of the studies report positive outcomes, a recent review of education/support group interventions (Toseland & Rossiter, 1989) notes that these results are often based primarily on clinical impressions, testimonials, and brief nonstandardized evaluation questionnaires. Much more equivocal findings are reported when more rigorous experimental and quasi-experimental designs are used.

Individual/Group Psychotherapy and Training

Psychotherapeutically oriented interventions for caregivers offer individual, group, or family therapy to those caregivers who self-identify as clients and request mental health services (Gallagher, 1985; Peterson & Hanna, 1988; Schmidt & Keyes, 1985). These programs aim to enhance the caregiver's ability to manage specific problems and to teach cognitive/behavioral skills within a time-limited framework. Specific treatment methods, such as cognitive, behavioral, and psychodynamic therapy, have been used in individual work with distressed caregivers, and these have been found to be effective treatments for caregivers with clinically significant depressive reactions (Gallagher, 1985). Much of the recent work has emphasized the use of brief, skill-oriented therapies for caregivers, such as stress and relaxation therapies, behavior management strategies, and collaboration and case-management training skills to improve the coordination of services.

A fairly broad range of skills or task-oriented interventions are represented in the literature. Some have advocated teaching family members to use behavior modification principles with family members who have impairments to reduce the incidence of negative behaviors and to increase positive behaviors, such as self-care and social activities (Haley, 1983; Pinkston & Linsk, 1984). A somewhat more recent focus has been improving the coping skills of caregivers through various training programs, such as assertion training, stress management, problem solving, social skills training, cognitive stimulation, communication training, and time management (Dellasega, 1990; Gendron et al., 1986; Haber, 1984; Quayhagen & Quayhagen, 1989; Robinson, 1988; Shulman & Mandel, 1988). One recent study reported on a program to enhance the involvement of families as caregivers to institutionalized elderly through the development of a training program to teach family members care planning and to familiarize and involve them in the overall operation of the unit (Hansen, Patterson, & Wilson, 1988).

Another theme in the service literature is the development of partnerships or collaborations among families, professionals, and agencies to enhance the coordination of formal and informal services for elders and their caregivers. One way of accomplishing this has been through the training of caregivers in case management techniques, usually by a social worker, to help them function autonomously and alleviate their burden (Silverstein, Gonyea, & King, 1989; Simmons, Ivry, & Seltzer, 1985).

Clearly, most task-oriented training programs for caregivers seem to be aimed at alleviating the burdens of caregiving. The rationale for these programs may come from research showing that tolerance of debility in demented patients is related to the number and types of problems presented by the patient (Gendron et al., 1986), and the likelihood of institutional placement may be increased as a result of behavior problems (Haley, 1983).

CONCLUSION

As is by now clear, the service literature is organized by *type* of intervention, presumably because caregiving has typically been decomposed into discrete tasks and needs, many of them seemingly amenable to particular types of interventions. Indeed, Clark and Rakowski (1983) divide caregiving into 45 separate tasks. The predominant forms of interventions are educational and training programs, which emphasize the acquisition of caregiving skills to alleviate the stresses of caregiving. However, some recent research has shown that a task-based definition of caregiving may be inconsistent with the experience of caregiving (Bowers, 1987; Chenoweth & Spencer, 1986). These studies point out that caregiving is distinguished by its purpose, not by its tasks. In fact, instrumental caregiving, which is studied most by gerontologists and policy analysts, is considered by caregivers to be the least important (Bowers, 1987), and this is often a source of conflict and tension between caregivers and health care professionals (Bowers, 1987, 1988; Hasselkus, 1988).

The incongruence between what caregivers and professional practitioners view as important may account for some of the apparent reluctance of caregivers to use available services (Barusch, 1988; Caserta et al., 1987; Montgomery & Borgatta, 1989). Researchers have noted that caregivers are independent and need to retain a sense of personal control over the caregiving situation. Caregiver comments such as "nobody knows her better than I do," "doctors can't keep up on everything," and "today doesn't look like a very good day," (Hasselkus, 1988) suggest that caregivers have a sense of possessing special knowledge that needs to be a part of the caregiving relationship.

Helping caregivers to manage their role without losing a sense of personal control may be an important component to consider in the design of future programs, which may need to recognize not only a balance of shared tasks but shared perspectives also. Moreover, future programs may be unsuccessful in reducing burden, delaying institutional placement, and reducing costs unless caregivers can be recruited early in their caregiving roles to have an effect on their future behavior (Montgomery & Borgatta, 1989).

Although a growing number and array of services are available to caregivers, such as education/support groups, respite care, and adult day care, it is not clear if these services are meeting the needs of caregivers. Underuse of these formal services and their relative lack of impact on outcomes such as caregiver well-being (Callahan, 1989) raise serious policy questions about continued expansion of community-based long-term care services. Before we conclude that these services produce benefits that are negligible, it is important to recognize that there are few longitudinal perspectives or models of the caregiving process on which to base appropriate interventions.

As noted by Pearlin, Mullan, Semple, and Skaff (1990), research into caregiving has become a flourishing enterprise. But do we know what the needs of caregivers are if we do not have an adequate understanding of the caregiving process? For example, there has been a recent proliferation of services for caregivers to dementia patients, ostensibly because such patients have been historically underserved and their caregivers experience considerable stress (Friss, 1990). However, data from a recent longitudinal study by Montgomery, Kosloski, and Borgatta (1990) suggest that the caregiving experience may be generic and that family members of those with Alzheimer's disease appear to have few unique service needs. A recent study by Fortinsky and Hathaway (1990) suggests that service needs for caregivers can be better assessed if we adopt a career or longitudinal perspective. Few studies have pursued a developmental approach to caregiver needs, yet caregiving is clearly a dynamic process characterized by changing caregiver and care recipient needs. In any event, much is yet to be learned about the caregiving process, and such research may lead to improved interventions.

It seems safe to say that despite a large number of studies, including some with fairly strong research designs, we do not know much in detail about the actual and potential effects of direct services on caregivers. We do know that people are grateful—those who complete group interventions are overwhelmingly positive in their assessment, reporting that their experience has been a positive one and that the service providers are people of remarkable merit.

However, on more objective measures of benefits, results are both more modest and more ambiguous. On standardized assessment measures, there seems a clear tendency to observe *statistically* significant reductions in indicators of psychological distress. However, whether these reductions are large enough to be *clinically* significant has yet to be carefully addressed under standardized clinical protocols in any otherwise rigorous study of which we are aware. In any event, the results are less dramatic than researchers had hoped when they set out to rigorously assess their effects over the past decade.

In our opinion, we are not likely to achieve any major breakthroughs in increasing the effectiveness of the standard modes of service provision: counseling, education, and social support, whether individually or in groups. These are well-understood interventions that have been used and tested in many settings over many years, and the modest effects we observe probably reflect what is possible to achieve. Although these interventions can probably be strengthened somewhat through more longitudinal research into the caregiving process, major gains in effectiveness are not to be expected. Because these interventions can often be accomplished relatively inexpensively, they may still be good candidates for expanded support. We see no evidence of need for specialized medical interventions for caregivers, although the participation of a community health nurse in support and education groups can be a means of casual monitoring. Caregiving responsibilities might also be recognized in routine medical work-ups, and physicians should be educated on the topic.

A further important consideration, and one that must be faced more squarely than it has been, is that little evidence has been found of a large unmet demand for direct caregiver services. A universal experience among those of us who conducted the earlier demonstration studies in this area was finding that when we threw open our doors, the response was by and large underwhelming. Community workers had assured us that large numbers of caregivers in dire need of services would be thronging to our interventions, but they never materialized. Instead, in order to recruit enough subjects to make our statistical tests work on any treatment effect smaller than a miracle, we were required to market the services aggressively, even at a price of zero.

What does this mean? At the most general level, we think it means that the provider community is ahead of family caregiving in its development as an important social fact. Such caregiving is not yet broadly recognized as an institutionalized dimension of social life (as in the case of, say, childrearing) that requires a collective or formal response (but see Brody, 1985). At the moment, family caregiving to elderly relatives is seen as an essentially private matter to be undertaken and resolved idiosyncratically within both the resources and the authority of the family. Only when the family fails dramatically do people regularly turn outside for help, and then only reluctantly and often too late for milder interventions to matter much. Although family caregiving to elderly relatives is becoming a statistical norm, it has not yet evolved as a social norm around which a clear set of shared values, standards, goals, and supporting services can crystallize.

As demographic reality inexorably moves us toward the Golden Age of caregiving, things will follow a predictable course. Much larger numbers of families will find themselves with one or more frail elderly relatives who require care from the family. They in turn will form a critical mass of people who will increasingly see themselves as participating in a distinct social phenomenon, and common experience and common interest will lead to an articulated set of norms, standards, and perceived needs.

At this point I think we will see a rapid buildup in explicit demand for services. This process is already under way, of course, with the provider community, as usual, leading the way. But it is still very early in the game.

For those growing numbers of caregivers who even now see a need for direct services, there are more prosaic reasons for constraints in their use of them. Primary caregivers, especially those with the heaviest burdens of caregiving, are busy people, often operating at the limits of their energy and logistical resources. Although they may want to use a support group or other direct service, they face the practical problems of arranging for transportation and alternative care for the care receiver. Also, the support group or other activity competes for scarce time and energy that could be invested in others to whom they have obligations. The painful irony is that often those whose conflicts are greatest and whose resources are least—and hence who may stand in greatest need of services—are precisely those least able to make use of them.

Can this problem be ameliorated by "packaging" services in mutually enabling combinations? To our knowledge, no published study has systematically addressed the question of service interaction for caregivers. Does the availability of respite services, for example, serve as an enabling factor for caregivers to make greater use of, say, support group services? It seems plausible, but we do not know that it has been clearly demonstrated in the published literature. It may be possible to use the data set assembled by Montgomery and Borgatta (1989) to address this issue, in that its conditions include educational and support group services both with and without respite services. Research that we currently have under way (Monahan, Greene, & Coleman, 1982) indicates that the availability of a secondary family caregiver significantly involved in care substantially increases the use of support group services, whereas a rough proxy for the availability of formal respite services does not.

In addition to issues of enablement in using direct services, there are also questions of predisposition. Extensive anecdotal evidence shows that caregivers resist using direct formal services because they dislike being put in the position of "patient" or "client." Few know better than these caregivers the hateful aspects of dependency, and interventions that cast them into the role of a care receiver rather than the giver are threatening to the very self-image that underlies their role, even though the demands of that role may often feel overwhelming. This propensity may also be a factor in another behavior that has been frustrating to researchers: an apparent propensity for caregivers to deny or understate the levels of stress and burden they are experiencing. We have found that caregivers who are obviously under great stress may give survey responses that mask or all but deny such stress. Some of this, of course, represents the unsinkable personality of some caregivers, but much of it clearly reflects a determined stoicism, or simply a whistling past the graveyard. Low pretest levels on target variables for the intervention make it more difficult to observe larger positive effects of treatment because room for improvement is limited.

Further expansion and enhancement of direct services to caregivers must better meet some of the problems that caregivers experience in using these services. Efforts must be made to reduce the real cost of access to these services by not imposing significant new time and trouble costs on people already short of time and long on trouble. New programs must not impose significant new time and care management demands on people already struggling for some order in their lives. They must offer services in a format that does not, however unintentionally, place the caregiver in a position of unwanted dependency. Finally, services must be offered efficiently and must be inexpensive on a service unit basis, particularly when their average positive effects are as modest as those for direct caregiver services appear to be. For this reason, it seems difficult to justify, much less to finance, broad use of relatively expensive services, such as paraprofessionals as respite providers, to release the caregiver to use direct services.

It is possible to operate traditional models of support groups and educational interventions relatively inexpensively from a budgeted-cost standpoint, particularly if capital costs (essentially space and furniture) can be held down by using existing community resources. Most churches, community centers, senior centers, and the like have furnished space that is underused and can be made available at nominal cost. We estimate that a busy and efficient service team (secretary, social worker, community nurse) can provide an 8-week (16-hour) support-training group service of good quality at less than $140 per individual intervention, if the system operates at full capacity. Using rigorous operations-management techniques, this figure could doubtless be reduced still further.

Models for future development and refinements of caregiver services will need to be still more responsive to the problems caregivers face in making effective use of existing ones. Here, we think, technology has an important role to play. First, it is not necessary for individuals to meet at a common location to function as a group. Modern telephone switching systems and handsets can make it simple to connect several households in a conference mode so that scheduled, professionally conducted group discussions can proceed telephonically, although this would require developing group leadership techniques adapted to this model. One might also consider less structured, and possibly anonymous, subscriber "caregiver conversation lines" that are continuously active with professionals on-line to guide discussions and help make referrals.

Along with this, the continued development of more conventional information and referral systems should be encouraged. Advances in artificial intelligence and "expert systems" methodologies offer the prospect of self-guiding, sophisticated information and referral systems that could respond in depth to telephone inquiries and be operated continuously at low cost.

It could also be useful to draw on the growing capabilities of cable and satellite subscription television services with community access channels to offer quality programming to and for caregivers and their families: for example, talk shows and panel discussions, perhaps with call-in participation. Educational, dramatic, and inspirational programming could be developed. Such programming should, we think, be committed more to affirmation than analysis. Caregivers often have more need for a combination of Leo Buscaglia and Ruth Westheimer than a conventional social service intervention. It could be very useful, of course, to build more conventional interventions around people's responses to technically sound but compelling media episodes. We believe that the imaginative use of the media and communications technology can only improve immediate services to caregivers, and it may also help bring family elder care along as a basic and positive dimension of our social existence. Such models seem to us worthy of committing substantial funds to demonstrate and develop.

As family caregiving to elderly relatives becomes more a norm, it is important that realistic but positive social interpretations of these relationships become a staple of popular culture, for which the mass media must be the primary vehicle. Good parent care, for example, should be defined, recognized, and presented as a normal and essential dimension of social maturity and responsibility, as natural and essential as the commitments of marriage and the rearing of children.

5

Compensation of Family Care for the Elderly

NATHAN L. LINSK
SHARON M. KEIGHER
SUZANNE E. ENGLAND
LORI SIMON-RUSINOWITZ

BACKGROUND

The most direct approach to helping family caregivers comes from policies that provide financial assistance or compensation to family members who have chosen to give care. In the United States, family compensation has most often been a last resort, although it is increasingly prevalent in a wide array of state programs.

In this chapter, we first briefly review the current state of the art related to compensation through cash, salaries, allowances, or vouchers for family care in the United States and in other countries. Second, we present a summary of our surveys of state programs for family compensation in 1985 and 1990. Third, we discuss implications for policy reform and suggest criteria for a model program. Our focus throughout is largely, but not exclusively, on poor families, who would most likely need publicly subsidized care if family care were not provided.

Three types of policies compensating family care include (a) tax incentives, (b) legal obligations on family members to be financially responsible for elderly relatives, and (c) direct compensation to family caregivers,

AUTHORS' NOTE: Portions of this chapter are adapted from our book, *Wages for Caring,* Linsk et al., © 1992 by Praeger, an imprint of Greenwood Publishing Group, Inc., Westport, CT. Reprinted with permission.

either through wages or cash grant. The first two are discussed briefly, and the third is the primary focus of the chapter.

Tax Incentives

The tax subsidy approach to increasing informal caregiving has included tax exemptions, tax credits, and tax deductions. The tax approach is based on the assumption that some families could do more for their relatives but choose not to do so. Policymakers see tax approaches as a way to support informal care and as a means to avoid expansion of government programs. The drawback is that higher-income households benefit more than lower-income groups (see Chang, Jonston, Mueller, & Swart, 1984; Minnesota Gerontological Society, 1984). The assumption that using the tax system may increase consumer choice overlooks some restrictions on benefits to dependents living in the same household. Tax approaches are also thought to allow simple administration, thus decreasing costs. Policymakers suggest that tax approaches include a built-in cost-sharing component because the subsidy depends on families contributing their caregiving services.

Tax subsidies may also present disadvantages. For one they fail to target the most needy, because determining eligibility by degree of functional need is complex and expensive to administer. Another criticism is that it is difficult to estimate the financial value of *volunteered* services. Tax approaches assume that all household members are employed, which would prohibit benefits to retirees and may be inappropriate for older families. Similarly, tax schemes may require clients and caregivers to live in the same household, which is the least preferred option for relatives and elderly clients as well as the most stressful caregiving pattern (Horowitz & Dobrof, 1982). Furthermore, all current and most proposed tax mechanisms offer too low a benefit to sustain continued family care above uncompensated levels. As an "incentive" benefit, it is unlikely to work.

The disadvantages of tax subsidies tend to outweigh the benefits and make this approach difficult to justify. Policymakers are interested in tax subsidies, probably because no direct expenditures are involved. However, costs are attached to lost tax revenue; for example, the Child and Dependent Care Credit cost $1.3 billion in 1981 (Burwell, 1986).

Legislated Financial Support From Families

Requirements that families provide financial support generally apply to families of nursing home residents. This shifts costs from government to families. Health Care Financing Administration (HCFA) 1983 directives allowed state Medicaid administrators to contain nursing home costs by mandating "family responsibility" laws. Proponents of this policy were concerned about higher income families not contributing to nursing homes costs for Medicaid-eligible relatives, and they assumed that families could provide more support for their relatives but would choose not to do so. Opponents were concerned the policy would prevent appropriate nursing home placements, create stressful family relationships, give children inappropriate decision-making authority over parents, and require adult children to make unreasonable sacrifices, such as deferring their own children's college education or depleting their retirement savings.

Primary supporters of legislative requirements for family support include state Medicaid administrators who need to "stretch" limited resources. However, the potential revenue raised from family responsibility laws would probably be minimal due to high administrative costs and relatively few available adult children (Burwell, 1986; Minnesota Gerontological Society, 1984). As mandatory contributions could deter new nursing home admissions and encourage families to find less costly long-term care arrangements, indirect savings might occur, but no evidence has confirmed this possibility (Burwell, 1986). Several states have attempted such programs; none have been successful to date. Legal technicalities and strong public opposition have prevented mandatory family payments from being considered a serious policy option (Burwell, 1986).

Direct Family Compensation

Family caregivers may be compensated in the form of unrestricted cash grants or vouchers. An unrestricted cash grant allows clients to use funds for any purpose, whereas payments are tied in some way to the tasks of care or hours worked. A voucher may be used only for a specific type of service (Habib, 1985). Arrangements to pay relatives have ranged from hiring family members as employees in existing community service programs to giving an allowance directly to elderly clients to purchase their own services. These arrangements differ in the amount of control given to home care agencies, clients, and families (Linsk et al., 1992).

Research on Family Compensation

Burwell (1986) reviewed 13 state programs to help the HCFA determine whether to alter the definition of "personal care services" under CFR

470.170(f) of Medicaid regulations, so that relatives could be caregivers. The programs studied varied in size, funding source, and benefit levels. The largest was the California In-Home Supportive Services Program; its family component budgeted $90 million to serve 29,000 clients annually. This program, established in 1951, was administered through the Department of Social Services, and recipients generally hired their own caregivers, rather than those available from home care agencies. The average monthly benefit was $262, with a maximum of $921.

The American Bar Association's Commission on the Rights of the Elderly conducted a study assessing consumer-directed approaches in home care (Sabatino, 1990). With support from the Commonwealth Fund, case studies were done in six states (California, Colorado, Massachusetts, Oklahoma, Oregon, and Wisconsin) believed to have a consumer-oriented program. All relied heavily on "individual providers" of personal care, and all but Oklahoma allowed family members to be providers. Sabatino noted two perceptions that led policymakers to endorse individual providers: It saved costs; and clients preferred families, friends, and neighbors when available.

Sabatino's (1990) review suggests that clients varied in the ability and desire to choose providers, and the states and agencies were concerned about liability for individual workers. None of the states actually experienced lawsuits with unfavorable outcomes, but a few suits had been brought and either were settled out of court or did not progress to litigation. Sabatino notes great variation in how *family* is defined for purposes of state and federal policy decisions.

Sabatino's (1990) major focus is consumer involvement and autonomy. Even among these states selected for a consumer-oriented stance, explicit policies protecting consumers are scarce, and general protections (e.g., a bill of rights) or specific protections to individual consumers (e.g., a care contract) are rarely provided. Consumer incapacity is a factor in limiting participation, but programs to assist capable consumers such as client training are limited to informal instruction and written guidelines.

Whitfield and Krompholz (1981) studied the Maryland Family Support Demonstration Project, which offered payment to family caregivers. This project served 1,500 clients, and the average 1981 grant was $1,824 yearly or $152 monthly per family. Clients hired their own caregivers and did not use home care agencies. A quasi-experimental evaluation of 60 subsidized and 60 nonsubsidized families found no differences in the rate of institutionalization, but the mortality rate was significantly lower in the subsidized families. The researchers determined yearly home care costs

for project participants and compared them to nursing home costs in
Maryland (average costs of $14,922 and $14,600, respectively). They
concluded that a family support program should continue because it was
more cost-effective and humane than institutionalization (Whitfield &
Krompholz, 1981). However, the Maryland program was phased out of
existence (D. Folkemer, personal communication, October 16, 1986).

Biegel (1986) conducted a national study of policy incentives to assist
families in caring for their elderly relatives; this research included direct
payments as one type of incentive. He defined direct payments as funding
provided to family caregivers or to elderly clients themselves for purchase
of services from family and nonfamily caregivers. He reported on programs in 20 states. Funding sources for family payments included Medicaid, social services block grant funds, and state-designated money. Some
states defined family broadly enough to justify using Medicaid funds (in
spite of regulations) or used other sources to reimburse relatives. Benefit
levels and eligibility requirements reflected a goal of minimal government intervention, that is, services designed to fill gaps unmet by families.

In 1985, Linsk and his colleagues conducted a study of Illinois home-
care agencies and their experience and perceptions about family care
compensation (England, Linsk, Simon-Rusinowitz, & Keigher, 1989;
Linsk, Keigher, & Osterbusch, 1988). These studies highlighted the discretion that agencies retain on whether or not to hire or compensate families,
even within the same state-funded programs. Of 76 responding agencies,
30 reported that they currently hire family caregivers, 2 reported they
provide family allowances to provide care, and 3 reported they provide
allowances to purchase care. Of those who hired families, 38% indicated
that families were used when no other caregiver was available or under
other specific circumstances, including when instructed by a state unit on
aging, when no one else spoke the consumer's language, when family members could not afford to give up employment to provide care without pay,
and as a temporary measure when no unrelated caregiver was available.

A number stated that families were hired at their request when it was
considered to be in the best interest of consumers. Two thirds of these
family members were assigned to provide care both to their own relatives
and to other clients who were not related. Fifteen agencies cited policies
against hiring family members, which highlighted problems with family
members meeting agency qualifications as employees (8 agencies), concerns about supervision (6 agencies) or dependability of care providers (5
agencies), perceived conflict of interest (5 agencies) or lack of objectivity
of family members (2 agencies), or lack of funds (6 agencies). A small

number of agencies voiced concern that families would accept funds and then provide inadequate care (3 agencies) or that hiring families would promote abuse or neglect (2 agencies).

There are almost no studies revealing the voice of the consumers and family caregivers on the family compensation issue. A major exception is the work of Keigher and Murphy (1992) on consumer responses to compensated family care in Michigan. Twenty-four family dyads from the Michigan Adult Home Help program who received family payments were interviewed, using structured qualitative interviews. These families generally had provided long-standing care, and half had previous full- or part-time jobs. Most of the caregivers were daughters, but sons, grand-children, a son-in-law, and a grandniece-in-law were also included. The caregivers used the payments in a number of ways, with more than half using the money for related caregiving expenses (medications, supplies, diapers, etc.) or personal expenses of the care recipient, including food, rent, utilities, and clothing. Some used the payment for their own needs. Residing together seemed to significantly increase the likelihood that the reimbursement would be spent on the consumer's needs.

Notably few caregivers reported providing care for the cash received, and most noted emotional reasons for providing care. Caregivers felt that the amount of money the state paid for care was not enough to make people get involved unless they truly cared. As one stated:

> If the state told me they would pay me to care for somebody else for the money I am getting, I would say forget it—for that amount of money for what I'm doing? . . . There has to be love involved because the money certainly wouldn't make somebody go in and do something like [I do]. (Keigher & Murphy, 1992)

Several consumers and their caregivers stated that the payments provide reciprocity in their care arrangement; if caregivers receive a payment, consumers feel they are offering help back to the people caring for them. The large amount of care provided raised questions about whether the caregivers were in fact exploited. Many of the caregivers said they felt the care they provided was "a job," and they saw this as a legitimate full-time occupation. And many consumers preferred having familiar caregivers come into their homes, instead of admitting strangers.

Objectives of Family Compensation Policies

If programs are designed primarily to contain costs, evaluators need to know the extent to which financial burden is a factor in family decisions to institutionalize a relative or sustain family care. Evidence suggests that the motivations to begin or continue giving substantial amounts of family care are more emotional than financial (Arling & McAuley, 1983; Burwell, 1986; Chang et al., 1984; Doty, 1986; Horowitz & Shindleman, 1983; Minnesota Gerontological Association, 1984). However, as Arling and McCauley point out, the role of financial factors in determining whether a decision is made to use a nursing home is likely to be complex. Cash grants probably do not prevent institutionalization by motivating families to provide home care they would not otherwise have provided (Doty, 1986). Some findings suggest that family caregivers prefer direct service programs to cash payments or tax incentives (Doty, 1986; Horowitz & Shindleman, 1983). Given a choice, some families might not accept financial incentives.

If the primary purpose of family compensation programs was to ease the burden on caregiving families, what benefit levels would effectively achieve this goal? The question is both practical and political and raises a number of issues. Should families receive sufficient support to allow a caregiver to stop working outside the home? Should family caregiving be relieved occasionally with respite services? Should families be paid to perform work they may otherwise do without any reimbursement? Is it exploitative to pay a relative less than an unrelated caregiver and to expect unreimbursed hours of service? Most family compensation programs have addressed this issue by defining benefits at a "stopgap" level.

The most frequently discussed disadvantage of family compensation programs is concern about public funds being used for services that family members would provide without reimbursement. This question has translated into two "postulated effects":

1. Substitution effect, the concern that families will decrease their involvement and substitute publicly sponsored care.
2. Woodwork effect, the concern that families will be "coming out of the woodwork" to demand services.

Despite these theories, many states have viewed family compensation as an attractive option to increase the supply of home care providers and stretch public funds. However, standardization of benefits may not be appropriate, given the varied needs and resources of older families. Budget constraints may require cautious service distribution, emphasizing a balance among informal and formal services for each family situation. A rigid policy, implemented in a bureaucratic fashion, could deny services to elders needing care or force people to hire family caregivers when a nonrelative would be better. The needs potentially addressed by family compensation might include lack of income. Families may not have other income sources or the resources of the elderly individual who needs help may be insufficient to purchase care.

International Perspectives

Government compensation for social care performed by family members and other informal caregivers may seem like an innovation in the United States, but the mechanism is not unusual in other Western countries. Virtually all industrialized countries have come to recognize the need for financial assistance to households that care for members who are dependent and disabled by making a variety of provisions through social security and social services. There is growing concern among nonindustrialized nations about how such work will be valued and supported. The social security systems of most nations support this care through "constant attendance allowances," supplemental payments to support the provision of personal care to those who are old or who have disabilities. General social security provisions for invalids currently exist in at least 57 countries, and work injury provisions are available in another 36 countries (Linsk et al., 1992).

Systems continue to evolve to protect workers and their families against the risks of market labor, industrial environments, and old age. In addition to constant attendance allowances, nations provide a wide variety of services and other benefits for those who are old or who have disabilities (Brocas, 1988) and for their caregivers, as well as other social supports that begin to relieve families of the potential burden of caring.

Provisions for constant attendance and invalid care allowances can be contained within any of the five separate branches of social security. The principal branches and their benefits include the following, with equivalent existing U.S. programs noted in parentheses:

- Old age, invalidity, death, and survivorship: covering long-term risks, providing pensions as income replacement (Old Age, Survivors & Disability Insurance, OASDI)
- Sickness and maternity: covering short-term wage replacement and/or medical benefits
- Work injury: providing wage replacement, compensation, and medical benefits (Workers' Compensation)

- Unemployment: providing partial wage replacement, training, and job placement (Unemployment Compensation)
- Family allowances: additional income for raising children

In actual practice, attendance allowances are usually included as a benefit under old age and invalidity, and sometimes under sickness or work injury protection. They can also be covered by family allowances, but such provisions are less widely available and often less adequate (Brocas, 1988).

Entitlements to benefits vary as to whether they are work-related (occupational and contributory) pensions or nonwork connected (social assistance and funded with general tax revenues). Entitlement to the former is based on earnings and contributions whereas entitlement to the latter is tied simply to the individual's disadvantaged status or need as indicated by age, incapacity to work, or possibly simple citizenship. (A third type of entitlement, veterans' benefits, are the only widely available provision for attendant allowances in the United States, but these are not a part of social security.) This basic link between benefits and market labor-generated contributions—the insurance concept—has been questioned in many countries, and it has eroded gradually in some places through expansion of flat grants, universal entitlements, and social assistance schemes. Prototypical models include the social insurance model in the Federal Republic of Germany and the citizenship model in Denmark. Jamieson (1990a, 1990b) points out that the German system is premised upon a *family care model,* benefiting breadwinners and their dependents as a group, in contrast to a *state care model* in Denmark, benefiting family members separately by virtue of their own contributions of either cash or labor or status as citizens. She notes that the former has starkly less attractive features for female family caregivers as individuals.

As this brief review highlights, virtually all nations in the developed world have had experience administering payments to help elderly people with disabilities to purchase care and services they need. Several nations have directly administered payments to relatives who provide care. We now turn to our findings regarding payments to families within the United States.

STUDY OF CURRENT STATE POLICY

In 1985, we conducted a study that systematically assessed state programs in all U.S. states and territories. It addressed the following questions:

> To what extent and under what circumstances do jurisdictions permit public payments for family caregiving?

> How do states use various sources of federal and state funding to pay families for providing home care services?

> What are the implications of programs paying families to provide care to the poor and the most needy elderly persons, particularly when program resources are scarce and there are limitations on how many clients can be served?

In 1990, we undertook a follow-up study to assess changes that may have occurred among state programs. (See Linsk et al., 1988, 1992, for detailed presentations of these studies.)

In 1985, we sent a 10-item questionnaire to the current directors of each of three agencies: the State Unit on Aging, Public Welfare, and Social Services in all 50 states plus the District of Columbia and four territories (American Samoa, Guam, Puerto Rico, and the Virgin Islands). Respondents were asked about programs for in-home services, under what circumstances programs allow for family payments, and reasons for or against allowing payments to families. Those in states with no provision for family payments were asked how they dealt with family members who wished to be paid providers. Of 165 questionnaires sent, 89 (54%) were returned, providing at least one response each from 46 states, the District of Columbia, and three territories (Guam, Puerto Rico, and the Virgin Islands), that is, 50 jurisdictions in total.

In January 1990, similar surveys were sent to five key agencies in the same jurisdictions. Added to the original three departments were the Medical Assistance (Medicaid) unit or agency and the umbrella human services agency, if one existed providing multiple services. Of 275 questionnaires sent, 151 (55%) were returned, providing at least one response from every state, the District of Columbia, and three territories (Guam, Puerto Rico, and the Virgin Islands), that is, 54 jurisdictions in total. Six states or territories returned only one questionnaire.

The expanded questionnaire asked agencies to report on specific programs within their purview, and a wide array of programs were reported. More detailed questions about family payments were asked: for example, whether family members were permitted to or prohibited from participating, what special limitations were placed on family compensation, and who chose the provider. Five states were selected from those that allowed family payments, and follow-up telephone interviews were conducted.

These interviews focused on the history, size, cost, and trends in their programs.

In 1985, 35 jurisdictions (33 states plus the District of Columbia and Puerto Rico), or 70% of those responding, indicated that they permitted some form of financial payment to relatives for providing home care to clients. In 1990, 37 jurisdictions (35 states plus the District of Columbia and Puerto Rico), or 69%, indicated they permitted some form of such payments. A jurisdiction was considered to have indicated "yes" if any responding agency indicated that a state program allows payment to relatives for providing at least one home support service or that it does not prohibit payment of relatives.

The percentage of jurisdictions did not change substantially. In 1985, 15 jurisdictions did not have any programs permitting family payments, and in 1990, 17 jurisdictions. Eight states remained negative. Moreover, there were twelve shifts, six from no or no response to yes, and six from yes to no.

States Prohibiting Payment
to Relatives Providing Home Care

Although only 17 jurisdictions prohibited family payments outright in 1990, 40 of the 54 jurisdictions had at least one agency citing program prohibitions. Although federal Medicaid regulations prohibit the payment of relatives through the definition of Personal Care Services, not all states cited the Medicaid exclusion of family members as a specific reason for disallowing payments to family caregivers. (It was noted by only 10 of the 15 states in 1985 and 27 of the 40 states with prohibitions in 1990.) Although the same constraining Medicaid regulations apply to all states, the perceived significance of the federal prohibition appears to vary.

The state's own prohibitions or conditions were mentioned almost as frequently as the federal regulations as reasons for disallowing payment of relatives. These nonfederal restrictions included state laws or regulations of programs funded with state monies, as well as Title XX (Social Services Block Grant) and Title III-B of the Older Americans Act. In all, 7 of the 15 states cited state rules as the reasons for not allowing payments to relatives in 1985. Eight states cited such prohibitions in 1990. These restrictions are largely related to cost-containment concerns of state governments.

States Permitting Payment to Caregiver Relative

The use of payments to relatives is typically restricted to very specific circumstances under which consumers are at high risk of institutionalization. In some jurisdictions, payments are also restricted by the program's locus in one agency rather than another and its reliance on certain funding sources. We found a continuum of restrictions on eligibility, ranging from granting the consumer total discretion in hiring a caregiver to the state agency's complete management of home care and protection of the interests of the consumer.

State cash grants, often supplementary payments (SSP) to supplemental security income (SSI) beneficiaries, are the most direct and universal means by which states can assist individuals and families and allow them maximum discretion. Because they do not specifically target individuals requiring home care, cash grants are a relatively inefficient mechanism. For example, Alabama officials stated in 1985 that the recipient may pay any related or nonrelated person who lives in or outside the home for personal care services, but the SSP is a maximum of $60 per month. In California, the 1983 SSP level was $794 per month for an individual living independently, $250 more than in any other state. About 10% of California's elderly received SSI/SSP, which is generous and widespread coverage when compared to 5.9% of the elderly nationwide. Because California's other home-based long-term care provisions are also relatively extensive, it is impossible to determine how much this provision alone contributes to keeping a greater proportion of clients independent.

To compensate for less available money, other states "target" their grants of discretionary funds more carefully. Rather than use SSP, Hawaii uses a special Title XX provision to pay for family care for the low-income frail elderly without other resources. As with SSP, payments are made to the recipient who, in turn, pays the chore provider, who can be any 'nonlegally responsible relative." Payments do not cover personal care or medical care. In 1985, Oregon allowed about 75% of its home care clients this same discretion to purchase care from whomever they chose. Michigan allows some 27,000 consumers to choose their own personal care providers, about half of whom are relatives. The payment check is written to both the client and provider. The kind of client discretion in these programs is quite similar to that provided by the Veterans Administration's Housebound Aide and Attendance Allowance Program, which currently serves about 220,000 veterans with disabilities nationwide (Grana & Yamishiro, 1987).

The administrative advantage of these arrangements is that, to varying degrees, the state (or its case management subcontractor) avoids direct liability for payment (responsibility for either rates, monitoring of quality, or making personal choices) by underwriting a financial transaction that occurs strictly between the consumer and a consumer-selected provider. Not employing providers directly has allowed some states to circumvent federal prohibitions under Medicaid and to avoid union bargaining and coverage of fringe benefits.

Grana and Yamishiro (1987) described the programmatic advantages of cash grants as follows:

> The advantages of cash compared to in-kind benefits have long been noted by economists. Competent consumers know best how to allocate their services to maximize the satisfaction of their needs and wants; they are more efficient than other persons in promoting their own personal well-being, happiness and independence. The cash equivalent of an in-kind transfer will permit a beneficiary to achieve a higher level of well-being and happiness, and in this sense, the cash transfer is socially optimal and more efficient. A cash benefit has the additional advantage (in most cases) of being easier and less costly to administer. (pp. 1-3)

On the other hand, total consumer discretion means that no case management protects the interests of the consumer and/or handles administrative tasks for the consumer. In this regard, critics of cash disability allowances assume that old people are not able to judge their own needs, that grants will be squandered, and that the beneficiaries of such cash allowances will end up dependent on public programs at even greater cost than would have been incurred with better initial management (Grana & Yamishiro, 1987). Subsidies in the form of in-kind services leave little decision making in the hands of the recipients, and the cash benefit would be more expensive given the greater number of claims and higher administrative costs. For example, in 1988, Michigan had to increase case management services because the courts declared that consumers must deduct FICA and taxes from payments to their caregivers, a process too difficult for many consumers. It also capped maximum monthly payments to avoid Workers' Compensation deductions. In avoiding liability as an employer, the state in effect passed that liability on to consumers.

Consumers, families, case managers, and agency staff are involved in choosing caregivers. Forty-four respondents from 30 states or territories noted the role of the consumers themselves. Twenty-three respondents from 18 states mentioned the importance of the family as a whole taking part in selecting the caregiver. Respondents from 17 states noted the involvement of case managers, whereas respondents from 15 states or territories reported agency staff involvement. Although almost all respondents said multiple agents were involved in choosing the caregiver, few respondents mentioned or clarified that it was a multistage joint effort, wherein a case manager chooses the worker, who must be approved by the consumer.

Restrictions on Which
Relatives Can Provide Care

Criteria for caregiver eligibility are various and can make programs complicated. Jurisdictional rules specifically indicate which relatives may receive payments. Because of the prevalence of spouses in family caregiving, a major question is whether or not a spouse is eligible for financial compensation. This issue raises many concerns about the needs and contributions of spouses as weighed against judgments about whether the spouse's care (and providing an incentive to sustain it) produces a benefit worth compensating by the staff.

Whether payments to spouses are allowed is related to the source of funding for home care programs. In 1988, public discussion was opened on the federal Medicaid regulations pertaining to prohibitions on reimbursement of relatives for providing personal care. Although the result has been a loosening of the prohibitions (largely because of the way states define *relative*), many states specify that spouses may not be reimbursed. Consequently, states that continue to pay spouses do so with alternative sources of funding, such as Social Services Block Grants (formerly Title XX), the Older Americans Act, state general funds, or Medicaid provisions other than Personal Care. The Medicaid Home and Community-Based Care waivers appear to be an increasingly important source of coverage for spouses in some cases.

In 1985, only 6 of the states allowing payment to family caregivers explicitly excluded spouses from eligibility, but this number increased to 15 in 1990. Because explicit kinship restrictions were not specified in all cases, we cannot be certain how many other states excluded spouses. The variation in policies regarding exclusion of spouses seems to be at least partially explained by whether Medicaid is used as a funding source. The 35 states that have family compensation and that purchase personal care (16 of them cover the medically needy) are precluded by this Medicaid restriction from including spouses and have had to find ways to keep adult children from being excluded as relatives since the 1988 HCFA rules were proposed.

Exclusion of adult children as caregivers is somewhat less widespread. In 1985, only Montana excluded them; in 1990, four jurisdictions excluded adult children—Alabama, Arizona, Missouri, and Puerto Rico. Other exclusions included underaged relatives (California, Washington), grandparents/grandchildren (Montana, Oklahoma, Virginia), foster parent/child, stepparent/child, stepbrother, stepsister, parents- or children-in law, or sisters- or brothers-in law.

Many states operating under Medicaid Home and Community-Based Care waivers seem to have allowed payment to spouses in their respective packages of Medicaid-eligible home care services, if costs could be kept within allowable ranges. The waivers allowed states flexibility in paying spouses, but of course they also imposed severe cost-consciousness (Weissert, 1986).

Other Restrictions

Several states imposed restrictions based on whether the caregiver and the consumer live in the same household. In 1985, four states restricted family payments to those who live together, but only one respondent indicated such a restriction in 1990. In 1985, four states restricted payments to those not living together, whereas in 1990 six states prohibited coresidence, with only one in common over the 2 years.

A number of restrictions referred to qualities of the caregiver. In Oklahoma, payments ware restricted to those situations in which another caregiver who spoke the consumer's language could not be found. In 1990, eight states indicated a "last resort" rule that families only would be paid if no other caregiver could be found. The number of states requiring family caregivers to meet a set of qualifications increased from one in 1985 to eight in 1990. This may suggest the caregivers were more likely to be considered as eligible for the program, rather than the exception, or that comparable programs especially for relative caregivers are emerging as an explicit form of in-home care on a more widespread basis.

In 1985, at least three states required caregivers to meet welfare income guidelines, and several states did so in 1990. In 1985, Washington state required relative caregivers to be otherwise eligible for general assistance for their own needs. Connecticut required that caregivers who qualified for public assistance must apply for it; then the essential services program would pay the caregivers an extra allotment for their services. In two out of three of these cases (Connecticut, North Dakota), these "categorical" restrictions on the caregiver appear to have been lifted by 1990 in favor of a more flexible and permissive policy that continues to recognize the value of family care to the consumer. In 1990, West Virginia required SSI income-related eligibility; Vermont required the family member to be in financial need but not eligible for SSI or Aid to Families with Dependent Children (AFDC). In the 1990 survey, several states mentioned caregiver financial difficulty as a criterion.

Caregiver employment was a common theme in both years. In both 1985 and 1990, nine states (about 25% of those who allowed family caregiver payments) required caregivers to give up outside employment if they were receiving caregiver compensation. Overall, this represents 17 different states between the 2 years, suggesting that this is a very common requirement. Two states mentioned financial criteria related to the consumer or caregiver, generally describing the standard in terms of "hardship" or an income floor.

Several state program staff described restrictions in hiring based on licensure and screening. In 1985, seven states required the caregiver to be employed by a county or Area Agency on Aging, whereas none did so in 1990. In both 1985 and 1990, four states required the relative to be employed by an agency contracting with the state. Only one state, Alaska, required licensure, and this was only in the 1985 survey. Requiring employment with a certified agency or licensure of all personnel is an attempt to ensure the quality of patient care. Several states restricted payment to specified types of services in 1985, but only one did so in 1990. Two states restricted family payments to temporary situations in 1990.

Variations occur depending on whether programs are administered by states directly, administered by local governments, or contracted by either of these through local agencies under state contract to provide care (vendor organizations). Responsibility for case management must then be tracked separately from actual service delivery. The means by which family caregivers are actually paid by a government or local vendor varies in amount, hourly limits, care plan, and so on. This is extremely difficult to track. As service becomes increasingly privatized, it could become impossible to follow, except in states with special programs of service for relative caregivers.

Implications

Officials' implicit concerns about costs and potential abuses have limited the otherwise great potential for growth of family payment programs. Most states have developed a variety of strategies to temper both woodwork and substitution effects. Although three states (California, New York, and Michigan) reported rather large programs that had clearly expanded availability, all included screening methods to contain eligibility.

The 1990 survey revealed the impact of Medicaid waivers and the concomitant growth in state programs. The number of states using Medicaid personal care funding increased from 22 to 26. Along with this came increasingly restrictive kinship rules: HCFA's restrictions against spouses receiving payments and efforts to exclude other family members, as well. But concern for community care appears to be focused on government providing only what it cannot get families to do for free; this is more a passive model than a proactive, entitlement policy.

The findings of these two surveys reflect several aspects of the states' current view of family caregiving compensation. Several states emphasized the importance of "gap filling" tasks in the total range of services they provided to the elderly, a "little bit of targeted assistance" that was believed to prevent institutionalization (Linsk et al., 1992, p. 91). For example, a respondent from Iowa noted, "Sometimes the price of gas is all that prevents relatives from providing care" (p. 91). The value of discretionary resources in the hands of caring families was widely noted. This is the rationale of the Pennsylvania legislation that reimburses families for out-of-pocket expenses only upon presentation of receipts for up to $200 per month. Payments are important "to support the existing service when the family is in danger of giving up" (p. 91). Some jurisdictions make family payments available on a strictly "by exception" basis after determining that payments will make the vital difference. All states emphasized the principle of not supplanting other sources of support, and most do not intend to make payments for existing levels of unpaid care.

The perception of state officials about whether relatives add to or reduce the hours of service required is basic to their decision to support paying relatives. Is pay an incentive that expands the amount of care already provided, or does it force a limit on the amount of care, because it only pays for a certain amount that agencies provide? Few states can afford to limit their reliance on family assistance. Almost universally they explain that family payments generate more care than what is specifically purchased, something no one could claim regarding agency care. Usually some notion of consumer vulnerability precedes the criteria of income.

Some states have recognized the penalty paid by poor, related caregivers by clearly targeting additional assistance to them or by requiring covered family caregivers to apply for welfare. The latter requirement may actually discourage use of the provision because welfare is usually seen as a stigmatizing program. Yet even those few states with relatively generous payments (California, Michigan, and New York) would not be likely to secure a family caregiver who had other employment options. Medicaid, low-cost meals, and shopping services are prototypes of alternative programs to support family care, but these are limited to the ill poor; much could be gained by extending such policies to the well poor.

Uncertainty remains about whether payment of relatives providing home care is cost-effective. In one sense the question is whether program support and services would be more valuable to caregivers than actual cash, but in another and wider sense the question comes down to how states can avoid spending any more money at all. Although compensation of family caregivers is certainly possible in most states, it is an underused option, complicated by the regulations and proposals in effect at HCFA. The hiring of "outsiders" might discourage one segment of the population from providing care themselves, but another group, at least similar in size, seems unable or unwilling to accept any help from outsiders at all. They would get no support if the state offers only agency-provided care. Yet, relatives of very poor frail elderly are often poor themselves, so that paying them may offer economies of effort as well as administration, maximizing the quality of care provided at the same time.

The findings reported here do not permit assessment of the results of specific programs or the optimal policy to create incentives for families to provide home care. A great deal more knowledge of the motivations and marginal vulnerability of individual caregivers, as well as those of states' individual caregiving systems, would enhance our understanding of the utility and the effects of this policy choice.

RECOMMENDATIONS

What would a fair and effective program to compensate family caregiving look like? We will present suggestions for who should receive which service and how the services would be made available and financed. (This analysis is loosely organized across dimensions articulated by Gilbert & Specht, 1986.)

Defining the Beneficiaries and Program Goals

Long-term care policy should include providing needed home care or institutional care for those who meet three criteria: (a) significant functional need, (b) inadequate social supports, and (c) financial need. The policy goal is to compensate for deficiencies in those three areas, and these criteria make up an entitlement standard for support of family caregivers.

In many states, compensating families is viewed as a last resort that will save the additional costs of institutional or 24-hour agency care. This view is doomed to failure as a long-range solution to care needs. When family compensation is provided only through a loophole, it will tend to be evaluated negatively, because families are unable to adjust to agency demands. Hiring family caregivers as a last resort is basically inequitable because families then do not have equal access to compensation. Our data suggest that the agencies will only hire family members when it is convenient for the agencies, and consequently families in greater need, or with more complex interaction styles, may be discriminated against. Therefore, we recommend against "last resort" hiring as the basis of family compensation.

Caregiver family payments could be based on care needed or provided, rather than on wages lost. Given the general structure of care and all that implies, it is not feasible in the United States to compensate caregivers for what they lose in wages. A state cannot equitably compensate both the caregiver who previously earned $50,000 a year and the caregiver who previously earned minimum wage. States should pay no more than the going rate for personal care, regardless of other options available to families. However, programs may focus on maintaining family caregiving efforts by partially offsetting losses caregivers experience by not being able to continue employment, pursue education, or provide care to other family members.

Alternative principles reframe the issue of cost and benefit. One alternative would be to reduce societal dependency on unpaid family labor and create a viable labor force for family care. Another would be to reduce the negative consequences of unsupported caregiving, including future dependency created for the family caregiver by being out of the workforce. For a number of reasons, there is increasing interest in reducing dependency on medicalized home care. These trends point in the direction of reframing the question of family care from reducing institutionalization to greater community (rather than institutional) capacity to meet the social dependency needs of citizens.

Another concern revolves around equity to family caregivers in allocating those services provided by the formal system. Home support programs often include an eligibility assessment of the "informal care network." This screening may discriminate against family caregivers because when a family caregiver is present, the eligibility level is discounted. There is no sound basis to discriminate against payment of family caregivers if they are as qualified to provide care as a nonfamily member working for an outside agency.

Benefits to Be Provided

We propose that the best form of benefit is a cash transfer to consumers combined with caregiver fringe benefits, which may be supplemented by complementary consumer services. This combination encourages maintenance of potential caregivers in the paid labor force. Existing structures drive the system as much as possible, so that the existing care system may be reinforced.

This program option is attractive politically because it ensures that services are provided with minimal intrusion to the family at minimum cost to taxpayers. Enhancement of caregiver capabilities is likely to be popular with voters, most of whom have such responsibilities for at least one older dependent relative during the course of their work lives.

This approach offers significant advantages over other options. Paying wages alone leads to many bureaucratic dilemmas in fitting families into an agency model of care. Whether families are employed by existing agencies or become employees under state or local governmental auspices, a wage alone requires creating structures for hiring, training, monitoring, benefits, coverage, performance appraisal, and dealing with attrition and turnover. We have not ruled out the possibility of home care agencies hiring family members, but our recommendation is that hiring relatives is best reserved for situations in which this action is in the best interest of the consumer.

An allowance alone without caregiver fringe benefits poses three problems. First, without benefits the work is compensated unequally when compared to paid home care work provided by nonfamily members, thus devaluing or failing to sustain family caregiving work. Second, without some basic fringe benefits (e.g., Social Security, health insurance, Workers' Compensation, disability payments), the caregiver may be forced to look for other work outside of caregiving simply to receive benefits routinely provided by the workplace. We also suggest that care allowances should be combined with other needed in-home services such as day or respite care, transportation, home health, or any other needed services.

Our proposals presume that individual (consumer) choices are the energy driving the system. The benefit is in the form of a cash allowance controlled by consumers when consumers are competent and only under the joint control of caregivers and the state when consumers are not capable. To maximize individual preferences and optimal privacy, the choice of caregiver is left to consumers. The Veterans Administration Aid and Attendance Allowance currently uses this system, employing strict criteria regarding competence and a clear process for having another make choices (Grana & Yamishiro, 1987). Not *all* family care will be compensated. Most families provide care beyond their service allotment, which can be seen as a form of cost-sharing. These in-kind supports create a "bonus care" contribution.

Strategies for Delivery

States would develop various plans for organizing and implementing a care allowance program, much as the states now provide for the array of services to the elderly. A key feature of the organization of the system focuses on how it integrates with existing systems of service for poor people who have disabilities.

A care allowance system, then, is the preferred delivery mechanism because it offers a system of joint responsibility: Families, consumers, and government would share in developing, implementing, and monitoring services. An allowance would enhance and support existing family responsibilities, maximizing the likelihood that existing family care patterns are maintained intact. It makes consumers responsible for participating in care planning and voicing need for care as well as capabilities. When possible consumers would provide their own care management, including reporting and fiscal management; spouses, other family, or guardians would share in this effort as necessary. The proposed system makes family caregivers responsible for provision of care and often for communication and liaison between government agencies and consumers. In particular, family caregivers take responsibility for personalizing the care given. At the same time the caregivers would adhere to necessary guidelines, which would operate like employee work and reporting rules to ensure that the care is given in the agreed on manner.

Through its chosen method of program decentralization, the state would be responsible to ascertain that the care is provided as agreed, that beneficiaries are financially eligible, and that reassessments and recontracting for care occur on a regular basis. The state might also administer benefit packages for consumers (as in Ohio) and assure training for caregivers. The state would operate protective services programs and assure that these are consumer based.

Administering the Benefit. States would select a unit to administer the care allowances, when possible, through an existing service unit for dependent elders. State units on aging and welfare or social service departments might be the service delivery entities, depending on the state organization for long-term care delivery. A single state office might directly administer the benefit, with a case manager responsible for implementing, monitoring, ensuring quality assurance, and providing benefits as the consumer agent.

An alternate wage model would require the state or the home care agency under state contract to provide the benefit directly. The caregiver becomes an employee, once either the consumer, the agency, or the state decides that this is in the consumer's best interest. Caregivers must become bona fide agency employees, receiving the same benefits as other employees. To do this, the state might need to include some protections for family caregivers in terms of ensuring equity of treatment. For example, the state might encourage the compensation of families, using a "right of first refusal" approach to screening whether families are appropriate paid caregivers before moving to other options.

Eligibility Criteria. Eligibility for care allowances should be based on consumer needs and income. States might determine cutoffs for functional disability and income for participation in the program. States would need to make decisions about whether their Medicaid eligibility criteria are high enough to use as a mechanism to determine eligibility. In 1984, this criterion varied from $775 per month in Alaska to $120 in Mississippi, whereas the national poverty level was $848 per month (Holahan & Cohen, 1986). Standards for the "medically needy" program (the protected income level) vary further. States have the option to increase these eligibility limits on both income and assets, and it is only in so doing that equity will be maintained among health care and social service benefits for persons of limited means.

Quality Assurance. Ultimately the state must certify that needed services are provided. Caregivers or consumers concerned that mandated services are not in place or being provided could request a review of the service needs and participate in that review. Caregivers would have the right to withdraw from the program, or services might be terminated at consumer request. Caregivers with complaints about their treatment by the state or case manager might be able to use the state's usual grievance or complaint resolution process.

Although some policymakers and agencies in our surveys expressed considerable concern about program abuse and elder abuse, many states with experience in family compensation had much less concern. Nevertheless, how to protect consumers must be considered. Protections might include bonding of caregiver-employees or prescreening for criminal activity or previous reports of elder abuse or domestic violence, as is already done in some states (e.g., Texas). A liability insurance-type program used for other informal caregivers might be adapted to the needs of family caregivers and consumers. Existing mechanisms, such as elder abuse reporting procedures, protective service programs, and ombudsman programs, might monitor program abuse and deal with problems.

A quality assurance system also might be used internally to review objectives met and particular consumer needs. The case managers' assessments could be analyzed to assure quality. Equally important would be consumer-based evaluation, using qualitative interview methods and observational evaluations from both consumers and caregivers (see Levit, 1989, for a model of such an evaluation). These methods would pay close attention to personal responses to the program, as well as its perceived meaning and value; the outcomes reported by consumers, families, and formal providers would be valuable in determining program quality.

Financing

Current federal and state matching arrangements in a wide variety of categorical programs offer options that states might adopt to operate the caregiver compensation program described above.

Supplemental Security Income (SSI). The most direct cash option is to increase SSI, a federal program, and the State Supplementation Payment

(SSP) of SSI. These payments are received by those elderly whose resources are so low that they do not qualify for Social Security. In one sense using this venue would target poverty most effectively, and for this reason SSI is basic as a floor on which our proposal must be built.

However, SSI payments need to be brought up to the poverty level. In addition, an SSI penalty for coresidence with others should be amended. Currently, if an SSI recipient receives food and shelter in someone else's household, the SSI payment is reduced by one third. Note that 26% of the elderly aged 85 or over live in a relative's household. This is the very population that tends to be most income disadvantaged and most in need of supportive services by available family caregivers (Bould, Sanborn, & Reif, 1989). This current provision is particularly punitive toward caregivers.

Both of these SSI proposals are necessary to enhance poor caregivers' ability to care properly. It makes little sense to pay caregivers for their work when consumers are still hungry, cold, or about to be evicted for nonpayment of rent. Family caregivers will not benefit from a payment scheme if they are forced in turn to compensate by putting all their pay into meeting the daily living expenses of their elderly family member.

However, after these basic deficiencies are resolved, SSI would become an excellent source for payments to informal caregivers for several reasons. Consumers receive the monthly grant with no strings attached. A share of the SSP could certainly be added and designated for an "attendant allowance," which consumers would be free to spend as they choose by hiring caregivers of their choice. Arizona, the only state that mentioned using this program in our surveys, makes clear in its SSP payments that this money is for the purchase of assistance.

Medicaid Options. The only "open-ended" federally matched funding source is the Medicaid program, which has been the source of most of the innovative home care support programs created during the 1980s. Only half of poor children and one third of poor elderly are covered by Medicaid. This key provision designed to provide health care to the poor elderly can only be available if the states increase the grant levels for welfare recipients. This is certainly an equitable approach; however, states rarely make such significant and costly changes as state policy alone. The alternative would be to acknowledge the special needs for care, including home care, among the elderly and to include such costs in Medicare or an alternative nationalized program.

In the absence of such a development, several state Medicaid options are currently still open for development of home care services, but states have not found Medicaid easy to tap to expand services. The most available option remaining is use of Personal Care under Medicaid for the hiring of informal (nonagency employee) care providers. The deterrent to states using this option has been HCFA's restrictions against hiring relatives and its insistence that personal care providers be "qualified"; in other words, that personal care be a medical or medically related program. However, several states do currently pay relatives with Medicaid personal care funding.

Our research suggests that use of the Medicaid Home and Community-Based Care waivers is not so promising as a funding mechanism. HCFA's review and approval authority over the state plans results in perceived interference with the operation of the state programs. Many states have encountered oversight problems with inclusion of relatives or even informal caregivers: HCFA objects to including relatives in the coverage plan, viewing the practice as "widening the net." This may be interpreted partly as reluctance to allocate services based on social rather than medical needs. Much of the personal care provided by relatives may be classified as social care necessary to maintain the person outside of an institution, and this may be viewed as less justifiable than medical need, especially if the individual was not recently discharged from a hospital or nursing home setting.

Many of the service units now authorized under Medicaid mirror what is provided by families, except that the agency-provided service has inflationary and other features that government shows no tendency toward controlling. Payments to families, on the other hand, are highly controllable. On a unit basis, the services provided by family caregivers can be equitably provided at far less cost and are more controllable and predictable in terms of annual increases.

Despite HCFA's concerns, some states are covering family caregivers under the Medicaid Home and Community-Based Care waivers. Given the varying use of the waivers, states should explore how they may define care or limit caregivers to receive reimbursement.

Social Service Funding. The logical funding source for family caregiver payments is with programs designed to purchase social care: the Social Services Block Grants (SSBG) and the Older Americans Act.

As a financing source, the SSBG already purchases all kinds of services from individual informal caregivers (e.g., child and adult foster care, family day care, and professional services), making this program easily adaptable to family payments. Ideally, a federal program of support designated within the SSBG would be used, as Congress used to designate a portion of Title XX for children's day care.

Block grants are already used for family caregiver compensation in many states, but on a limited basis and often restricted only to those who are not otherwise eligible for Medicaid: for example, caregiving spouses. There is no federal prohibition against paying family caregivers in the SSBG. In fact, payments can even be made to a spouse, but usually this is done in a very restrictive fashion as the exception rather than the rule.

Both SSBG and Older Americans Act funds have ceilings on federal matching funds, so that current payments and services cannot be expanded without the states reallocating current programs or spending additional state dollars to supplement them. Due to the social pressures as well as the restrictions on even these federal moneys, we tend to favor state supplementation.

State Revenues. Considering the limitations of other options, use of state-only funding is rational, despite severe fiscal constraints and reluctance to adopt new programs without federal incentives. We argue that some of these considerations have changed. Chasing limited federal moneys has become counterproductive. Public support is likely for proposals with tangible benefits to affected families.

Many states have developed coordinated long-term care planning and service departments and have already turned extensively to state funding to fill the gaps. In this sense, family compensation is a most significant gap that should be filled. This approach would be especially attractive as a complementary part of long-term care systems planning because of its low opportunity cost and potentially high political payoff in terms of public support among a vast number of potential beneficiaries. Stone and Kemper (1990) estimate that although the immediate caregiver group is only 3.5 million, the total potential constituency is much larger.

CoPayments. We propose that the program be provided without cost to all elderly whose incomes are below the Medicaid protected income standard (currently $4,320 a year for single persons). Those with higher incomes would make a copayment based on their income adjusted for medical costs. The copayments would be set between 5% to 50% for those elderly consumers below the median income for the elderly, which was $14,334 in 1987 (U.S. Bureau of the Census, 1990). Those whose income is higher but less than the median income for all households, which was

$25,986 in 1987, would make copayments between 55% and 95% of the benefit.

CONCLUSIONS

Two issues continue to preoccupy policymakers, program leaders, caregivers, and consumers. These are the moral issue of whether family caregivers should be paid and the cost issue. The attitude about these two concerns will determine whether family compensation is facilitated by state and federal policy.

How relevant are cost issues, given the perceived value of family care? Clearly a policy that costs more money will not be as feasible politically or practically. However, the cost issue may be a smokescreen for the fact that care is needed, regardless of who provides and pays for it. The real question is not what will be the cost but who will bear the cost. If public sources will not bear the costs, they will be absorbed up to a maximum by families and communities. The gap between what families can provide and what is needed will indeed be costly in terms of personal suffering and inadequate quality of life for our nation's elders.

What do we really know about the cost of family compensation? The objectives, structure, and design of programs would determine whether family payments save or cost additional money. The wage or allowance level, administrative arrangements, and eligibility criteria all would affect costs and savings. Good studies are needed to document cost savings and excesses, using different models of compensation, efficiency, and administrative arrangements.

Financial supports for family care need to be available when family care is shown to be in the consumer's and caregiver's best interests. Kinship should not be the basis for discrimination. Federal barriers to family involvement, such as the proposed Medicaid regulations prohibiting family compensation for personal care, have real negative consequences for families.

In fact, we know disturbingly little about family caregiving, beyond its sheer scope and prevalence. It is important to establish social indicators of family care, so we can document its extent and trends. Federal initiatives could encourage demonstration programs across several states using different models.

Given the current national debate about family values, family compensation offers a practical partnership between government and families to meet long-term care needs of dependent elders. Our findings suggest that this mechanism reflects consumer and family preference, may maximize family care, may reduce the long-term care load on government, and may reduce or contain costs, or at least some states believe it does. Concerns that families may exploit these programs have not been substantiated. The existing potential for family compensation in three quarters of the states, given disincentives from federal sources to offset family costs, speaks to the pervasive need to further consider and develop family payment policies.

In fact, family compensation potentially can address several of the underlying values currently confronting both policymakers and families. Family compensation may respect the issues of family privacy and integrity by maximizing choices by consumers and their families about how to arrange care. Family compensation also may support the value of individual and family independence, in that offsetting family contributions and costs may delay the need for formal services or institutional care. Family compensation, correctly structured, may be a lower-cost alternative than more complex agency-based or facility-based services. Properly targeted, programs may also have the benefit of providing income maintenance support for the poor, or even of creating employment for elders and women.

One would think a program that offers these advantages—maintaining families, respecting consumer choice and privacy, sustaining independence, containing costs, reducing poverty and unemployment—would be a serious contender in the debate over how to address national issues of long-term care provision. Although caution is needed to ensure that we do not overstate the promise of family compensation, compensation should be a universally accessible option for families in need. Family compensation cannot substitute for an overall long-term care system, but it appears to be a very useful tool for sustaining duration of family care and improving quality of life for all involved.

6

Family Caregiving and Access to Publicly Funded Home Care

Implicit and Explicit Influences on Decision Making

PAMELA DOTY

The theme of this chapter is the role of family caregiving and other informal supports in determining access to publicly funded home-care benefits. How informal resources interact with and influence public provision of formal services will be described, and the consequences of various approaches will be evaluated via examples from home care financing and service delivery systems in the United States and abroad.

The main analytic dimension to be compared and contrasted is between implicit and explicit approaches to incorporating family caregiving into allocative decision making with respect to public benefits. By implicit approaches, we refer to systems that take informal caregiving for granted and assume that care needs not served by available public resources will be taken care of by family, friends, and neighbors. Also included are systems in which availability of informal support is taken into account outside of—typically prior to—formal decision making and is, therefore, an influential factor but one that is not openly acknowledged. In contrast, explicit approaches characterize systems in which an active effort is made to

AUTHOR'S NOTE: The views expressed in this chapter are those of the author alone and should not be construed as representing the official position of the U.S. Department of Health and Human Services.

integrate publicly funded services with informal supports—or their recognized lack—in developing a total care plan.

SYSTEMS IN WHICH EXPECTATIONS
FOR FAMILY CAREGIVING ARE IMPLICIT

The Influence of Selectivity Biases

Availability or unavailability of family supports influences access to formal home care in myriad subtle ways. First and foremost are the *selectivity biases* that determine when health professionals—such as doctors and hospital discharge planners—choose to refer and recommend individuals for home health and home care services and that influence when clients and families decide to self-refer by contacting local social services departments, area agencies on aging, and so on. These decisions obviously take place prior to and quite separately from the formal processes of assessing eligibility for benefits under particular programs.

At first glance, for example, one might think that availability of informal support at home would have little to do with access to Medicare home health benefits: From a formal eligibility perspective, this decision is supposed to be based on medically determined "need" for skilled nursing and therapy services. However, in practice, professional judgments about whether these services can be safely and effectively delivered in a home setting depend very heavily on whether or not adequate informal support seems to be available in the home to meet the patient's nonmedical care needs.

During a week spent observing the discharge planning process at a Washington, DC, hospital, I noted that the first questions posed concerning each case taken up at the weekly discharge planning conferences on every ward were:

Who is listed on this patient's admission sheet as "next of kin" or "person to notify in an emergency"?

What responsibility is this person prepared to take when the patient is discharged?

The answers to these questions played a key role in determining:

Who was referred for an assessment for Medicare home health eligibility by the hospital's contract home health agency?

Who was referred to Medicaid and services funded by Social Services Block
Grants (SSBG) available from the city?

Who was referred for a skilled nursing facilitiy (SNF), rehabilitation hospital,
or nursing home placement.?

In order to be referred for Medicare home health benefits, elderly
patients generally had to have family caregivers who were judged to be
involved and reliable. If the patient lived with at least one highly involved
and reliable family member, the patient was not usually referred for
supplemental home-care services. However, if a family member was only
visiting temporarily to provide for the patient's post-acute needs, questions were asked about how long the family member could stay, and an
assessment for longer-term supplemental Medicaid personal care or SSBG-
funded homemaker/chore services was often recommended. Elderly patients with physical disabilities who lived alone or had only some rather
weak informal support were routinely referred to the city's SSBG- and
Medicaid-funded home-care programs—as long as they were cognitively
intact.

Decisions became more difficult when cognitive impairment and possible vulnerability to exploitation were suspected; when family members
were perceived as unreliable, hostile, or uncooperative; or when the patient
was very old, with severe disabilities, and had only weak informal support
available. For example, in one difficult case, a patient who lived alone
and had no close relatives appeared to have a fluctuating level of mental
impairment that the discharge planner found difficult to evaluate. Phone
calls to the patient's lawyer and her upstairs neighbor elicited conflicting
views. The lawyer, who considered the patient to be mentally incompetent
and in serious danger of financial exploitation, recommended nursing home
placement, whereas the upstairs neighbor said the patient was "not that
bad" and offered to look out for her if she returned home. The discharge
planner was left to decide which of these two views was the more trustworthy—all the while considering the hospital's potential liability if the
patient went home and the lawyer's concerns about exploitation turned
out to be justified. The discharge planner reluctantly decided to recommend nursing home placement when she learned that a monetary court
settlement the patient repeatedly referred to as recently awarded had actually
been received several years earlier and that the patient had squandered or
been "conned" out of much of the money.

In making their recommendations and referrals, the hospital's discharge
planners were well aware of the financial eligibility requirements for the

District of Columbia's home care programs, as well as the maximum amounts and types of services these programs made available. Because this was an inner-city hospital, patients judged to be in need of formal services very rarely failed to qualify on financial grounds, if not for Medicaid, then at least for the SSBG-funded program, which had a higher income threshold.

More problematic were the maximum service hours available—10 hours of homemaker/chore services weekly in the SSBG program and 20 hours per week maximum of personal care attendant services under Medicaid. Many of the very elderly, low-income black women who were typically subject to discharge planning at this hospital had large extended families who were willing to care for them. In these cases, the limits on available formal help posed no problems—if, indeed, formal help was considered necessary at all.

However, in those not-infrequent cases in which patients had only weak or unreliable informal support at home, discharge planners were aware of a likely gap between the patient's total care needs and the amount of care they would get from the combined efforts of informal helpers and the maximum level of formal services available from Medicaid and SSBG-funded programs.

Accordingly, discharge planners implicitly factored their awareness of available service limits into their judgments about whether elderly people with disabilities who lived alone or had weak informal supports would face an acceptable level of risk, if recommended for home care and referred to the city programs. For example, consider this case:

The patient was a woman with disabilities and cognitive impairments who lived with her husband and adult daughter. The patient had a history of several hospital admissions for acute medical problems brought about by dehydration and poor nutrition. Following her most immediate previous hospitalization, she had been discharged with extended Medicare home health visits, including 4 hours daily of home health aide services and 2 hours daily of SSBG-funded homemaker/chore services.

In addition, her daughter had given up a good job in California and moved back to Washington, DC, to take care of her. However, the daughter worked during the day, so the woman was left in the care of her husband for several hours daily. The husband was described as "strange"—possibly early Alzheimer's but, in any case, too "macho" to be willing to help out with any household tasks or otherwise participate in his wife's care. The home health agency personnel often had a difficult time getting him to open the door and let them in when they arrived for work.

The hospital discharge planner felt that the daughter was unhappy and resentful about giving up her life in California and took this out on the home health attendants, whom she constantly berated as incompetent and asked to have replaced. The home health agency and the discharge planner did not believe that the aides were incompetent and felt that the daughter "expected too much" from the home health agency.

In view of the situation, the discharge planner felt that it was time to recommend nursing home placement. The main elements of her reasoning appeared to be: Because of her cognitive impairments, the patient may never know the difference. The husband doesn't really care. The daughter feels trapped and miserable but won't admit it directly: I can get her off the hook. The situation is placing unreasonable demands on the home health agency and demoralizing its workers. If I don't break the cycle by sending the patient to a nursing home, she is likely to keep bouncing in and out of the hospital.

In another case, this same discharge planner cast herself in the role of the patient's champion in arguing for home care against the wishes of some members of the patient's informal support network who favored nursing home placement.

The patient was a 90-year-old woman who was very frail and nearly blind. She could walk, but her walking consisted of a very slow shuffling movement. A grandnephew in his 20s lived with her, but he worked during the day and was often out in the evenings. The woman had a long-time involvement in her local Baptist church, and now that she could seldom get out of her house, church members visited her and constituted her primary informal support network, apart from the grandnephew. The church pastor felt that it was too risky for the woman to continue to live in the community and thought she should be placed in a nursing home. However, the discharge planner had known the patient for several years—the woman had previously received formal help from a community-based program for which the discharge planner had worked— and strongly disagreed with the pastor and the church members.

In this case, the discharge planner's reasoning was as follows: I know her. I know she wants to stay at home. Her mind is still intact and it would demoralize her go to a nursing home; she could die as a result. She is tough, and she is more functional than she looks. She still cooks—it might drive you crazy to watch her do it because it takes her half an hour just to shuffle across the room to the stove. But what else has she got to do all day? This keeps her alert and occupied. If we get her the maximum available in-home help from both Medicaid and Title XX, she will only be alone for a couple of hours during the day. True, one of these days she may die when she's home alone, but she's 90 years old, and every extra day she lives is "gravy" anyway. Even if she had no disabilities she'd be likely to die soon. I think she should be allowed to take the risk. Why should she have to go to a nursing home just because the church is worried that someone will blame them if she happens to die unattended?

Two cases that came up during my observation week posed particular problems for the hospital discharge planners because available public resources fell significantly short of what was necessary to meet patients' needs for care in the community—yet, ironically, in neither case did the patient have sufficient or, more accurately, the right kind of medical and functional disabilities to be considered appropriate for nursing home placement. In the first such case, the details were as follows:

> The patient was a recovered "skid row" alcoholic who had been sober for 10 years. Prior to hospitalization, he had for many years lived and worked as a cook in a halfway house that provided alcoholism treatment. He had multiple medical problems; his kidneys, liver, and other major organs were dysfunctional as a result of his years as an alcoholic. He had also suffered brain damage that eroded his intellectual capacity, and he had a passive, dependent personality.
>
> His follow-up care plan required short-term rehabilitation and, for the longer term, staying in compliance with a medication regime and having frequent physician visits to monitor medical conditions that if untreated, could lead to acute problems and otherwise unnecessary hospitalization. The hospital staff did not believe that he could handle this level of self-care.
>
> Nevertheless his case would be easy to decide if the man had had a home and a family who could take responsibility for seeing that he took his medicine and saw a physician regularly or at the first sign of problems. The man was asked if he had any family; he replied that he had two brothers in the area whom he had barely seen in 20 years. He made it clear that he did not want to show up on their doorsteps asking to be taken in at this late date, and the discharge planner did not press him to do so.

The hospital discharge planner was extremely angry at the director of the halfway house, who refused to take the man back. She felt that the halfway house was the man's surrogate family and had an obligation to take him. The director took the position that the man had not been a client but an employee required to pull his load and that the halfway house was "not a nursing home." The discharge planner was particularly incensed that the halfway house director would not come to the hospital to break

the bad news directly to the patient but expected her to tell the patient that
he had now lost both his home and his job as a result of his illness.

The discharge planner was also concerned that she could not place the
patient in the rehabilitation hospital owned by her hospital's parent corpora-
tion. The rehabilitation hospital required a guaranteed discharge destina-
tion prior to admission, and the patient had none. Medicare-certified
nursing home beds were in very scarce supply.

Board and care was considered but rejected because the discharge planner
did not feel that a board and care operator could be trusted to take sufficient
personal interest in monitoring the patient's medical needs. Asked what
would likely happen to the patient, the discharge planner replied:

> We'll probably have to bend the rules—exaggerate his medical instability—
> and get him into a nursing home. We have a nursing home in Baltimore where
> we send these kinds of cases. I hate to send people there because it is so far
> away, but this man won't have visitors so it doesn't matter that much. This is
> where I usually send patients who have come from homeless shelters—and we
> get quite a few admissions from shelters because this area has several. It's not
> what I would call a good nursing home, but it's also not as bad as you might
> expect considering the population this nursing home serves.

In the second problematic case, the facts were as follows:

> The landlady at a neighborhood boarding home where an elderly man lived
> called an ambulance and sent the man to the hospital's emergency room. There
> was nothing physically wrong with him and therefore no medical reason for
> hospital admission. It turned out that the man was severely cognitively im-
> paired with Alzheimer's disease but was physically strong and aggressive. He
> had nearly burned down the boarding house, apparently not for the first time,
> and the landlady was fed up. She packed his bags and threw him out, but her
> conscience required that she send him somewhere, so she called an ambulance
> and sent him to the hospital emergency room. The hospital discharge planning
> staff was in a panic and an uproar. They had to find a place for this man because
> the hospital would have to bear the uncompensated costs of an unnecessary
> admission if they could not. It turned out that the man had three children living
> nearby.

The younger and less experienced discharge planners, in particular,
expressed quite judgmental attitudes toward the family; they were out-
raged that the family could have allowed this situation to develop and felt
that proper family behavior would have been for the family to show up

immediately and very apologetically to relieve the hospital of this troublesome case.

However, by the end of the day, the children were still hemming and hawing; none had either flatly refused or made a firm commitment to take the father in. One child said that she would take the father into her home if the discharge planner could promise to arrange daily in-home care while she was at work. She was afraid her father might burn her house down if left alone. The discharge planner replied that she could arrange 6 hours of in-home care at best. When asked why the family couldn't use the man's own income from Social Security and SSI to pay for the extra hours needed, the discharge planner said she believed his relatives were low-income and wanted to use his check to cover the extra household expenses his presence would bring.

The discharge planner did not believe that the man would qualify for nursing home placement, given his lack of physical impairments or medical/nursing needs. In her view, the only real solution was for the hospital staff to work on family members until by cajoling, browbeating, shaming, and bribing them with services to the extent possible, they could be convinced to "do their duty."

When elderly clients with disabilities seek formal services from the community rather than from a hospital, a different kind of selectivity bias operates. It also works to ensure that public program officials are rarely confronted with cases in which applicants do not need help because they clearly have sufficient informal care resources to meet their long-term care needs. When family members are available and able to provide care without experiencing undue burden, neither the client nor the family is likely to perceive a need for help that would lead them to seek formal services. This is because family caregivers typically subscribe to societal values and norms about family responsibility that dictate when it is appropriate or legitimate to seek help and when it is not.

These family norms are so deep-seated and so widely shared and upheld that they seldom need to be written into formal processes of eligibility determination for publicly funded home care. Spouses, for example, know that they are expected to take care of each others' needs—especially in the areas of housekeeping, cooking, laundry, and so on, but including personal care, as well, unless they themselves are too frail or ill to help. Similarly, adult children and other relatives know that once they have decided to move in with an elderly relative with disabilities or to bring an elderly relative to live with them, they have tacitly obligated themselves to assume, and be held to, a higher level of caregiving responsibility than that borne by family members who do not live with these relatives. Few families violate these implicit rules.

Nurses and social workers who do eligibility assessments for publicly funded home-care programs can cite few examples in which they denied services because the family was capable of providing all necessary care. A fieldworker in Washington state related an anecdote about a "multi-generation welfare family" who, she said, "knew all the angles" and looked on a grandmother with disabilities as another opportunity to "milk the system." Because the state authorized paying family members as providers under certain circumstances, a younger member of the household applied to get paid for providing the grandmother's care. The fieldworker turned down the request because, as she put it: "I knew she was going to be there anyway. It wasn't that she was refusing to provide care if we didn't pay her—she just thought she'd see if we'd go for it."

The fieldworker made it clear that this case was so rare she found it more amusing than offensive. More common are the stories fieldworkers tell about children who call expressing concern for their elderly parents, but when the fieldworker contacts the parents, the caregiver-spouse is angry that the son or daughter has gone "behind their backs" to public authorities. The social workers go on to relate how they proceeded to talk caregiver spouses into recognizing their need for and accepting help— speaking with a certain amount of irony, because one of the tacit norms of their profession is that social services workers are not supposed to be in the business of "pitching," let alone "foisting," services on reluctant clients.

The effects of self-selection bias on the use of home care services are quantifiable. Use of formal services (both public and private pay) among the noninstitutionalized elderly living in the community has been analyzed recently, based on the 1982 and 1984 National Long-Term Care Surveys (NLTCS) and the 1987 National Medical Expenditures Survey (NMES). The findings indicate that factors statistically related to weak informal support are almost as powerful as severity of functional disability in predicting formal services use (Coughlin, McBride, Perozek, & Liu, 1990; Short & Leon, 1990). For example, Coughlin et al.'s logistic regression analysis of 1984 NLTCS data found that the probability of using formal home-care services during the prior week among sample members was .362 for those with three to four dependencies in Activities of Daily Living (ADL) and .481 for those with five ADL dependencies; the probability of formal service use during the prior week was .281 for sample members living alone and .342 for those with no informal helpers. This and other analyses of NLTCS and NMES data suggest two principal patterns of formal services use among the impaired elderly living in the community.

The most common pattern—that is, the most numerically frequent one—involves use of formal services by elderly women living alone. Typically, this group has only impairments in Instrumental Activities of Daily Living (IADL) or, at most, one or two ADL impairments; the formal help they receive mainly involves homemaker/chore services. The second pattern involves elderly persons with severe ADL impairments—often demented and incontinent besides—who live with family caregivers and receive substantial amounts of informal help. The formal services used by this second group tend to be more expensive personal care attendants and/or professional home nursing care.

Clearly, in the first instance, formal help is being used primarily to compensate for lesser availability of or less immediate access to informal care, whereas in the second case, formal services are supplementing a high level of informal support. Among informal caregivers who seek formal help to supplement their own efforts to provide care, adult children and other nonspouse relatives are disproportionately represented vis-à-vis spouses. In addition, studies of the elderly's self-reported unmet or undermet needs for ADL and IADL help have found that those relying on spouse caregivers are much less likely to report such needs than those receiving care from other family members (U.S. General Accounting Office, 1986).

An analysis of National Channeling Demonstration data (Kemper, 1992) found that, even in the context of an experimental expansion of access to publicly funded home care, availability of family help was associated with use of less formal care, more informal care, and more care overall. The author notes that

> the analysis has shown that informal caregivers are not only the most common providers of care in the community (which is well known), but they also provide far and away the greatest amounts of care. Moreover, the amount of informal care received increases with disability at a much greater rate than does formal care under the same circumstances. This suggests that as care needs increase, family and friends step in to provide the bulk of care.
>
> These findings concerning informal care highlight difficult equity choices that must be made about who should receive public long-term care benefits. How informal care is valued affects—either explicitly or implicitly—the choice of eligibility criteria and benefit levels for home care programs. Those with immediate family are endowed with a source that others do not have, and

the estimates presented here suggest that the differences in endowments are great. Those with a spouse and one or more children receive on average 23 hours more care per week than those with neither. (pp. 447-448)

Kemper (1992) goes on to point out that taking the availability of family into account in determining eligibility or benefit levels conflicts with the values of many people and poses difficult implementation problems. Nevertheless, in allocating long-term care benefits, it is impossible to avoid judgments about how to treat differences in the availability of informal care.

Inadvertent or Unintended
Consequences of Eligibility Criteria

At first glance, the fact that selectivity biases operate so powerfully may appear to make a strong case for not taking the availability of informal supports into account in formal determinations of eligibility for publicly funded home care. Why fix something that isn't broken? Why insult families by questioning their need for help when so few families seek to take unfair advantage? This kind of reasoning probably explains why long-term care professionals often resist, sometimes with outrage, the idea that availability of informal support could be a legitimate criterion in assessing eligibility and assigning benefit levels for publicly-funded home and community-based care. Their reaction makes a lot of sense, too—so long as it is assumed that the purpose of establishing eligibility criteria is to distinguish applicants who do not need home care services from those who do.

However, if we examine how eligibility criteria are set and function existing home- and community-based service programs, it quickly becomes apparent that screening out "nonneedy" applicants is not their purpose. Rather, the purpose of eligibility standards, as with coverage and reimbursement limits that apply to benefits subsequently authorized, is "triage"; that is, deciding who among the needy will and will not be served and to what extent their needs will be met, given available public resources.

The criteria chosen to assess need for services, the relative weights assigned to particular criteria, and the cutoff points selected to screen individuals in or out of program eligibility, as well as the set of decision rules used to allocate benefits to particular levels of need and the types of services offered— all of these have subtle but nonetheless very powerful differential consequences for clients in different family situations.

For example, programs that require high severity of functional disability for eligibility (e.g., three or more ADL dependencies, severe cognitive impairment, or medical needs often associated with nursing home placement) can be expected to serve higher proportions of elderly who have extensive family support but need supplemental help, as compared to elderly living alone, particularly when service hours are limited. This is because individuals with severe disabilities have a very difficult time remaining in the community unless they have the very intensive support that is more likely to be provided by family members than public programs. Some experts have suggested, for example, that 25 hours of weekly attendant care is the minimum level of service that public programs must be prepared to authorize to promote "independent living" for people with moderate to severe ADL impairments (Litvak, Zukas, & Heumann, 1987).

At the other end of the scale, home care programs that only require an elderly person to be "disabled" but have no specific threshold requirement for severity of impairment and that provide only a few hours weekly of homemaker/chore help can be expected to serve mainly the mild to moderately impaired elderly living alone or frail couples.

These relationships make intuitive logical sense but are not easy to document because most home care programs do not keep good descriptive statistics on beneficiaries and do little analysis with the statistics they do keep. However, a few illustrative examples can be provided. For example, statistics from the National Channeling Demonstration (Christianson, 1986) can serve as a proxy for home care programs with high disability requirements for eligibility and moderate benefits. Roughly 80% of participants in both experimental groups had ADL-impairment levels characterized as "severe" to "extremely severe" and nearly half were incontinent.

In the "basic case-management" model, clients received an average of 8 hours of service per week and, in the more generous "financial control" model, clients received an average of 16 hours of service weekly. The percentage of clients living alone ranged from 34% in the basic model to 39% in the financial control model—and the percentage of those living alone who had no informal support ranged from 7% to 8%, respectively.

In contrast, the Connecticut Promotion of Independent Living (PIL) program has targeted clients with less severe disabilities: 60% of those served between 1981 and 1986 had one or fewer ADL dependencies (Lusky, 1990). Forty-seven percent of PIL clients lived alone. Unfortunately, no data are readily available about service types or average service hours accorded PIL clients.

Data from New York's In-Home Services program suggest that intensive service packages can compensate for stringent disability criteria in enabling a public program to serve clients living alone (United Hospital Fund, 1987). In this program, clients must have enough disabilities to qualify for nursing home admission. In New York City, as of 1985, 52% of the caseload received more than 50 hours of personal care attendant service weekly (including 17% who received round-the-clock in-home care). Over two thirds of the New York City clients lived alone.

As a final example, 1989 statistics from Indiana's Choice Program suggest that clients living alone tend to enter public home-care programs at lower levels of disability than those living with others. Thus the mean score on the disability assessment instrument (scale of 0-100) for those living alone was 64, as compared to 73 for those living in two-person households, 77 for those in three-person households, and 82 for those in households of four or more (Saywell, Kinney, Rosentraub, & Steinmetz, 1989).

It is not clear how consciously aware public program administrators are of the relationship between eligibility criteria, maximum benefit levels, and the ability of their programs to serve people with no or weak informal supports. The design features of most public home-care programs appear to be mainly determined by perceived budgetary and other resource constraints or political considerations (such as the desire to create a highly visible program that serves a large number of clients, even if that means spreading resources very thinly in terms of per capita benefits). Most programs also set goals of preventing institutionalization, including in many cases, the intent to provide cost-effective alternatives to institutionalization.

However, understanding of the variables that affect institutionalization is poor—particularly among program administrators as opposed to researchers. As a result, programs across the country have come up with very different notions of what eligibility screens will best target the population "at risk" of nursing home placement and what types and levels of service can deter nursing home placements. In any case, the "bottom line" for most program administrators is to structure a program that will cost no more than policymakers have determined they can afford and are willing to spend.

Politicians—particularly at the federal level—often commission policy research to define and measure the extent of population "need" for services based on disability measures and to estimate the costs of a program that will "meet the need." However, when it comes to actually legislating programs into existence, politicians are inclined to redefine "need" and the levels of service required to meet the need to bring projected program costs into line with budgetary goals. Indeed, it could be argued that when policymakers become unwilling to do this—that is, when they or influential interest groups become wedded to a definition of need for services that is likely to produce costs far in excess of the amount perceived to be available or affordable—decision making tends to become paralyzed. This may explain why most home-care program expansion over the past 10 years has taken place at the state and local level in nonentitlement programs (Intergovernmental Health Policy Project, 1988).

The difference between entitlement and nonentitlement programs is not so much that the former are legally bound to serve all in need and the latter are not. Rather, it is that once the criteria of need have been established as an entitlement, they are more difficult to change, and are particular to retrench. In an entitlement program, changes in eligibility, coverage, and even reimbursement limits often require legislation or formal rule making with public comment periods. For example, in the Medicare home health program, who is entitled to care and who is not is determined by the definition of such terms as *skilled* care, *homebound,* and *part-time* and *intermittent* services. In order to be eligible for home health benefits, Medicare beneficiaries must demonstrate a need for skilled care and must be confined to their homes, but they cannot require services on more than a part-time, intermittent basis. Any effort to change the definitions of these terms in ways that are perceived to restrict eligibility immediately arouses stiff resistance from provider groups and, through them, from consumers. In contrast, administrators of state-run home-care programs— including Medicaid-financed programs but especially those that are only state funded—have far wider discretion to restructure the size and scope of their effort by making changes in eligibility and benefit criteria.

Indeed, a striking feature of state and local home-care programs is their tendency to constantly review their assessment criteria for eligibility determinations and benefit allocation and to revise the formalized assessment/care planning instruments used to apply these criteria to particular cases. When state and local economies are doing well, policymakers often look to expand popular programs, such as home care for the elderly. The legislature votes higher appropriations for home care, and eligibility and benefit criteria are liberalized accordingly. Conversely, when the state economy takes a downturn or when program costs start creeping up beyond levels required to stay within the annual budget, program officials are directed to scale back. Their typical response is to invoke such strategies as redoing the assessment form to screen in fewer eligibles and lowering the maximum authorized or average service hours and spending limits per client.

Massachusetts, for example, has responded to its fiscal problems of the past several years by directing the home care corporations that administer state- and SSBG-funded home- and community-based services for the frail elderly to tighten eligibility criteria. As a result, by 1989, 70% of clients being served were in the highest three disability categories, as compared to 38% in 1986. However, average hours of service did not increase commensurate with the higher disability levels of the caseload (as of 1989, clients in most impaired category averaged only 7.6 hours of service per week), and the program continued to emphasize homemaker/chore rather than personal care services (Wilner, 1989).

We can only speculate on the effects of such changes in patterns of service allocation on clients with no or weak informal supports. However, the findings of a longitudinal study of Massachusetts elderly and their formal/informal services use are suggestive of what those effects might be. The study (Morris, Gutkin, Ruchlin, & Sherwood, 1989) found that from 1982 to 1986, the incidence and the intensity of formal services use was greatest among the elderly residing in senior housing and lowest among the elderly in private homes, with those living in private apartments showing intermediate formal service use. The elderly living in senior housing composed only 5.8% of the total Massachusetts' elderly population.

Compared to those in the other housing settings, particularly those in private homes, residents in senior housing were disproportionately older, poor, less likely to be married, and more likely to live alone. For example, 85% of residents of senior housing were unmarried, and two thirds lived alone, compared to 42% and 22%, respectively, of those living in private homes or apartments.

Although most residents in all three settings received informal help, such help was available in much greater amounts to those living in private homes. On average, residents of private homes received 4 hours of informal help per 1 hour of formal help, and among those with ADL impairments, in particular, the ratio was almost 5 to 1. In contrast, among residents of senior housing, the ratio of informal to formal services use was 1 to 1, even among those with ADL impairments.

Thus, even though intensity of formal service use was greater among residents in senior housing and increased with disability levels, the availability of formal help (most of which was provided via the state through the home care corporations) did not come close to compensating for the comparative unavailability of informal support for residents of elderly housing vis-à-vis elderly living in private homes.

In 1988, the Colorado legislature became concerned about rising costs in the state's home-care allowance program, which provided cash payments to elderly with impairments to help pay for supportive services or, in some cases, to compensate family caregivers for support provided ("Direct Payments," 1990). In response, program administrators replaced the previous system, which had largely left eligibility and payment authorization decisions to the discretion of case managers, with a standardized assessment tool that specified benefits by disability level.

Generally speaking, the benefits authorized under the new system proved to be considerably less generous than those authorized under the discretionary system. Consumer advocates filed suit but lost the case. The court ruled that program administrators had acted within their authority in designing and implementing the new standardized eligibility and benefits assessment tool and could not be said to be exercising their authority in a manner that was "arbitrary and capricious." The court's reasoning appears to be that the standardized assessment system was scientifically based (it accorded benefits on the basis of ADL levels) and operated according to objective rules that prohibited case managers from discriminating in favor of one client versus another on grounds other than disability. In other words, the state was under no obligation to ensure sufficient public resources to meet the care needs of the elderly with disabilities who lived in the community; rationing was acceptable so long as the rules were objective and based on scientific measures of disability such as ADL scores.

Cost increases in Indiana's Choice program in the summer of 1989 prompted the Department of Human Services to reconsider eligibility criteria and earlier plans for program expansion. According to researchers hired to evaluate the program's cost-effectiveness vis-à-vis nursing home care, eligibility had become the most controversial issue for the Choice program. Particularly difficult was defining who was truly at risk of entering a nursing home. State Officials were aware that if they tightened the definition for risk of institutionalization, they would automatically save money because the Choice program covered only those defined as disabled enough to qualify for nursing home.

Preliminary results from a DHHS-sponsored study of changes in Medicaid personal care programs between 1984-1985 and 1989-1990 (Litvak & Kennedy, 1991) suggest that in most states, where comparative data are available, the trend has been toward tightening the disability criteria for eligibility for Medicaid personal care programs and toward fewer average hours of service per client. Ratcheting up the disability scores required for program eligibility is often explained and justified as a means of ensuring program cost-effectiveness by more closely targeting the population likely to require nursing home placement in the absence of publicly funded home care.

Higher ADL and cognitive impairment scores are, indeed, statistically associated with higher likelihood of nursing home placement, but so is lack or lesser availability of family support. Higher impairment levels and low family support do not necessarily go together. As a result, to the extent that home care programs with high disability thresholds for eligibility end up screening out persons with fewer disabilities who are at risk of nursing home placement due to lack of informal support, they have not truly improved their targeting of the "at-risk" population. A longitudinal study of clients discharged from Connecticut's Program for Independent Living between January 1, 1981, and December 31, 1986, sought to understand the factors associated with discharge to nursing homes. Although age, ADL score, Mental Status Questionnaire (MSQ) score, and living alone were all found to be significant predictors of discharge to nursing home care, the most statistically powerful of these factors was living alone (Lusky, 1990).

This is not to say that tighter eligibility standards or cutbacks in benefits are always unjustified. If they are not applied as a reflex response to rising costs but are based on actual analysis of use patterns in relation to client characteristics, they may be warranted.

In 1988, the Board of Supervisors in Fairfax County, Virginia, became alarmed by an unexpectedly large increase from the previous year in the caseload size and costs of the "companion care" program (a Title XX homemaker/chore service program receiving 80% of its funding from the county itself). More sophisticated than most municipalities, Fairfax County decided to analyze data from its management information system to determine the reasons for the increases and develop a longer-term strategy for cost containment.

However, the problem was considered too serious to defer all response until the results of the data analysis were in. Rather than put clients on a waiting list, which the supervisors believed would spark public protest, program administrators adopted an immediate reduction in maximum service hours from 40 hours weekly down to 32.

When the data on service use were analyzed, it was found that 19% of companion care clients lived alone, whereas over two thirds lived with "able-bodied" caregivers. The latter group were nonetheless being author-ized to receive relatively generous benefits (compared to available data on typical benefits in other states and in the adjacent areas of the Wash-ington metropolitan area).

Then after some revisions were made to the assessment instrument and the formula used to authorize service hours according to disability level, clients with able-bodied caregivers were being recommended for an average of 20 hours of companion service. Fieldworkers argued that these levels were, in fact, necessary. At first glance, the rationale for such high service intensity was not at all clear. For example, the "companions" were only authorized to perform housekeeping and other IADL tasks, not "hands-on" personal care, so the connection between higher ADL impair-ment levels and the need for more hours of companion care was not apparent. After all, the amount of time it takes to do housekeeping, shopping, and laundry depends more on the size of the residence and the proximity of shopping and laundry facilities than it does on the severity of the client's disabilities.

Moreover, no one believed that the proper role of the program was to support family caregivers who had brought elderly parents into their homes by supplying them with 20 hours weekly of free "maid service." What became apparent on closer analysis was that—without quite realiz-ing it—the county had become involved in providing a "sitter" service to watch over elders with disabilities who would otherwise be alone all day while their family caregivers worked. In many cases, clients and families were supplementing program services by paying privately for additional hours of companion care.

Once the meaning of the program's service pattern was understood, program administrators were left to ponder a number of value-laden policy questions. There was no doubt that many of the program's clients did in fact need some level of protective surveillance or that many could benefit from services to address their social isolation. However, was com-panion care—which cost on average of $5 per hour from independent providers and $10 an hour from agencies—either the most cost-effective or the most appropriate way to meet the socialization needs of these elderly?

Moreover, was it appropriate for the county to be subsidizing what was, in effect, a rather expensive model of one-on-one, in-home day care for elderly clients—many of whom might themselves be low income, but whose family caregivers were often middle class—when no such services were being made available to help working parents meet their child care needs?

A number of recommendations emerged from the study. One was that Fairfax County should consider lower-cost technological solutions to provide protective supervision, such as offering elderly clients who lived alone or were home alone while their family caregivers were at work subscriptions to the local hospital's electronic "lifeline" service. In addition, it was recommended that efforts be made to meet clients' socialization needs through other means than companion care; for example, by arranging for transportation to local senior centers and developing liaisons with agencies running Older Americans Act programs, local churches, and community service groups that could provide volunteer companions and "friendly visitors" (Takemoto, personal communication, 1988).

SYSTEMS THAT EXPLICITLY TAKE INTO ACCOUNT INFORMAL SUPPORT RESOURCES

Focusing on "Unmet Needs"

In recent years, a number of state home-care programs for the elderly—particularly those that are generally regarded as being on the cutting edge of innovative practices—have incorporated availability of informal care explicitly into their program designs. Availability of informal care may be a factor in determining both eligibility and benefits or in determining benefits after eligibility has been established on the basis of functional disability. For example, in Oregon, eligibility for in-home services financed under the Medicaid home- and community-based care waiver program or under Oregon's Project Independence is contingent on (a) meeting a financial means test; (b) meeting the established priorities for service, which are defined and ordered by severity of functional disability; and (c) being judged unable to maintain independent living on the basis of one or more criteria, including "relatives/friends and neighbors cannot meet all the client's needs."[1]

Applicants to Wisconsin's Community Options Program (COP) may establish eligibility for home- and community-based care without regard to availability of informal support if they have a long-term or irreversible illness or disability resulting in at least two severe medical needs or if they have developmental disabilities, Alzheimer's disease, a related dementia disorder, or a history of hospitalization for chronic mental illness. However, applicants seeking to qualify for COP services on the basis of functional disabilities (ADL and IADL dependencies) not associated with severe medical needs must also be determined to have inadequate informal support to meet their needs, based on at least one of the following criteria:

1. The person has no friends or relatives who are able or willing to provide needed assistance, support, and personal or chore services.
2. Friends or relatives who have been providing needed assistance are no longer able or willing to continue to provide help.
3. Friends or relatives who have been providing assistance are not able or willing to increase the amount of help needed to meet changing conditions.

Similarly, Washington state's comprehensive assessment form used to assess applicants for all aging and adult services programs includes an evaluation of the availability of informal (or privately paid) caregiving resources. In the section dealing with psychological/social/cognitive functioning, the assessment asks whether the client currently has a primary caregiver (unpaid or paid privately) who is able and willing to continue to provide care. If yes, the assessor is directed to enter the name and telephone number of the primary caregiver. In the section dealing with functional impairments, scoring is based on points assigned, not to ADL and IADL dependencies, but to "unmet needs"—that is, ADL and IADL needs not being met or not considered adequately met by existing informal and privately paid caregivers. The codes for unmet needs include:

O = all help required is already provided
M = minimal help needed
S = substantial help needed
T = total help needed

Unmet needs coded as M, S, or T are accorded different point values based on the presumed importance or urgency of having a particular functional need met.

For example, unmet needs with respect to toileting are scored higher than unmet needs with respect to bathing and dressing. Interestingly, some unmet IADL needs are scored higher than some unmet ADL needs. For example, unmet needs with respect to preparation of a main meal are scored as high as unmet needs for assistance with eating and toileting and, therefore, higher than unmet needs for assistance with bathing and dressing.

The service plan that is developed on the basis of the assessment identifies "problems," not only with respect to unmet needs for ADL/IADL assistance, but also with respect to medical care and needs that arise from impaired psycho/social/cognitive functioning. It specifies the mix of formal and informal help proposed to address each problem. In addressing the problems identified, case managers are encouraged to develop strategies that go beyond program boundaries; that is, to pursue liaisons with other public programs that provide specialized services, to identify volunteer or charitable resources in the community, and to recruit or help the client recruit additional informal services.

This holistic approach can be illustrated by the service plan for a Washington state COPES (Medicaid home- and community-based care waiver) client.

The main service being supplied by COPES was in-home attendant help with ADLs and IADLs. The attendant was to provide live-in care, partially paid for in wages by the state, with the remainder of the payment being provided "in kind" by the client in the form of free lodging to the aide and the aide's two children. Because of the client's mobility impairments, she lived on the first floor of her house and could no longer access the entire second floor, which was to be used by the aide and her children. The client recruited her own attendant—subject to program approval—and she chose a young woman from the neighborhood whom she had known for 20 years—because the attendant was a child whom she regarded as a surrogate "daughter."

The attendant had been a substance abuser, and her children had been placed in foster care as a result; but she had recently completed a rehabilitation program and was in the process of regaining custody of her children. The client herself was a recovered alcoholic—with many years of sobriety—who felt that because of her own experience she could help the attendant stay drug- and alcohol-free.

Although this might otherwise have been considered a risky situation, the case manager agreed to authorize the attendant because the client's disabilities were all physical rather than mental—indeed, the client was considered to have an unusually feisty and independent spirit—and because the client assured the case manager that she would dismiss the attendant and call the case manager in to make other arrangements if any problems arose. (Importantly, the case manager made clear that she would respond immediately to help arrange alternate care if necessary—reassuring the client that she need not tolerate abuse or neglect from the attendant.)

Other elements of the care plan included transportation to the doctor (to be funded via the regular Medicaid program), referral to an ACTION-funded senior companion program, and attendance at a day health center, which was recommended partly for socialization and partly for medical monitoring of the client's several potentially unstable medical conditions and complicated medication regime.

In planning care for this client, the case manager was concerned about the client's social isolation: The woman was long divorced, childless, and apparently had only one living relative in another state; in addition, she could not leave her house without help due to her mobility impairments and the steep stairs that had to be negotiated to get in or out of the house. The case manager was also concerned that the client might become depressed without sufficient mental/social stimulation and also did not want the client to become overly dependent on the attendant for companionship, a situation that might make the client tolerate poor performance by the attendant. The service plan also included two other unusual elements:

1. Furniture for the live-in provider, which was to be obtained with social services discretionary funds (because, without this job, the provider was a candidate for welfare assistance).
2. Veterinary care for the client's dog, whom the client regarded as her main friend and protector. The dog's veterinary care was not paid for by Medicaid, but out of supplemental funds for special needs donated by a local charitable organization.

Even in Washington's COPES program, program design features sometimes pose frustrating administrative barriers to achieving the desired flexible response to what both the family and the case manager agree are significant unmet needs. Consider the following case, for example:

Two sisters in their 70s were caring for their 57-year-old niece, who had severe disabilities from birth due to cerebral palsy. The aunts had been caring for the niece in their home for nearly 15 years, following the death of her mother; they had been COPES clients for about 2 years. The sisters received some financial assistance from COPES, as authorized family care providers, but their most pressing need was for help with transportation. They had already spent several thousand dollars on ramps and related equipment, but they could not afford the hydraulic lift they needed to get the niece in her wheelchair/bed in and out of their van more easily. Both sisters were concerned that they might harm their own health in continuing to do this hard work themselves. Previously, one of the sister's sons, who lived across the street, had helped, but as a result of an industrial accident, he was himself suffering disabilities and terminally ill.

The case manager had been trying for over 6 months to obtain the lift, thus far without success. The problem was that equipment of this type was not on the list of COPES services. In principle, the equipment was available under the regular Medicaid program, but the individual in charge of authorizing durable medical equipment refused to grant authorization. His reasoning was that there was not a sufficient medical rationale for the lift: It would be more cost-effective for the client to call an ambulance for physician visits, and it was not appropriate for Medicaid to pay the costs of equipment to be used for nonmedical transportation purposes.

Indeed, the main reason the sisters wanted the lift was because they were highly involved in community volunteer projects and social activities as members of the local Lions Club. They usually included their niece in these activities, which she enjoyed very much. They had also just completed a month-long visit—with the niece—to relatives in California. Although COPES would have paid for respite care, the sisters had no interest in "sitter services" that would allow them to continue their active schedules while leaving the niece at home. Although the case manager was confident that she would eventually win the day at a Medicaid hearing by showing that the lift would pay for itself vis-à-vis ambulance expenses within 3 to 4 years, she estimated that obtaining approval for Medicaid coverage of the lift would probably take at least another 3 to 6 months.

The highly individualized approach of COPES to addressing particular problems or unmet care needs can be contrasted with a case illustrating the more traditional "formulaic" approach to assessing eligibility for and authorizing a given level of service under a categorical program. Ironically, this example is also from Washington state, which, in addition to the COPES Medicaid waiver program, also operates several other home-care programs, including a recently established Medicaid personal care optional benefit and a long-standing SSBG-funded program for home-maker/chore services. In these latter two programs, only one service is offered and clients do not have case managers; rather, they are visited at home by a social services caseworker who performs an initial assessment and periodic reassessments. At least in the instance observed, caseworkers in these programs seem to apply the assessment tool in much more of a "rote" or traditionally bureaucratic manner.

For example, in the case in question the facts were these:

> The client, who was being visited for a regularly scheduled reassessment, complained that she was receiving far more hours of in-home attendant care than she wanted or felt she needed. The client said that the aide was there too often and that she was forced to spend too much of her own time supervising the aide and telling her what to do. The client felt that the aide could perform the housekeeping tasks that really needed to be done in far fewer hours. Under

this program, all in-home attendants were supplied by agencies, and the client was not very satisfied with the current and previous workers assigned to her case. The client also mentioned that her daughter was moving to the area and was prepared to help out with many of the tasks that the paid provider was currently doing.

The caseworker appeared somewhat taken aback and unprepared to respond to the client's statements. She said that the client was receiving an appropriate amount of service based on the initial assessment but a reassessment was due. After going through the form, the caseworker announced that because the client's functioning had improved, she would now be authorized for somewhat fewer hours of in-home care.

The outside observer was also struck by comments the client made suggesting that she was very uncomfortable with having a stranger help her with bathing. The client only needed stand-by assistance, and it would have been appropriate to explore using adaptive devices in the bathroom that would reduce the risk of independent bathing. The client and the observer had a brief conversation about some adaptations the observer's mother had made to deal with a similar situation. However, there was no discussion of incorporating this other approach into the care plan, apparently because the program was only set up to pay for in-home, agency-employed aide and attendant care, nothing else.

After the visit, the caseworker remarked to the observer that she had felt very uncomfortable and ill-equipped to respond to the client's comments. The caseworker had been trained to "go by the book" in determining eligibility and authorizing services according to the assessment form and did not know how to or whether she ought to negotiate a service plan in response to client and family preferences.

PROGRAM PHILOSOPHIES: PITFALLS
VERSUS POSSIBILITIES FOR IMPROVED SERVICE

Interest in taking availability of family support into account in providing publicly funded home care is not limited to the United States. Indeed, a recent study (Baldock & Evers, 1992) of innovations in home care for the elderly in three European countries—the United Kingdom, Sweden, and the Netherlands—identified as a major trend the shift "from implicit to explicit interaction with informal care systems." The authors of the study see personal social services for the elderly as being on the cutting edge of innovation in social welfare policy generally:

> It appears that the public services developed in the forty years after the second world war, consisting largely of highly centralized and standardized forms of care, with residential institutions playing the major role, are breaking down under ideological and resource pressures and are being replaced by more flexible, more individualized and often home-based forms of care. We call this the shift from "Taylorist" to "tailor-made" personal care services. A fundamental and logically necessary part of this shift is a renegotiation and reorganization of the relationships between formal, public care services and the informal, mainly family, sources of care for the dependent. (pp. 290-291)

Developing an explicit policy to coordinate the provision of publicly funded home- and community-based care with informal resources can take at least two forms:

1. Willingness to allocate public resources sufficient to compensate for absent or weak informal supports
2. Willingness to tailor the amounts and types of help provided by the public sector to the preferences and self-perceived needs for help of the elderly clients and their caregivers

Some program administrators may decide to opt for one or another of these strategies rather than both.

For example, policy papers describing the goals of the Israeli home-care insurance program make clear that the program's intent is to prevent institutionalization by supporting and rewarding informal family care, but not to provide enough formal help to prevent institutionalization of elderly persons who lack family caregivers. It is acknowledged that the formal help authorized under either of the program's two benefit levels is inadequate to meet the care needs of people without informal support. On this basis, Israeli policymakers make no apology for continuing to build nursing home beds toward a target ratio of 45 beds per 1,000 elderly, because institutional facilities are believed necessary to accommodate the elderly with impairments who lack family caregivers. Interestingly, Israeli legislators are also concerned that the local social services workers who manage the program and authorize and arrange for specific services might attempt to save program costs by authorizing fewer services to clients with more family support available.

Accordingly, in Israel, clients and families are authorized to choose which services they want from a "basket" of available services, but, by law, the services chosen must be worth at least 80% of the authorized monetary value of the benefit level authorized (i.e., benefit level one or two, based on the severity of the client's functional disabilities). During the planning stages, many experts had argued in favor of a cash benefit option that would compensate families for providing in-kind services or allow families to purchase services from independent providers, particularly friends and neighbors. However, the decision was made to authorize only agency-provided services of specific types, with cash benefits permitted only if agency-provided services were not available. Due to these and other features, many long-term care experts in Israel were somewhat disappointed with the design of the new home-care insurance program because they did not believe it truly embodied the kind of flexible interaction of public benefits with informal resources that they had advocated (Israeli National Insurance Institute, 1988).

In contrast to Israel's emphasis on support for family caregiving, British policymakers in charge of local services such as home help for the elderly have traditionally chosen to direct formal services predominantly toward elderly persons living alone—although this policy is the subject of increasing criticism. As of 1980, the British system has provided almost no formal services to elderly people with impairments who live with younger caregivers, especially younger married couples both with and without children. (Knowledgeable readers may protest: What about the career allowances? These cash payments to family caregivers are available to persons who have given up paying jobs to care for an elderly person with impairments; however, the allowances are currently set at £28 per week. As such, they constitute more of a symbolic token of appreciation than anything else.) Until recently, the British policy of directing local home-help services almost entirely toward the elderly with no or weak informal supports was implicit rather than explicit.

Baldock and Evers (1992) suggest that the reality of service allocation in Britain was hidden under the facade of a commitment to state-funded universal services and a continuing, if unrealistic, commitment to the ideology of universalism on the part of professionals and managers in the public sector. Only recently have policymakers been forced to confront and acknowledge the chronic underfunding that has meant that public authorities in practice have never been able—and are becoming increasingly less able—to meet the needs of more than a proportion of those nominally entitled to care. Now that public authorities have given up the pretense, as it were, of commitment to a universal disability-based entitlement, it is yet to be determined to what extent they will explicitly endorse a "rationing" scheme that continues to direct home care resources primarily to those with no or weak informal support.

In the United States, it seems unlikely that policymakers at federal, state, or local levels would want to be identified with policies that consciously and explicitly exclude elderly people because of the presence or absence or family caregivers. Indeed, our review of how informal resources are taken into account in the Oregon, Wisconsin, and Washington programs found that assessments of need for service in these state programs typically encompass both situations: those in which functional needs are determined to be unmet because informal caregiving is unavailable, and those in which needs are unmet or incompletely met because informal caregivers cannot provide all the help required.

Whether it is possible to develop a policy that adequately serves both groups is another question. Under severe budgetary constraints and pressure to spread resources thinly to accommodate rising numbers of elderly with impairments, it is obviously much easier—and perhaps the most politically safe and popular strategy—to pursue a policy that emphasizes small amounts of formal service in support of existing and substantial family caregiving efforts. Some home-care program administrators at the state level are aware of this problem and have developed benefit allocation policies intended to accommodate both groups.

For example, in Wisconsin's Community Options Program, per capita monthly spending limits are applied as an average across the caseload rather than per individual case. Moreover, counties are directed to spend a minimum of 20% of their COP allocations on high-cost cases, defined as those costing more than twice the allowable average (McDowell, Barniskis, & Wright, 1989). Similarly, California's In-Home Supportive Services Program has two separate per-case cost limits: one for cases requiring under 20 hours of service weekly and another much higher limit for cases requiring more than 20 hours of service (Litvak et al., 1987).

A very different approach to accommodating the heavy and high cost formal service needs of elderly clients with no or weak informal supports is to develop sheltered housing options such as adult foster care and assisted living, which Oregon is currently doing. Often, in-home supportive services can be delivered with greater economies of scale in sheltered housing settings. For example, one of the recommendations that came out of the Fairfax, Virginia, program management study discussed earlier was to develop a "shared aide" program. Analyses of client data showed that large numbers of companion care clients living alone were concentrated in a few low-income, HUD-sponsored senior apartment complexes. It was thought that clients in these buildings might be able to share their companion care program aides. This would cut costs but also provide for more efficient, effective coverage: If needed on an emergency basis, the aide would be somewhere in the building and potentially "on call" to all clients for a longer period.

In addition, program managers saw potential in using the shared aide concept to facilitate getting clients living in the same building acquainted and spending time together so that they could provide for each other's socialization needs and look out for one another during off hours. Here again this would promote more efficient, effective use of paid aide time because the aides could then put more effort toward performing IADL tasks rather than being sitters.

Baldock and Evers (1992) note that administrators in the European home-care programs they studied often have very different ideas in mind when they speak of integrating and coordinating public benefits with informal long-term care resources. They identified three distinct strategies, which may be pursued singly or in combination:

1. Providing incentives or creating conditions intended to strengthen and sustain family caregiving efforts
2. Actively managing the contribution of informal caregivers
3. Shifting costs from the public to the private sector

According to Baldock and Evers (1992), all three strategies pose risks or dangers in the sense that they are not necessarily benevolent in intent or effect and may ultimately be perceived by family caregivers as more exploitative than supportive. In particular, they note,

These risks of inappropriate cost-shifting are most evident in the United Kingdom where availability of institutional care for the old in state hospitals and residential homes has been allowed to decline substantially relative to the numbers over 75. Public domiciliary care services are primarily the responsibility of the local authorities, who, because of budgetary constraints have not been able to expand their services in line with numbers. They have responded with new rationing or targeting devices designed to concentrate their services on the most needy. In some parts of the country this has meant actually withdrawing home help services from dependent old people who have become used to them on the grounds that they are not amongst the most needy. The gap then has to be filled by voluntary or family care. In the process the whole public system may have moved to better targeting and a more efficient use of its resources but it has also shifted costs to the informal sector. (p. 302)

Similar risks are apparent in the U.S. context, particularly insofar as policymakers continue to insist that the main purpose of publicly funded home care is to prevent and postpone nursing home placement. Many states are both developing or expanding home care programs and actively pursuing policies to reduce their supply of nursing home beds relative to the size of their elderly populations. Yet the results of research and demonstrations carried out over the past 10 years indicate that publicly funded home care has very limited potential to substitute for nursing home care in individual cases or to reduce institutional use in the aggregate. Research and demonstration results also call into question the ability of publicly funded home-care programs to provide incentives or create conditions under which families will choose to continue to provide informal care longer than they would have otherwise. Evaluations of respite care have found modest effects at best ("The Evaluation," 1988; Kaspar, Steinbach, & Andrews, 1990; Lawton et al., 1989; Miller, Berg, Bischoff, & Sachlenker, 1989; Montgomery, 1988a).

CONCLUSIONS

The emerging conclusion from the past decade's worth of policy research on home- and community-based long-term care and its effects on family caregiving appears to be that the family responds to its own dynamics, which, by and large, are remarkably impervious or invulnerable to manipulation via public policies—whether for good or for ill. Thus the good news is that families rarely withdraw their efforts or substitute formal for informal help when publicly funded home care is made available. However, by the same token, improved access to formal help via public programs only rarely inspires or encourages families to provide more informal care or to maintain family caregiving for longer periods than they would have otherwise.

If, indeed, the family tends to "do its own thing" with or without public support, this further suggests that the possibilities for case managers in public programs to actively "manage" family contributions are also quite limited. The best that they can hope to do is to acknowledge informal resources in such a way that publicly funded help does not mindlessly duplicate or wastefully supplement care already being provided while failing to meet other needs that the family is unable or unwilling to serve. Thus, instead of attempting to manage family caregiving, case management in public programs more properly entails molding and adapting public help around the informal support system.

It can be very expensive to provide the kind of professional case management necessary to develop a holistic care plan that efficiently and effectively integrates public and informal care resources. As a result, such an approach may not be less expensive than an approach that allocates a defined set of authorized services according to a formula based on disability measures. Whether it costs more, the same, or less, the distribution of expenditures will clearly be different. With an explicit focus on "unmet" needs, lower expenditures in cases in which families are providing most care informally will not represent funds saved—but rather funds reallocated to cases in which less informal support is available. Similarly, the emphasis on tailoring help specifically to consumer and family preferences involves more attention to the quality and appropriateness of help, not simply to controlling costs.

Given scarce resources, policymakers do not really have a choice of whether or not to consider family caregiving in the provision of publicly funded home care for the elderly in need of long-term care. The choice is between doing so implicitly or explicitly. When family caregiving is taken into account implicitly, there is an unspoken expectation that any gap between the amount of help supplied via public programs and the total amount of help needed will be met by informal caregivers. This tacit assumption works to the disadvantage of those who have no or weak informal supports, a group that constitutes a minority of elderly with disabilities who live in the community but a much higher percentage of those who use public home-care programs. Moreover, no public home-care programs— or even proposed programs—promise sufficient resources to meet all the long-term care needs of elderly with disabilities who live in the community, such that providing informal care becomes a purely voluntary activity that may enhance the person's quality of life but is not strictly necessary.

Many advocates of publicly funded home care favor determining eligibility and allocating benefits on a "need" basis, with need being defined in terms of disability levels. In practice, this typically translates into the recommended use of standardized assessment instruments that measure severity of functional disability and/or degree of cognitive impairment in terms of scores on the Katz scale of ADL or the MSQ. This chapter has argued that the apparent egalitarianism of this approach is illusory. If eligibility and access to public benefits are determined according to disability levels alone, then individuals with substantial informal support from family and friends are likely to receive more formal help than they actually need, whereas individuals with no or weak informal support will receive less than adequate help. Indeed, many in the latter group are likely to be excluded from public programs altogether, if they do not meet the disability severity threshold for program eligibility. A more truly even-handed approach is for public home-care programs to take the availability of family caregiving explicitly into account by focusing their interventions on "un- or undermet" care needs and tailoring the types and amounts of help provided to client and family preferences.

NOTE

1. Oregon Administrative Rules, Chapter 411, Division 30—Senior Services Division, Revised 6-29-88, Section 411-30-01 (2)(a)(B).

7

Legal and Ethical Issues in Family Caregiving and the Role of Public Policy

MARSHALL B. KAPP

INTRODUCTION

In contemporary America, it is a virtual article of faith among those involved in the planning and delivery of long-term care services that older persons requiring health care or other assistance with the activities of daily living would prefer to receive that assistance while residing in the community, in their own homes or those of relatives, rather than in an institution. In fact, most long-term care is provided outside of institutional walls. But most frail, vulnerable elderly people are cared for in the community by family members (usually spouses and adult daughters). This informal, unpaid caregiving may or may not be supplemented by formal, paid caregivers.

Some attention recently has begun to be paid to the constellation of legal and ethical issues confronting formal service providers delivering paid care to older persons in their own homes (Haddad & Kapp, 1990). In the informal long-term caregiving arena, substantial work has been done in the past 2 decades examining the psychological (Brody, 1985), social (Hooyman & Lustbader, 1986), and economic implications of relying heavily on family members to keep elders with disabilities at home. However, little effort has been made to identify and analyze the unique ethical questions surrounding family caregiving (Pratt, Schmall, & Wright, 1987), and useful literature addressing particular legal ramifications of family caregiving is exceedingly sparse (Kapp, 1991b, 1992).

This chapter briefly catalogs some of these ethical and legal issues. It must be noted at the outset that, in terms of practical impact on the lives of dependent older persons being cared for at home by their families, ethical considerations will tend to predominate over legal ones. Most of the dilemmas arising in the sphere of long-term family caregiving are basically interpersonal and social in nature, the kinds of problems that the law often is ill-suited to resolve successfully.

This chapter identifies several hypothetical legal issues involving client rights and family responsibilities. However, frail, homebound older people will find it difficult if not impossible to enforce their theoretical legal rights. In our "claims-based" legal system, individual liberties and entitlements that have been transgressed are vindicated only if the injured party possesses sufficient physical, mental, emotional, and financial wherewithal to engage the processes of the formal legal system. These include the retention of an attorney willing to work on the basis of a contingency fee agreement (Cohen, 1986). Few people depending on long-term family caregiving for their daily existence will possess such capacity. Thus violation of a client's legal rights by family members in the home care setting usually will go unvindicated. In practical terms, family behavior affecting the client's rights will be influenced primarily by the way in which the family conceives of its ethical role and resolves perceived ethical quandaries through its behavior (Cicirelli, 1992).

THE DEFINITIONAL ISSUE

In many contexts (e.g., proxy medical decision making for incapacitated people), family members ordinarily are afforded a preferential legal and ethical status, on the theory that they know best the client's values and preferences and will respect them or that, alternatively, the family will usually act in the client's best interests (Rhoden, 1988). As an increasing number of people choose to engage in close nontraditional relationships with others (e.g., same or opposite sex lovers) to whom they are unrelated by blood or marriage, public policy makers must address the question of whether to include such relationships in the concept of family, where that concept carries special legal and ethical significance (Brown, 1990). This issue becomes especially pressing as more and more older people outlive their traditional relatives, outlive the mental capacity of their traditional relatives, or grow older and dependent never having married or borne offspring.

WHY FAMILIES GIVE CARE

Before discussing rights and responsibilities that arise within the family caregiver/client relationship, we must identify the most salient legal and ethical motivations for family members of dependent older persons to enter into such a relationship in the first place. Legitimate countervailing influences are also noted.

No law compels family members to personally provide direct, hands-on care to dependent relatives. Totally ignoring the dependent individual's basic needs to the point of extreme physical endangerment may constitute elder neglect (Subcommittee on Health & Long-Term Care, 1990), which is criminally condemned by statute in virtually every state (Quinn & Tomita, 1986). However, relatives may fulfill their obligations by securing formal caregiving for the dependent person rather than by providing the caregiving themselves.

A number of states, under the authority of the federal Medicaid statute (HCFA, 1983), have passed "family responsibility" statutes attempting to recover from delineated relatives the state's costs in providing long-term care services to a dependent person (Byrd, 1988; DeJong, 1983). These laws are questionable ethically because of their potentially deleterious impact on family interpersonal relationships. Operationally we question them because they are rarely successful on balance in capturing significant dollars (Durso & Marshall, 1985). Legally we question them because they arguably violate constitutional safeguards of equal protection and due process (Kapp, 1978). Even when family responsibility laws can be enforced, they permit family members to "buy out" of their family caregiving responsibilities rather than satisfying them in a hands-on manner.

Thus the substantial number of families that provide long-term caregiving to relatives with disabilities must be inspired primarily by ethical, rather than legal, considerations (Zuckerman, Dubler, & Collopy, 1990). One relevant ethical principle is a belief in reciprocity, that care provided to an older relative is a form of payback for benefits that person earlier conferred on the family. Family caregiving in this view is a way of evening the ethical score. Family caregivers may also be motivated by compassion for the present vulnerability of the relative, a phenomenon that has been labeled the "power of dependency" (Callahan, 1985). The ethical principle of beneficence (Pellegrino & Thomasma, 1988), or doing good, militates against abandoning dependent elders precisely at their hour of greatest need.

Countervailing, ethically defensible pressures militate against families entering into or staying within long-term direct caregiving relationships with relatives who have disabilities. These include attention to potential caregivers' personal, professional, financial, and social needs and desires, including responsibilities owed to their spouses and children (Callahan, 1988). Many family caregivers endure tremendous sacrifices in terms of these legitimate interests by voluntarily (at least in the legal and ethical, if not the psychological, sense) choosing to accept family caregiving responsibilities for parents, aunts, uncles, siblings, or spouses that trump those other interests (Cantor, 1983).

PUBLIC POLICY AND QUALITY CONTROL: THE ROLE OF CIVIL LAWSUITS

One major objective of public policy ought to be to assure that the quality of services provided to dependent older persons by family caregivers meet minimum standards. An important legal mechanism of quality control in acute health care settings (e.g., hospitals and physicians' offices), and to a much lesser extent in nursing homes, is the civil malpractice lawsuit brought by the patient against a provider. Such suits allege injury proximately caused by the provider's negligence (i.e., substandard care) and seek monetary damages to compensate the patient for the injury suffered. For several reasons, as a practical matter, this legal mechanism is not available to help assure the quality of family caregiver services provided in the home to dependent clients.

Even when professionals are the ones providing services to older individuals, few successful lawsuits arise out of the home care environment. This is not a venue to which the much-publicized "liability crisis" has spread (Johnson, 1989).

Theoretically, a family caregiver could be held legally liable to a client for (a) substandard care rendered by the caregiver directly, (b) negligence in selecting and hiring an incompetent, formal, paid caregiver whose error or omission injures the client, and/or (c) mismanagement of the client's financial assets. Research reveals no judicial decisions in which this sort of liability has been imposed, and realistically such claims are extremely unlikely.

First, dependent older people being cared for by family members in one or the other's home will be dissuaded from initiating civil lawsuits in most circumstances by bonds of loyalty and affection to the caregivers. Even if the relationship has not been one of affection and loyalty, there is little financial incentive for the client to pursue such actions. Family members cannot purchase and do not carry "family caregiver liability insurance" and hence their personal economic pockets are unlikely to be sufficiently deep to enforce the payment of judicial judgments. Even if the pockets were deep, what would the dependent elder do with the money awarded? It would probably be spent on formal, paid caregivers to take the family's place. Having the proceeds of a significant legal judgment would make the client ineligible for publicly funded means-tested programs such as Medicaid or Supplemental Security Income. Even if the psychological climate and economic incentives pointed toward litigation against the family, few clients who are dependent on family caregiving would have the physical, mental, emotional, or economic ability to gain access to the civil justice system to vindicate their theoretical rights.

Second, even those home care clients who are willing and able to pursue a civil action for damages against a family caregiver would have an exceedingly difficult time successfully proving their case in court. In any negligence action, the plaintiff shoulders the burden of proving by a preponderance of the evidence (greater than a 51% likelihood) four separate elements:

1. That a duty as defined by a standard of care existed.
2. That this duty was violated.
3. That an injury occurred.
4. That there was a link of proximate or direct causation between the defendant's breach of duty and the plaintiff's injury.

In the context of family caregiving, the standard of care is not a professional one, but only that degree of care and skill commonly possessed and exhibited by other average, reasonable families in similar circumstances. In the unlikely event a client could prove a violation or breach of this standard of care, it would be difficult to establish that this negligence was the most proximate or direct cause of injury to a client who was already dependent as a result of disabilities. Finally, even assuming the elements of proof could be satisfied, the measure of damages would probably be small in which no future lost wages or immense new medical expenses were involved and life expectancy is limited.

If the civil lawsuit that is ubiquitous as a purported quality control device in the acute medical care context is not useful to deter poor quality of care in family caregiving situations, how then can and should public policymakers employ legal mechanisms to assure the quality of such care? Government could require that families providing home-based services be bonded or insured to provide compensation for negligently injured clients. Government could strengthen external regulatory oversight and monitoring of family caregiving through legislative and budgetary empowerment of ombudsmen (Freeman, 1990) and through advocacy programs and regulatory agencies that heretofore have been concerned almost exclusively with policing formal caregivers.

Expanded government involvement in family caregiving would be very problematic. It would raise fundamental questions about the limits of the state's *parens patriae* power to protect citizens who are unable or unwilling to protect themselves against harm, especially when state intervention occurred without the client's permission or even over the client's objection. An expanded government role in this sphere would have significant budgetary implications. Problems would abound regarding placement of people whose families refused to care for them in the wake of government intervention, especially when clients refused transfer to a nursing home but were unable to care for themselves without a great deal of outside assistance. Damage to the psychological and social aspects of interpersonal relations within the family caused by third-party monitoring and intervention would also need to be taken into account.

The next section of this chapter looks at two areas in which states do impose themselves within the family caregiving context in the name of quality assurance. However, before moving to that discussion, the impact of family caregiving on a client's potential legal remedies against a negligent formal caregiver is noted.

For most home care clients, formal and informal caregiving occur in combination. For many clients, formal home-care services would be impossible in the absence of supplementary informal caregiving, and those clients would need to be placed in institutional settings if family caregivers were not available (Doty, 1986; Horowitz, 1985). Thus public policy ought to encourage maximum coordination between formal and family caregivers.

However, fear of legal liability sometimes inhibits formal caregivers, especially home health agencies, from training family members to perform certain home care tasks (e.g., operation of some medical machinery or delivery of some medications). Formal caregivers may be apprehensive that they will be held legally responsible if the family members perform these tasks poorly and injure the client in the process. This apprehension may impinge on the most effective use of family caregivers to maximize the benefits of investment in formal caregiving.

This apprehension about potential legal liability for errors of family caregivers is vastly overblown (Kapp, 1991a). Even if clients could somehow get into a courtroom, the performance of family caregivers, and therefore of the agency that trained them, would be held to a very minimal standard. The errors of family members probably would be considered intervening causes that broke the chain of proximate or direct causation between any negligence on the part of the formal caregiver and the injury incurred by the client. If the family inaugurated a civil action on behalf of the client, the family's own errors could be construed as contributory or comparative negligence, blocking recovery against the defendant. In addition, the family may be held to have voluntarily and knowingly assumed those risks that actually materialized to harm the client, absolving the formal caregiver of liability in the absence of negligence.

Thus involvement of family caregivers actually decreases the liability exposure of formal caregivers, although this is a point sometimes misunderstood by the latter group. The challenge for public policy is to encourage formal caregivers to maximize the use of available, competent family caregivers by reducing liability fears, while also encouraging formal caregivers to exercise due care in the training and monitoring of, and the delegation of tasks to, family caregivers. Especially nettlesome legal and ethical issues arise when the client complains to the formal caregiver about the quality of the family caregiver's services; the extent of the formal caregiver's obligations in such circumstances is uncertain. This leads us to a discussion of external regulation and intervention within the family caregiver/client relationship.

GOVERNMENT REGULATION AND QUALITY CONTROL: ABUSE AND NEGLECT

As previously noted, external regulation and monitoring of the family caregiver/client relationship is, and should be, minimal, with this relationship generally presumed to be a private one between people drawn together by natural bonds of loyalty and affection. However, to characterize the relationship in such terms in every case would be quite naive (Wolf,

1988). Some families are dysfunctional, and judgments and behavior of family members may be adversely affected by conflicts of interest or unbearable psychological strains. Thus, although society cannot legislate loving kindness among family members, it can attempt to prevent or remedy egregious behavior at the other end of the attitudinal scale. State statutes prohibiting and criminally punishing elder abuse and neglect represent an exercise of the state's *parens patriae* power to protect vulnerable older persons from the worst kinds of mistreatment at the hands of their caregivers, even when those caregivers are family members.

Enforcement of elder abuse and neglect statutes against family caregivers raises a number of legal and ethical questions. Those who suspect elder abuse or neglect by family members must ask at what point that suspicion is reasonable, such that mandatory reporting requirements and accompanying provisions providing immunity against defamation claims come into operation. Ethically, should suspected abuse or neglect be reported, even over the client's objection? That is, should the potential reporter act as the state's agent in benevolently protecting the client rather than as a respecter of the client's autonomous choice (assuming it is an autonomous choice) to remain in the home environment, even at risk of familial abuse or neglect? Will reporting suspected abuse or neglect really promote the client's welfare if the only realistic remedy is placement in a nursing home that the client resists? Formal caregivers must also consider their own possible legal liability for failure to comply with elder abuse and neglect reporting requirements, especially if subsequent injury to the client can be directly connected to the failure to report, and thereby notify authorities of the need for timely intervention.

Once a violation of the client's rights to be free from abuse and neglect has been reported, realistic remedies available to underfunded protective services offices and to the courts are severely constrained. Even when sufficient proof of elder abuse or neglect is adduced, ethical dilemmas are presented by placement decisions regarding the dependent client whose family life—such as it was—has been disrupted by the legal system, often over the client's objection. The situation frequently devolves to the troubling decision between condoning continued placement in an abusive or neglectful household or involuntarily imposed transfer to an institution and severance of family ties.

Public policy makers must search for a more complete array of remedies for situations of family caregiver abuse and neglect of dependent relatives. The focus must be shifted away from the punishment of offenders, which rarely accomplishes any valid societal objective, and toward solutions that safeguard the client from harm while respecting the client's autonomous preferences and preserving the positive aspects of family relationships.

GOVERNMENT REGULATION AND
QUALITY CONTROL: LICENSING ISSUES

Another area of government regulation with potential implications for the role of family caregivers concerns professional licensure statutes. Every jurisdiction has enacted professional licensure statutes that restrict the performance of certain services to those individuals who, based on demonstration of specified education, training, and knowledge, have been licensed by the state to perform those services. Licensure statutes are exclusive or monopolistic, in the sense that unlicensed personnel ordinarily are not permitted to perform services that are restricted to licensed professionals. The public policy rationale for these licensure statutes is the inherent state police power, that is, the inherent authority of society to take action to protect and promote the general health, safety, and welfare of the community.

In the home care context, professional licensure laws of greatest immediate importance are those relating to physicians, nurses, and various therapists (e.g., physical and occupational). Professional licensure laws apply for the most part solely to the health-related portion of home care activities. However, some states also require a minimum number of hours of training before a home health aide, homemaker, or certified nurse assistant may provide personal care or homemaker services. New federal regulations governing home care agencies participating in the Medicare program also contain provisions on minimum home aide training (Code of Federal Regulations, 1989).

When willing and able family members are available, home care agencies typically train those individuals to provide certain personal care and homemaker services for the client. Most state Nurse Practice Acts explicitly exempt from their coverage services provided by family (and in most cases friends also) to relatives in their own homes.[1] The home care agency has the professional duty to assess the capacity of family members to perform specific tasks and to properly instruct and monitor those persons to assure the client's safety.

The legal picture is most complicated in the area of medications. No state explicitly empowers unlicensed family members to administer medication;

neither do most states expressly prohibit family from doing so. It is generally accepted that family members may assist the client to take over-the-counter medications (e.g., by opening, holding, or even emptying medicine containers). The ability of family members to administer prescription drugs without technically violating Nurse Practice Acts is more problematic, although as a practical matter relatives do assist dependent relatives to take prescription medications thousands of times a day around the country without any reported prosecutions for practicing nursing without a license. The picture becomes cloudier still when other health-related tasks are at issue. Again, there is a dearth of reported case law on this subject. Formal home-care providers thus far have generally proceeded to delegate tasks to family members despite some anxiety about liability associated with acts and omissions of those individuals, a practice validated by practical experience reflecting an absence of reported legal cases.

Public policymakers must recognize the value of using professional licensure laws as a regulatory tool to contribute to client protection. At the same time, such laws should not be written and enforced so restrictively as to unduly impede access of clients to preferred and appropriate family caregivers. This overarching tension between the policy goals of protection or well-being, on one hand, and maximizing client autonomy—including the right to take risks—on the other, runs throughout any consideration of the proper degree of governmental involvement in the quality assurance of home-based informal or formal services.

ACCESS AND FAMILY
CAREGIVER COMPENSATION

Creating incentives to enhance access of clients to desired and appropriate family caregiving in the home environment ought to be a central public policy objective. Financial compensation is one kind of incentive that might further this objective (Arling & McAuley, 1983; Linsk et al., 1988).

At least 23 states, in the exemptions to their respective Nurse Practice Acts, expressly require that home care services by family members or friends be provided free, whereas other states are silent on the question of compensating relatives. Even when no compensation is available, families who can financially afford (and are physically and mentally able and live in close enough proximity) to provide free home-care services may find this the best way to optimize the client's freedom and choice.

Even clients who would prefer not to use a relative may decide that family caregiving is acceptable as the only realistic alternative to nursing home placement.

However, many relatives who are able and otherwise willing to serve in the caregiving capacity may find their personal financial needs preclude working without compensation. In response to this problem, some states that do not legislatively require that family caregiving services be free (e.g., California, Oregon, Wisconsin) have devised methods of paying family members as independent providers for home care clients. Under home- and community-based waivers, Medicaid home-care monies may not be paid to a spouse of an adult client or the parent of a minor child, but they may be used to compensate other relatives for their services (WDHSS, 1988). Specific state appropriations for home care may be used to compensate any family member, including spouses and parents of minor children, and several states have implemented specific standards and methodologies for doing this.[2]

As an adjunct to its home care program, Oregon also operates a sizable (approximately 7,000 beds) Adult Foster Care Home program (Kane, Kane Illston, Nyman, & Finch, 1991) using state appropriations, Medicaid waiver money, and Supplemental Security Income.[3] Under this program, the consumer is cared for in someone else's home. About one third of Oregon's Adult Foster Care Homes are licensed as Relative Foster Homes, meaning that the consumer is cared for in a family member's home. Public funds can then be used to pay the relative as a foster care provider.

Most of the objections to expanding public financing for family caregivers serving dependent home-care clients revolve around economic factors (Arling & McAuley, 1983). However, some of the arguments are ethically grounded, claiming that society should not have to pay families to engage in activities to which they are already morally obligated. A complete analysis of the competing arguments for enhancing access to family caregiving through public financial incentives, on one hand, versus preserving a conception of family responsibilities based on morality rather than pecuniary motivations, on the other, is beyond the scope of this chapter. It is a tension that public policymakers should resolve clearly and quickly.

ALLOCATION OF SOCIETAL RESOURCES

The issue of paying public funds to family caregivers leads to a consideration of the even larger, and more fundamental, policy question: How much in the way of scarce societal resources ought to be devoted to home care for the elderly, as opposed to being used in other social pursuits? Deciding upon the appropriate allocation of financial and human resources for this purpose entails serious value choices about social justice and equity, both within and across generations. A more thorough discussion of the respective roles and responsibilities of the private versus public sectors in fulfilling (and indeed in defining) the needs of the dependent elderly is sorely needed, as is a deeper analysis of how home-based family caregiving fits into the overall health-care system in terms of the proper allocation of resources (Callahan, 1990).

BENEVOLENCE AND
AUTONOMY: FINANCIAL MANAGEMENT

Homebound clients may be physically unable to fulfill their financial obligations (e.g., unable to get to the bank or to write out and mail checks), even though they are capable of understanding their obligations and engaging in a rational decision-making process about the management of their finances. For people in this category, a variety of legal devices make it possible for the client to retain a degree of decisional control while authorizing a family member to act on the client's financial decisions. These include (a) the ordinary power of attorney, in which a competent principal delegates authority to another person to act as his or her agent; and (b) the joint bank account (joint tenancy) in which both parties own the account and either party may engage in transactions. These legal devices work well in most situations in which the client has physical but not mental disabilities.

Legal and ethical difficulties may arise within these arrangements when family caregivers take advantage of a power of attorney or a joint bank account to abuse the client's finances. Legal challenges to such abuse are unlikely, and courts and public agencies are essentially powerless to intervene if the client is mentally competent and fails to object to the family member's actions. In legal theory, competent clients could terminate a power of attorney or joint account at any point, but they may lack the physical capacity to effectuate that legal right. Only when clients lack decisional capacity to manage personal finances is the law empowered to intervene on their behalf without the clients' permission.

When decisional incapacity regarding financial management is present, any party may petition the local probate court (or its equivalent) requesting a finding of incompetence and appointment of a surrogate decision maker. The nomenclature of this substitute decisionmaker for financial affairs varies among jurisdictions (e.g., guardian of the estate, guardian of property, conservator). Usually, a family member initiates the petition and is appointed as substitute decisionmaker, although (especially when there are no available relatives or the motives of available relatives are suspect) a third party, such as a public agency, may initiate the conservatorship proceedings, requesting appointment of a nonfamily surrogate.

For a number of reasons, invoking the probate court system for formal appointment of a surrogate financial manager ought to be pursued only when other reasonable options are unavailable. In pragmatic terms, this process ordinarily is time-consuming, expensive, and emotionally traumatic for all involved parties. There is a substantial danger that the probate court will issue a sweeping order of general magnitude, depriving the client of decision-making rights altogether, rather than basing its inquiry just on the client's ability to make specific types of decisions and fashioning its empowerment of a surrogate decisionmaker in a precise and limited way. When no family member is available to serve as surrogate, appointment may be made of an individual or public agency that has no prior knowledge of the client's history or preferences or that lacks the resources or inclination to handle the surrogacy duties conscientiously.

When a family member, who, after being appointed conservator, abuses the client's financial affairs for personal gain, the *pro forma* periodic reporting requirements imposed by most overworked probate courts are unlikely to detect any but the most flagrant violations of fiduciary (trust) responsibility, and third parties are unlikely to bring objections to the probate court's attention despite the court's continued jurisdiction over the conservatorship. Although state law provides that a conservatorship may be terminated if the ward (client) regains decisional capacity, cases in which a ward has successfully overcome the presumption of continued incompetence are very rare; hence, conservatorship tends to last forever.

Ethically, the imperative to maximize the autonomy of the client (even the client whose decision making is impaired) while protecting the client against self-inflicted harm compels exploration of the least restrictive alternatives for accomplishing legitimate societal objectives in the financial as well as the medical and personal realms (Nathanson, 1990). One alternative to conservatorship that works well for incapacitated persons whose chief source of income is federal government benefit programs is the "Representative Payee" program. Under this plan, the government mails the monthly benefit check to a designated representative payee rather than to the incapacitated beneficiary. Some state benefit programs offer similar arrangements. Some clients, while still mentally capable, have planned ahead—often with family support—for their eventual inability to manage personal finances. For them, legal devices including the creation of living (*inter vivos*) trusts and durable powers of attorney can provide for an orderly exercise of surrogate financial management authority by family members without formal intrusion by the legal system (Gilfix, 1988).

Under any of the surrogate financial management devices discussed here, abuse and exploitation of the client may occur at the hands of unethical family members who are influenced more by economic self-interest than by their fiduciary or trust responsibilities to a dependent relative. Such abuse is unlikely to be detected or effectively remedied by the current legal system. Public policymakers must devise ways to protect dependent clients from financial exploitation by unethical family members, while encouraging the use of informal alternatives that work well in the vast majority of cases. In addition, public policy must discourage, too, the ready resort to the cumbersome probate court system or erection of regulatory intrusions (Subcommittee on Housing and Consumer Interests, 1988) into the family caregiver/client relationship unless less restrictive alternatives have been explored and found to be inappropriate.

BENEVOLENCE AND
AUTONOMY: MEDICAL DECISION MAKING

It should also be an important goal of public policy to balance fairly competing social commitments to individual autonomy, on one hand, and to protect vulnerable persons against harm, on the other, regarding medical decision making within the family caregiver/dependent client relationship. Family caregivers may be involved in the medical arena either as enablers and supporters of client decision making or as surrogates acting on the client's behalf (Adelman, Greene, & Chavon, 1987; Brody, 1978; Jecker, 1990).

The threshold inquiry is whether the client is capable of making voluntary, informed, authentic, and autonomous medical choices. The phrase "decisional capacity" is used to describe nonjudicial judgments about an individual's ability to engage in a rational decision-making process; "competency" denotes a formal judicial ruling about an individual's ability to make legally binding choices. A thorough analysis of the concept of decisional capacity is beyond the scope of this chapter (Kane & King, 1990; Kapp, 1990a). Suffice it to note here that legally and ethically valid decision making requires capacity only at a minimally sufficient level, and that assessing a home care client's possession of such minimal capacity accurately may be a very imprecise exercise. Decision-making capacity often varies for an individual over time and depends on environmental factors such as drugs taken, physical surroundings, methods of communication used, and other persons nearby. Decisional capacity is not a global, all-or-nothing matter, but rather depends on the complexity of the particular decision confronting the client at the time. Perhaps most important, decisional capacity depends on the person's functional ability to engage in a rational thinking process, and not necessarily whether formal or informal caregivers agree with the result or outcome of that thinking process.

Against this backdrop, the legal system is a rather blunt, crude instrument for dealing with questions relating to decisional capacity. When a client is decisionally capable, the legal doctrine of informed consent and the ethical principle of personal autonomy dictate that the client act as decision maker (President's Commission, 1982). Although the dependent client may certainly solicit and accept advice from family caregivers, ultimate legal and ethical authority to make valid decisions rests with the client exclusively. When this ideal process of collaborative decision making does not occur in practice, decisions may be imposed on the decisionally capable but physically dependent client by family caregivers and acted on by formal health care providers. However, the realistic risk of legal repercussions to the family or formal providers is slight in such cases; legal rights are not self-executing, and people dependent on family caregiving are among the least likely to assert themselves effectively in a claims-based society. Thus the main safeguards to assure that medical decisions of dependent clients are not overridden by family caregivers with their own agendas rests with the ethical commitment to the client's autonomy by family caregivers (Cicirelli, 1992) and by the formal care- givers who are asked to carry out the family's instructions.

Of course, many mentally capable clients voluntarily choose to include their family caregivers extensively in medical decision making. The client may formally delegate decision-making authority to a specific family member by executing a durable power of attorney document. Usually such a delegation will be unspoken, with the patient ostensibly making the decision (and exercising his or her legal authority) but in actuality relying completely on the family caregiver's judgment. Capable clients may also rely on their families to various lesser degrees without explicitly or implicitly delegating decisional authority to them completely. Many people with cognitive impairments may have difficulty making adequately competent decisions on their own, but they may be rendered capable "enough" with the support and assistance of family caregivers (Kapp, 1990b). The voluntary, informed reliance on family members of a decisionally capable individual, or one who can be made capable with sufficient family support, is fully consistent with an ethical commitment to the client's autonomy (Collopy, 1988; Kapp, 1989).

The law, in its crudity and bluntness, deals poorly with subtle, nuanced concepts such as assisted consent and informally delegated decisional authority, on the rare occasions that it is confronted with such concepts. The law prefers instead clear, definitive answers to issues, and it is a belief in the judiciary's power to render decisions with such characteristics that leads parties to submit their disputes to courts in the first place. Thus the courts are equipped to deal with issues of medical decision-making capacity only within the context of formal guardianship proceedings and to provide only either/or answers to those issues. In the law, only one person at a time can be an authorized decisionmaker, even when the reality is one of joint or assisted decision making. As long as a competent client is apparently the one agreeing to or refusing medical interventions, the law is satisfied. Hence, as previously indicated, the client's best protection against abuse of the assisted decision-making process by family caregivers is the ethical commitment of those caregivers and of the formal health care providers implementing the medical decisions to respect and maximize the client's own autonomy.

When the dependent client lacks decisional capacity, the family caregivers ordinarily act as surrogate decision makers. The traditional preferred status of family members as proxies for the incapacitated is grounded in the ethical presumption that families are most likely to know and follow the values and preferences of the client or, if the client's wishes in a specific situation cannot be deduced, relatives are most likely to make decisions in the client's best interests. The special legal stature of family members is reflected in the law in, for example, state family consent statutes,[4] state living will statutes that authorize family decision making in which no living will has been executed, state autopsy permission and organ donation statutes, and in judicial decisions (Areen, 1987; Krasik, 1987). One commentator asserts that the tradition of seeking consent and advice from family members is "so well known in society at large that any individual who finds the prospect particularly odious has ample warning to make other arrangements better suited to protecting his own ends or interests" (Capron, 1974, p. 425).

Formal health care providers generally rely on the wishes of family members of decisionally incapable adults without insisting on any legal formalities or judicial oversight. In most instances, this is a desirable reflection of the least restrictive alternative philosophy; the psychological, financial, and administrative burdens of formal legal involvement would be great without corresponding benefits in terms of meaningful client protections. Even where the probate courts are petitioned for a formal guardianship order, they almost automatically appoint a willing and available family member as surrogate decisionmaker, unless compelling evidence is produced of the family member's unsuitability for the role and the availability of a more appropriate surrogate.

Family caregivers may make at least four different kinds of medically related decisions as surrogates for their mentally incapacitated relatives:

1. Decisions to accept or reject particular medical interventions within the home
2. Decisions to transfer the client to a hospital or nursing home (Bayer, Caplan, Dubler, & Zuckerman, 1987)
3. Decisions to hire or fire formal caregivers to assist with the client, and the identity of those formal caregivers
4. Decisions to provide family caregiving services in the first instance

Formal judicial authority to make these types of decisions should be sought only in rare circumstances in which definitive legal delineation of respective rights and responsibilities is needed. At the same time, it must be acknowledged that family caregivers may be subjected to conflicts of interest based on financial concerns (e.g., the desire not to spend assets that would eventually come to them as their inheritance) or psychological factors (e.g., the stress of caregiving and consequent inability to care sufficiently for oneself or one's own spouse or children) that may interfere with carrying out the family's ethical commitments with full fidelity. Decisions may be made that are inconsistent with the substituted judgment and best interests principles. In such rare but real circumstances in which family caregiving as an avenue of surrogate medical decision making breaks down, public policy must provide an efficient but effective mechanism for intervening on behalf of the dependent client.

BENEVOLENCE AND
AUTONOMY: EVERYDAY ACTIVITIES

Previous sections argue that the formal legal system is likely to be of extremely limited effectiveness in promoting client autonomy or benevolently protecting the client against abuse or exploitation in the areas of financial management or medical decision making, in which the family decisionmakers and formal health care providers succumb to conflicts of interest and act unethically. The weakness of legal intervention and the centrality of ethical goodwill on the part of involved parties is even greater when the decisions to be made and actions to be taken concerning a dependent client are of a more mundane, everyday, personal variety.

Family caregivers may take many everyday actions that threaten the autonomy of dependent clients under the justification of protecting them, and most are effectively shielded from legal monitoring and intervention. Family caregivers who hide car keys so that clients cannot drive, alcoholic beverages so they cannot drink, cigarettes so they cannot smoke, or candy so they cannot upset their blood sugar are protecting clients in a way that clients might choose not to protect themselves if physically and mentally capable of incurring risks. Even more problematic are behavioral management strategies (e.g., physical restraints, tranquilizers, locked doors) agreed to by family caregivers to enable them and formal caregivers to manage clients longer at home, rather than being forced to transfer clients to an institutional setting.

Everyday ethics have drawn little attention from professional commentators, and virtually none from public policymakers. Excellent but limited exploration of the "morality of the mundane" has been undertaken recently in the nursing home context (Kane & Caplan, 1990). Although many of the issues and principles identified in that work cross over to the family caregiving arena, the latter also presents its own unique ethical questions that demand substantial independent investigation.

CONFIDENTIALITY
AND TRUTH-TELLING

Whether dependent clients are decisionally capable or not, family caregivers usually control the flow of information to them. Family members are in a position to monitor mail, telephone calls, television, radio, visitors, and other sources that might provide clients with information.

Family caregivers are also situated as a potential barrier between formal caregivers who possess information about clients' medical condition and the clients themselves. Reports, anecdotal but abundant, are frequently heard about families who are given medical information about a client by the health care provider before the client is told, and who request (or demand) that the information be withheld from the client (Christie & Hoffmaster, 1986). The purported justification for this conduct is protecting the client from the adverse affects of hearing distressing personal news. This scenario, which if anything occurs more often in the home care setting than in institutional environments, implicates at least two kinds of client rights violations: breach of the client's reasonable expectations regarding confidentiality and deviation from the ethical principle of truth telling.

Clients may choose to waive these rights, to have information imparted first to their families, and to have information withheld completely from themselves. However, to be effective, such a waiver of rights should be voluntarily, knowingly, and competently made. The problem is not that such waivers occur, but that health care professionals too frequently, too automatically, assume them. Withholding information from clients also arguably offends the ethical principle of beneficence: Some claim that for most patients, providing relevant, truthful information about their medical condition confers therapeutic benefit rather than a deleterious effect (Post & Foley, 1993).

The realistic liability risk to family caregivers or the health professionals who participate in the sort of scenario described here is exceedingly small. Even assuming clients have the wherewithal and inclination to seek legal redress (and even assuming clients find out that their rights have been violated in the first place), the likelihood is slight of proving the existence of nonnominal damages of the kind for which the tort system traditionally compensates plaintiffs financially. Hence, for this topic as for others discussed in this chapter, the client's hope of being treated with respect and dignity lies mainly with the ethical commitment of family and professional caregivers to the principles of confidentiality and truth telling.

CONCLUSION: PUBLIC POLICY OPTIONS

This chapter has cataloged a number of legal and ethical issues arising around and within the family caregiver/dependent client relationship and the public policy implications of those issues. Quite purposely, many pressing needs but few definitive solutions have been suggested. Without departing from this basically descriptive format, this conclusion outlines three public policy options relating to the issues identified in the preceding pages.

First, increasing the role of external regulatory standards and standard-monitoring bureaucracies within the family caregiver/dependent client relationship, to assure advocacy for clients who are not situated to assure quality of services and respect for rights on their own behalf, is an idea that public policymakers should entertain only with the greatest caution. Unless substantial data establish that overwhelming benefits would be achieved by such intrusion, the costs in terms of dollars diverted from other social purposes and undue disruption of traditional relationships that work well in most circumstances militate heavily against this course of action.

Second, more empirical research on relevant client and family attitudes and behaviors should be sponsored. Is it true, for example, that families really do know best the values and preferences of their dependent relatives? Are families more likely to follow the substituted judgment of their relatives or to act in their relative's best interests, rather than being subject to excessive influence by self-interests? What is the actual impact on dependent persons of intrusions into personal autonomy, in matters dramatic and mundane? Public policy, in this area as in others, should be informed by data instead of speculation as much as possible.

Third, many (but by no means all) of the legal and ethical dilemmas previously enumerated may be anticipated and planned ahead for by clients and their families while clients still retain sufficient mental capacity to formulate, discuss, and document preferences about the conduct of their future medical, financial, and personal matters. Policymakers should encourage professional and popular education about such advance planning devices as durable powers of attorney, living (*inter vivos*) trusts, and living wills. These devices can inform and empower the client's chosen agents—within or outside of the client's traditional family—to act for the client once the client's personal ability to make and carry out autonomous choices has receded. Policymakers should adopt strategies (the Patient Self-Determination Act of 1990 is one example)[5] to encourage greater reliance on these devices to assure people some degree of continued control over their own lives while recognizing that, for most of us, dependency will be a natural part of the life course and a state in which, if we are very fortunate, loving family caregivers will help us to live out our days in comfort and dignity.

NOTES

1. For example, Florida Statutes Annotated Sec. 464.022 (1); Georgia Code Annotated Sec. 43-26-11 (5); Massachusetts Laws Annotated Sec. 80B; New York Code Article 139, Sec. 6908.1.a.

2. For example, California Department of Social Services (DSS)-Manual-SS, Service Program No. 7: In-Home-Supportive Services, Chapter 30-763.24 (e); Oregon Administrative Rules Sec. 411-30-027.

3. 42 United States Code Sec. 1381 et. seq.; 20 Code of Federal Regulations Sec. 416 et. seq.

4. Alaska Stat. Sec. 9.55.556 (b)(3)(1983); Arkansas Stat. Ann. Sec. 16-1142D206 (b)(2)(A)-(B)(1987); Delaware Code Ann. tit. 18, Sec. 6852 (a)(2)(Supp. 1988); Florida Stat. Ann. Sec. 766.103 (3)(a)(1),(4)(a)(West Supp. 1989); Georgia Code Ann. Sec. 88-2906.1(b)(2),(e)(3)(Harrison Supp. 1989); Hawaii Rev. Stat. Sec. 671-3(a)(1985); Idaho Code Sec. 39-4303(1985); Iowa Code Ann. Sec. 147.137(3)(West 1989); Kentucky Rev. Stat. Ann. Sec. 304.402D320(Michie/Bobbs-Merrill 1988); Louisiana Rev. Stat. Ann. Sec. 40:1299.53,.55(West 1977); Maine Rev. Stat. Ann. tit. 24, Sec. 2905(1)(Supp. 1989); Minnesota Stat. Ann. Sec. 144.651(9)(West 1989); Mississippi Code Ann. Sec. 41-41-3(Cum. Supp. 1989); Missouri Ann. Stat. Sec. 431.061(Vernon Cum. Supp. 1990); Nebraska Rev. Stat. Sec. 44-2808(1988); Nevada Rev. Stat. Sec. 41A.120(2)(1979); North Carolina Gen. Stat. Sec. 90.21.13(a)(1985); Ohio Rev. Code Ann. Sec. 2317.54(C)(Anderson Supp. 1988); Texas Rev. Civ. Stat. Ann. art. 4590i, Sec. 6.03(a),6.04(a), 6.05(Vernon Supp. 1990); Utah Code Ann. Sec. 78-14-5(4)(1977); Vermont Stat. Ann. tit. 12, Sec. 1909(c)(3)(Supp. 1989); Washington Rev. Code Ann. Sec. 7.70.050(4), 7.70.060(Supp. 1989).

5. Public Law 101-508, 4206, 4751 (1990).

8

Toward a Caregiving
Policy for the Aging Family

ROSALIE A. KANE
JOAN D. PENROD

In Chapter 1, we asserted that the United States lacks a coherent policy on family care for the elderly. This is hardly a startling or insightful observation. After all, the United States cannot yet be said to enjoy a coherent long-term care policy, and long-term care policy is de facto family policy. A more difficult task is to sketch out the content of an optimal long-term care policy in its effects on family members who give care. We undertake that task in this concluding chapter. In the first major section, we draw together the background information that should inform policy, and in the second part of the chapter we discuss specific policy controversies. The chapter concludes with recommendations for policy and policy research.

BACKGROUND FOR POLICY

Throughout this book, many facts have been aired. The pages of references attest to the volume of research done about family caregiving, with resultant findings, hypotheses, and pleas for more research. Given all this, what "facts" are particularly important as we grapple with public policy? How confident can we be about the basic informational building blocks? What information is still needed?

Before suggesting public policy directions on this or any other topic, basic questions need to be examined. First, how many people are involved with the issue, and in what ways? In other words, how many people are giving family care and what are they doing? What is the prevalence of family care? Second, who in particular is involved—that is, what subsets of the population are engaged in family care? What, if any, particular characteristics of caregivers or subsets of caregivers are important? Here we consider household configurations and various ways that family caregiving is or could be shared among family members.

Then the policymaker needs to analyze the problem that public policy would address. For family care, that exploration takes us in two directions. What problems, if any, exist in the quality of the care that family members give or the ensuing relationships between the one who gives and the one who receives the care? What effects does giving this care have on those who do so? What role can public policy play in accentuating the positive and eliminating the negative in this regard? Finally, and to complicate matters, the policy analyst needs to take into account any likely trends and changes in all the above aspects of the issues.

Prevalence of Family Care

Policy analysis should always be grounded in the scope of the problem or issue. But the most basic questions are among the most elusive to answer:

How many adults are giving care to older family members?
How much care are they giving?
How much time are they committing to this enterprise?

The answers to these questions will suggest whether a set of policies is needed that applies to all citizens, or whether a narrower "fix" for a subset of people will do. The answers will also suggest how much it might cost to replace family care with so-called formal care, and how much current obligations to give care cost the family caregivers in lost opportunities.

Unfortunately, these questions are not answered easily. Estimates in the literature of the prevalence of family caregiving diverge widely. For example, Stone and Kemper (1989) found that 2% of American workers have elder care responsibilities, whereas Scharlach and Boyd (1989) put the figure at 23%. Estimates of caregiving in general also range considerably. In part the differences are definitional.

In some studies, the stage-setting question asks caregivers whether they are presently giving care and assistance to any adults in their family, and how much time they spend on such endeavors. These studies may collect painstaking information on the time spent by the family "caregivers" in a wide variety of activities (e.g., household help, personal care, transportation, emotional support) without inquiry as to the actual needs of the person receiving care. The results take account of family care regardless of whether the person receiving it has a disability and regardless of whether the contributions of the family member go toward filling "unmet needs." These studies overestimate the population of caregivers that is relevant to most policy considerations.

Other studies count as family care only care given to people with specific levels of functional disabilities. To get into these prevalence estimates, caregivers must be providing care and the people receiving it must "need" that care by some operational definition of need. As Robyn Stone (1991) pointed out editorially, this more stringent definition yields much lower prevalence estimates.

To make policy use of the data on family caregiving, one needs to decide which activities count for an operational definition of family caregiving. For instance, visits to one's parents (whether or not they have disabilities) would be considered social support in most sociologists' frameworks, but many public policymakers would decline to replace this help for low-income people at public expense if no family caregivers were available. On the other hand, even the most decided opponent of governmental social programs is likely to support helping low-income people with disabilities who have no family caregivers to help them get in and out of bed, to bathe, to use the toilet, and to put food on their tables or into their mouths. Indeed, for many decades, low-income people in nursing homes (who are disproportionately people without spouses or adult children available to help) have received public subsidies to support this kind of basic care and attention.

Many different numbers can matter. When expanded publicly subsidized community long-term care benefits are considered, policymakers need to estimate the numbers of eligible people (based on defined impairment criteria) whose care is now largely provided by family. To project the costs of the benefit, they also need to estimate how many would take up the new benefits. A starting point for estimating the size of the so-called "woodwork effect" (i.e., people who will "come out of the woodwork" to take up community long-term care benefits although they would consider entering a nursing home only as a last resort) is the estimated 13.3 million potential family caregivers who have a spouse or parent age 65 or over with disabilities (Stone, 1991). However, not all adult children provide help and not all elderly people with adult children receive help from them, so the number of people formerly cared for by family who would be added to any new benefit must be smaller than the actual number of potential family caregivers. Also, the way any new benefit is keyed to disability and income will shape the size of the eligibility pool.

If the main goal of public programs is to support family caregiving with respite services, training, and counseling programs, then one must estimate the smaller subset of active caregivers who would be the target group for each program. Employers who may face a loss of productivity because of workers' anxieties about their parents or who are contemplating adding employee-assistance programs to counsel and assist such workers may need to estimate how many worried workers are in the labor force, regardless of whether these workers are likely to bear major responsibilities for direct care.

Caution is also needed in drawing the boundaries of a long-term care problem and thus a caregiving response. For example, some suggest that the help given to family members with chronic mental illness is a form of family caregiving that should be considered in the same policy breath as other forms of family care, yet others might not recognize services to the mentally ill as long-term care. For example, Parmalee and Katz (1992) suggest that the typical oversight provided to the average person with severe depression, schizophrenia, or bipolar disorder differs so markedly from "mainstream" long-term care that the definition of family care for these conditions is stretched beyond reason. We tend to concur in this view. Unless those with chronic mental illness are unable to perform Activities of Daily Living (ADL) or Instrumental Activities of Daily Living (IADL), then formal services (and related assistance to the involved family members) should surely flow through the mental health system.

Characteristics of Family Caregivers

Demographic Characteristics. As Elaine Brody states in Chapter 2 of this volume, family caregivers are as varied as are human beings themselves. However, central tendencies can be identified. Family caregivers are usually middle aged or themselves old. Not atypically, the average age in samples of family caregivers hovers around 60, with sizable numbers in their 70s and 80s. This is partly due to the large number of wives and husbands who provide care. In Marjorie Cantor's (1991) hierarchical compensatory model for family care, the spouse is the first recourse, with adult children drawn upon only if no spouse is available or if the demands exceed the spouse's capacities.

The vast majority of family caregivers are the wives, husbands, daughters, and sons of the person with disabilities. Using the 1984 Long-Term Care Survey, Robyn Stone and Peter Kemper (1989) estimate that 75% of primary caregivers are spouses or adult children, and most are the wives and daughters of the older person. Although the image of the sandwich-generation woman, juggling the demands of children, elderly parents, and a job has caught the imagination, only a minority of family caregivers fits this profile. Stone and Kemper (1989) note that when the definition of care is limited to help with basic activities of daily living or with instrumental tasks, the number of spouses and adult offspring who provide elder care simultaneously with child care or employment responsibilities is relatively small. As noted earlier, they estimate that approximately 1.5 million people, or only 1.9% of all full-time workers, are active caregivers for a family member.

Indeed, most caregivers are at the age when their children are grown, and spousal caregivers are likely to be out of the labor force. The woman in the middle, to use the term popularized by Elaine Brody, is as likely to be caught between care of an aging spouse and an aging parent, or the competing demands of family obligations and plans for retirement. However, demographer Christine Himes (1992) projects that as a result of increased labor force participation by women and the recent trend toward delay in age of childbearing (into the 30s), the probability of overlapping child care and elder care responsibilities may increase over time. Public policy must be designed with the current profile in mind, but an eye toward the future is also prudent.

Household Characteristics and Proximity. Although multigenerational households are rarer than 100 years ago, most older people with disabilities are not isolated in the community or abandoned in nursing homes. Seniors remain a vital part of the American family well into their old-old age, and many live alone or with a spouse. Both older and younger adults prefer the intimacy at a distance that comes from separate households—if they can afford the luxury.

Family caregivers need not reside with the person receiving care. Although 22% of older people in the community live alone and another sizable group lives with a husband or wife, an estimated 76% of all older people have an adult child living within an hour's distance from them

(Crimmins & Ingegneri, 1990). Sometimes, the needs of the older person force a merger in one or the other's household, but, as Steinmetz (1988) illustrates, such arrangements may bring tensions. Moreover, some family members who live even farther away may be heavily involved in family care through long-distance arrangements and frequent flights home. The extended family is not dead—it is just apt to live in separate households.

Family caregivers also provide substantial assistance to relatives who live in group residential settings, including nursing homes. Using data from the Post-Acute Care Project, Kane (1994) found that 91% of the caregivers of a sample of older people discharged from the hospital to a nursing home or rehabilitative facility provided some tangible assistance that went beyond visiting or making care arrangements. In our own study of family members of older people in nursing homes, family caregivers provided hands-on help with personal care, such as eating, transferring from bed or chair, and walking, and help with instrumental tasks such as laundry, shopping, and cooking (Kane et al., 1993). The policy implications of this finding depend on whether nursing home costs would rise (or quality of life of nursing home residents would decline unacceptably) without the added family labor.

Although data are sparse, direct family care activities may be even greater for older people with functional impairments who are living in the thousands of licensed and unlicensed board and care homes, adult foster homes, and other group settings where staff assistance is less than in nursing homes. Based on a large-scale national survey of board and care residents in 10 states (currently being analyzed), Catherine Hawes[1] indicates that the majority of board and care residents with relatives in the vicinity do get help from those relatives with basic personal care and instrumental care. Perhaps as a reflection of cognitive disability among board and care residents, more than 75% receive family help with money management.

Shared Caregiving. Much of what is known about family caregivers comes from someone whom the older person or a researcher has designated as the family member or friend most involved with his or her care. The term *primary caregiver* was coined to depict this relationship, which has been studied in some depth. Indeed, most of the prevalence figures above refer to a primary caregiver; counting the so-called secondary caregivers is a heroic task. Observers have come to believe that one family member (by choice, designation, or default) bears the brunt of caregiving responsibilities for each older person, with others occupying secondary roles. Undoubtedly, this is true for some family situations, but it is hardly the only pattern.

Using the large National Long-Term Care Channeling Demonstration data set, Stephens and Christianson (1986) found that almost 60% of the elders in the study had secondary as well as primary family helpers. The average number of helpers for each older person was two, one primary and one secondary support person. Tennstedt, McKinlay, and Sullivan (1989) reported 75% of their sample of frail elders had secondary caregivers, and most had between two and four helpers. Stoller and Pugliesi (1991) found each older person had approximately four helpers, including a primary caregiver in his or her care system. In our study of 307 Medicare beneficiaries who were discharged from hospitals after being treated for a stroke or a hip fracture, we found that 93% of primary caregivers reported at least one secondary helper (Kane et al., 1993). Some family caregiving arrangements seem to be rather equal partnerships, and others involve sequential shouldering of responsibility. Of course, when the person needing care lives in the same household with a helping family member, the model of a primary family caregiver is most likely.

Perhaps the availability of secondary caregivers is associated with the decision to give care in the first place or with the willingness to continue caregiving. Not much information is available that directly relates to this topic, although Boaz and Muller (1992) suggest that families are more likely to stop giving care when the family caregiver has no backup from other family and the person needing care has severe impairments.

Effects on Care Recipient—
Quality of Family Caregiving

The kinds of activities that family caregivers undertake range widely. They include familiar household tasks (cooking, cleaning, laundry, driving) and personal care and nursing tasks that can be learned readily. For example, most adults can readily master the intricacies of giving oral medications or preparing special diets. Other tasks require manipulation of unfamiliar equipment—catheters, oxygen, intravenous infusions, even ventilators and feeding tubes. Some family care entails interpreting changes of condition and judging when medical attention is needed. Family members may need to learn about specific conditions and how to manage them—for example, how to prevent bedsores for a mother who is confined to bed and chair; how to minimize the agitation, anxiety, or angry outbursts of a husband with Alzheimer's disease; how to minister to a father with emphysema, causing weakness, shortness of breath, and intermittent hyperventilation and gasping for breath.

How well do families do these jobs? This would be useful to know to establish the boundaries of the professional sphere and the family sphere. If family care tends to be generally inadequate, leading to complications and bad results for the person receiving care, then the argument for paid care can be made rather easily. If family care cannot reach an adequate quality standard for some people with some combination of conditions without initial training or without regular monitoring from health care personnel, then care systems should include these provisions. Home care nurses typically consider the training of families to be part of their jobs. In a study of multiple perspectives on quality of care, we found that representatives of home care agencies were reluctant to be held responsible for their patients' health outcomes because they could not control the interventions of families or other helpers whom families might pay (Kane, Kane, Illston, & Eustis, in press).

Despite societal dependence on family care, information about its quality is sparse. Perhaps the subject has not captured the researcher's imagination. Perhaps policymakers would rather leave this subject unexplored, lest the answers aggravate a policy dilemma. Also, putting family care under a quality microscope seems somehow an inappropriate invasion of family life, analogous to studying the quality of the way parents care for young children.

In our own study, we found that only 6% of the family caregivers looking after relatives who left the hospital reported difficulty in doing technical tasks; they were much more likely to report difficulties in managing their time and feelings. Similarly, when we asked them 6 weeks after the discharge what they needed to learn to be good caregivers, almost half said they needed to learn nothing; at the 6-month interview only about 20% reported that they had needed to learn anything further in the interim.

Of the 166 who reported that they learned something to help them be good caregivers in the immediate posthospital period, 29% mentioned medical or technical skills, 27% personal care skills, 25% knowledge of the patient's condition, and 15% knowledge about services. Equally often they cited more generic learning; for example, 28% mentioned controlling their own feelings and reactions, 12% needed to learn previously unnecessary financial management skills, 10% mentioned time management skills, 5% cited communication skills, and another 5% behavior management skills. Six months after the hospitalization, the new learning of technical skills dwindled, and the 57 people who still reported gaining new mastery almost always cited the more general areas.

Of course, this hardly helps us understand the actual quality of care as experienced by the person receiving it. Care given by family is generally assumed to be more loving, attentive, and emotionally satisfying than care given by strangers. Eugene Litwak (1985), who has theorized about the kinds of social tasks best performed by formal organizations and those best left to kin and informal communities, would place family care for the elderly squarely in the latter category. Formal organizations could not, in this view, be any better than second best for the resilient, flexible, labor-intensive, and emotionally committed care that families can give.

Litwak's skepticism about the capacity of formal organizations to replicate the quality of care provided by families may generally be warranted. Yet, there is a quality downside to family care as well. Anecdotally, we also know that some persons receiving care would rather not have intimate family members perform certain intimate duties, such as bathing or toileting. This is particularly true of younger people with disabilities, who prefer to separate the task aspects of care from the emotional relationship of caring. Case managers for home care services report that adult children who do *not* live with the older client often have preferences at odds with those of the client. Indeed, case managers perceive an ethical dilemma in deciding how to position themselves when family members are urging that older people receive more formal care than they want or even enter a more protected residential setting (Kane, Penrod, & Kivnick, 1994). Occasionally, family caregiving roles engender the kinds of stresses that can lead to neglectful or even abusive care, such as the high levels of potentially life-threatening problems found by Steinmetz (1988) in a sample, albeit unrepresentative, of daughters caring for their mothers in shared households.

Plenty of information does exist to support the view that people dread being burdensome to their families, particularly their children. In her book with the evocative title *Counting on Kindness,* Wendy Lustbader (1991) showed that those depending on care strive whenever possible to keep the relationships reciprocal by compensating for help given to them; sometimes they do so in subtle self-effacing ways or in efforts that the family caregiver may not readily detect.

To summarize, the effects of family care on the person receiving it have been measured in broad terms with questions about whether family care keeps the older person from entering a nursing home. The quality of family care itself in terms of process or care-specific outcomes (e.g., rehospitalizations and relapses) or satisfaction of the older person is still an untapped research area.

Effects on Families

Much more attention has been paid to how family caregiving affects those who do it than those who receive it. The way family care affects the family caregiver is, indeed, an important question for policy. Policymakers need to know whether giving family care has temporary or lasting negative effects on those who do it, and under what conditions this is the case. Also of interest are the effects of family caregiving efforts on the entire family unit and larger societal effects, for example, on labor force participation, housing arrangements, and so on.

Caregiver Burden. Older people who dread being a burden would be demoralized by the family caregiving literature and policy dialogue. The effects of family caregiving on the caregiver are almost invariably summarized in terms of burden. Variously defined and measured, caregiver burden has been analyzed with respect to its correlates, its relationship to rates of institutionalization, general family relationships, caregiver labor force participation, and clinical depression. Burden is perceived as multidimensional and is recognized as having an objective and subjective component. Indeed, the unwieldy literature on the burden of caregiving has spawned a large number of review articles, critiquing methods and summarizing findings. Biegel, Sales, and Schulz (1991) assembled elegant models that various researchers have used to explain caregiver burden or stress.

The attention to negative effects of caregiving on the caregiver is justified because caregiving is clearly stressful for some family caregivers, even though a less pejorative umbrella term than *burden* is to be desired. But by whatever name, we also need to understand how stressful family caregiving is and how many family members experience destructive levels of burden. Methodologically, this is a difficult number to come by because human stress is multiply determined. In the words of the comedy figure, RoseAnn Rosannadanna, "If it's not one thing, it's another. It's always something." Those not stressed by family caregiving may be stressed by something else.

Much of what we know about caregiver burden comes from samples of caregivers drawn from clinical settings, such as caregiver support groups and Alzheimer's programs, often with no comparison groups. Although providing information about a subset of caregivers involved with the most time-consuming, emotionally wrenching, and potentially burdensome care situations, data thus derived do not permit estimating burden in the general population of family caregivers, many of whom never come to the attention of clinicians or researchers. Another source of information is the many demonstration projects on the cost-effectiveness of formal home-care services on the institutionalization of the elderly that were done in the 1970s and 1980s, culminating in the well-designed, multistate experiment known as the National Channeling Demonstration. Those studies typically identified both experimental and control groups of elderly people with characteristics that resemble nursing home residents. Measures of family burden at baseline for the total experimental group offers some indication of the burdens of care.

In the Channeling Demonstration, almost 2,000 family caregivers were interviewed; negative effects of caregiving on the caregiver were examined in five dimensions:

1. Time with other family members
2. Personal privacy
3. Free time and social life
4. Requirements for constant attention to the care recipient
5. Disturbances with other close relationships

The number of people attributing serious problems in these areas to family caregiving ranged from 22% who found caregiving hard on other close relationships to 32% who found the constant attention required to be a serious problem. When asked about their general life satisfaction, 38% reported that their life was "not very satisfying," in contrast to 41% who said that life was "pretty satisfying" and 21% who said life was "completely satisfying." These life satisfaction figures were markedly lower than comparable studies of the general public, but no data for noncaregivers over age 50 were reported (Stephens & Christianson, 1986). Thus it is difficult to be certain that the life satisfaction of caregivers is lower than a comparison group of similar people without caregiving responsibility.

In our study of 307 family caregivers who were caring for people discharged from hospitals with hip fractures or strokes, we coded open-ended comments about impacts on several dimensions and further classified them as positive or negative. Fewer than one third reported any financial impacts (all were negative), and 40% reported impacts on other family relationships. Most of those who reported that caregiving affected other family relationships characterized the effects as positive or mixed. Interestingly, all caregivers at all follow-up time periods in the year after hospitalization reported an impact on relationships between the caregiver and the family member they were caring for, and the direction tended to be negative. For example, at 6 weeks after discharge, 72% reported entirely negative effects and 28% reported mixed effects; a year later, 79% of those continuing to act as caregivers reported all negative effects on their relationships with the care recipient, and 21% reported mixed effects (Kane et al., 1993). The kinds of effects reported were greater distance in the relationship, anger, worry, pity, role reversal, and a sense of the older person's dependency. This finding suggests that a source of stress in family caregiving may be its effect on the relationship between the caregiving pair.

Positive Effects. In an experience that is generally regarded as burdensome, it is interesting to chronicle the positive sources of satisfaction. In our own open-ended study (Kane & Penrod, 1993), these included a sense of achievement, pleasure in seeing the family member improve, closer bonds between caregiving family members, affection for the care receiver, and the more dour satisfaction of doing one's duty. None mentioned anticipated financial rewards, and only 14% reported little or no satisfaction.

These findings are consistent with a current stream of research on the positive features or "uplifts" of family caregiving for people with Alzheimer's disease as contrasted with the aggravation or "hassles." Holding the tragedy of Alzheimer's disease constant, items in the uplift scale include pleasant interactions; receiving affection from the care recipient and understanding from friends and other family members; and smiles, responsiveness, and general cooperation from the care recipient. The hassle scale includes items reflecting care recipient characteristics, such as confusion, agitation, forgetfulness, repetitive questions, bowel and bladder accidents, failure to sleep through the night, and lack of responsiveness or cooperation, as well as the need to assist specifically with toileting, dressing, and bathing. Kinney and Stephens (1989) among others suggest that the net relationship of uplifts and hassles is a better predictor of well-being than either one separately.

Finally, a huge volume of descriptive and intervention studies suggest that caregiver characteristics are more related to perceived burden or stress than objective features of the situation, such as how much care is given. Spouses, for example, put in more labor with less perception of stress than do adult children.

What can we make of these kinds of data? An important message seems to be in the approximately two thirds of people in the various studies who fail to report stress related to caregiving or general life dissatisfaction, rather than in the one third who do. If caregiving is often a part of family

life that caregivers take in stride, then perhaps the policy efforts should
be aimed at alleviating difficulties for a particular subgroup rather than
everyone.

Employment Effects. The minority of family caregivers who are employed adjust work schedules to meet caregiving demands (Stone & Short,
1990). There is also evidence that the prospect of having to accommodate
work with caregiving keeps some caregivers out of the labor force
entirely. On the other hand, not all caregivers would choose to work if
they had no caregiving responsibilities. Thus there is some evidence for
a process of self-selection of working and nonworking family caregivers.
Researchers have found little evidence that employees and employers
suffer large costs associated with lost work time and emotional distress
due to elder care. However, the workers who anticipate these problems
may self-select out of labor force participation before they occur.

In our own study of caregivers for hospital dischargees, 44% were
employed full- or part-time, and only 9% of these perceived that caregiving
had negative effects on their work (Kane et al., 1993). These effects tended
to be somewhat subtle, such as poorer concentration and inability to seize
interesting opportunities or seek advancement. On the other hand, our
working caregivers did report increased difficulties in managing caregiving responsibilities, especially finding time to make arrangements by
telephone and to convey or accompany their relatives to appointments.
Thus, if policies encourage caregivers to be employed, both workers and
employers will likely need to accommodate the competing demands to a
greater extent than they do now.

White, younger, and more highly educated caregivers are more likely
to choose to combine work and caregiving (Stone & Short, 1990). Rationally, those who choose not to work so as to give care have less earning
capacity and lower opportunity costs for caregiving. Those who earn more
tend to purchase more caregiving services. Forecasts of changes in
caregiving costs associated with changes in labor force participation need
to take the range of salary levels into account.

Future Caregivers

Widespread concern has been voiced about who will be available to
give family care in the future, given declining family size in the United
States. However, as Himes (1992) notes, those now reaching older ages
are the parents of baby boomers. The majority have children, and most

families have more than one child. Thus the availability of family caregivers is likely to increase before it decreases. In a similar vein, Stone and Kemper (1989) note that the next generation of elders will have more potential caretaking children than the current group. Women aged 45 to 64 in 1980 had 2.8 children on average, compared to 2.3 for those 65 and older in 1980. Nevertheless, it is also true that recent declines in fertility will eventually have an impact on family care of older people with disabilities.

The message from these studies is that we must design policy with a clear sense of time horizon and constituency. Stone and Kemper (1989) contend that there is a large constituency right now for long-term care reform among people who are not old and who have no disabilities: These are the 13.3 million potential and active caregivers for 4.4 million elderly people with disabilities.

For the near future, we should worry about the fewer adult children who will be available when the first baby boomers turn 65 in 2012.

Such projections assume that everything else is held constant, but there are compelling reasons to consider what might change as the population ages. Baby boomers, having grown up with access to and use of a well-developed service sector, may be more willing to rely on formal home-care services and less on family care compared to the current cohort of older people. In addition, baby boomers have been the marketers' dream because they have money and are conspicuous consumers. Thus, as the number of people over 65 swells after 2012, we can expect the service sector to respond to whatever aging boomers demand and can afford.

POLICY CONTROVERSIES

Policy discussions about family care often fixate on specific controversial issues about which opinions are sharply divided. Indeed, even the authors of chapters in this book sometimes disagree with each other on such issues. In this section, we briefly identify and discuss some policy perennials, as well as some controversial issues that are less often raised.

When Paid Care Is Available, Does Family Care Erode?

Elaine M. Brody (Chapter 2), Nathan L. Linsk and colleagues (Chapter 5) and Pamela Doty (Chapter 6) all discuss the issue of substitution: the concern that families will withdraw their efforts when free or low-cost home care is made available. Both Doty and Brody assert that hard evidence for substitution cannot be found. In a recent review in *The Milbank Quarterly*, Tennstedt, Crawford, and McKinlay (1993) agree that cross-sectional studies of the demonstration literature provide little evidence to support policymakers' constant concerns about erosion of family care. However, their own longitudinal study found some evidence for substitution, but they assert that it is limited and transitory. The Channeling Demonstration found similar low levels of substitution; family members in the demonstration settings, on average, provided slightly less care than family members in the control sites, and the care they did provide involved a reallocation of attention from the more medically oriented and more intimate personal care services to more instrumental care.

Many researchers are eager to close the book on the substitution question. But the continued concerns among policymakers about the withdrawal of family care hinder the introduction of more extensive home care benefits and should not be dismissed too quickly for several reasons (Penrod, Harris, & Kane, in press). First, most of the information comes from demonstration projects with stylized, time-limited benefits that have per-person cost caps. We have little experience with the take-up rates of flexible, desirable home-care programs that have become established and trusted in the community. In addition, the most established and flexible community-based long-term care programs, such as Oregon's client-employed home-care program, have grown rapidly in clients served and total costs. (In this program, clients who are assessed to need care and authorized for a specific number of hours of reimbursed care may select and employ the caregiver directly. Once the person giving care is approved by the state, the state acts as a fiscal agent, cutting the checks and performing the necessary federal withholding.) The client-employed program in Oregon has much lower hourly costs than does the agency program, which is also covered by the state, but it is also a flexible and popular benefit with a high take-up rate and a high potential for induced demand.

A similar experience occurred in Canadian provinces, once socially oriented home care became a universal benefit, and Massachusetts' popular state-funded universal benefit for homemaker services also has grown rapidly over the past decade. We can safely predict that families will remain involved with their older relatives, continuing to offer emotional lifelines, when home-based services are more available, but we also have to expect that the public will be paying for some of the hands-on care that families now provide free. Multiplied over a whole population, these costs will not be negligible.

Perhaps what needs to be put to rest is any lingering view that a precise answer to the substitution question is needed before proceeding with policy. It is enough to know that the costs of community care can, through judicious definitions of benefits, be kept low, and that community care for the elderly is the overwhelming preference of older people and family caregivers alike.

Do Programs That Support Family Caregivers Work?

Another nagging question concerns the effectiveness of programs to support family caregiving. Do they do any good for anybody? Are they worth funding through public dollars? Rhonda J.V. Montgomery (Chapter 3) and Vernon L. Greene and Patricia D. Coleman (Chapter 4) note that scientific evidence gives little comfort to practitioners in the respite care or family support business. The more controlled the study, the fewer benefits the programs show. Yet those who use respite services and those who attend support groups wax ecstatic about their benefits. How do we reconcile this contradiction?

Testimonials typically come from current satisfied customers. Those who perceive the programs as beneficial are the ones who tend to use them and report their satisfaction, whereas the overall success of family caregiver programs in research terms is blunted by the large numbers of people who use them sparingly or not at all. Also, if a program generally achieves no results compared to a control group without access to the program, but it is helpful for a small subgroup, that subgroup could constitute large numbers within the nation as a whole. Thus well-targeted interventions, say to new caregivers of people with stroke, or respite day care to spouses of people with Alzheimer's disease, may still be worth pursuing.

Most important is whether family caregiver interventions are defined properly, delivered effectively, and targeted to the right people, and whether we hold realistic expectations for their effects. Apropos of the latter, a respite program may offer a useful security fallback for a family caregiver, allowing her to leave her post for family emergencies, even if the program isn't associated with dramatic effects in overall well-being. Both the Brody and Mongomery chapters suggest this. The family caregiver who uses respite care while having a surgical procedure or attending an out-of-town funeral is unlikely to report improved spirits, yet the respite care served its function. Apropos of defining caregiver programs, Rhonda Montgomery[2] has long argued that studies of social interventions such as respite care should take a cue from pharmaceutical trials. One would never study the efficacy of a drug without consideration to dosage, duration, indications, contraindications, and other conditions for use. Similarly, one should work to determine and refine through testing the proper dosage, duration, conditions, and indications for a caregiver program to have an effect.

Does Respite Care Make Sense?

Respite care tends to be the legislator's favorite long-term care benefit. It offers something tangible to constituents. Social conservatives can support respite care and still demonstrate that they favor the verities of family responsibility and family values. Fiscal conservatives can support respite care to shore up families and encourage their uncompensated labor. Most important, respite care is inexpensive compared to the price tag of making benefits directly available to older people needing care.

Respite care is an ambiguous programmatic category, and one that is hard to price or define. Instead of connoting a particular kind of service, it connotes a reason for the service—that is, to give relief to family caregivers. In their nature, respite services are identical to long-term care services— they can include home care, day care, board and care, and nursing home care. The respite services may require a mixture of skilled and unskilled services or strictly refer to the latter. Given that family members already provide most home- and community-based long-term care services and that more than half of those receiving formal home-care also receive family care, much of the formal care now being delivered could be considered to serve a respite as well as a direct function (NCHS, 1990). That is, if the services are delivered by paid personnel, then family members need not provide them. Despite the great popularity of respite services, policy discussions might be clarified if we stopped using the term and stopped trying to distinguish respite care from ordinary paid care. For one thing, this strategy would make the point that all subsidized formal in-home services for people with families are designed to augment rather than supplant families, and all have a potential respite function.

How Different Is Dementia?

Alzheimer's is often thought to be the cruelest disease. Its long course and tragic end, its ability to rob its victims of their memories, histories, personalities, and life savings, and its relentless demands on the time, patience, and energy of family members make it a severe test for any family. Family caregivers often suffer the additional anguish of doing the difficult, sometimes physically strenuous, sometimes unsavory tasks of care without being rewarded by the appreciation and companionship of the person receiving care. For these reasons and also because the advocates for people with Alzheimer's disease and similar dementing illnesses have constituted a politically effective interest group, some states have already developed programs earmarked for families with dementia.

In 1990, the Office of Technology Assessment (OTA), a research arm of Congress, released a commissioned report on the need for and merits of a special system to help family caregivers of persons with dementia locate and gain access to services. OTA described the varied needs of family members for health services, long-term care services, counseling, financial planning, and legal services, and it described the pros and cons of developing a specific system to help families locate and arrange services for people with dementia versus a general system that serves those families along with other family caregivers. OTA pointed out that by establishing a nationwide linking system for dementia services, "Congress would risk duplicating or disrupting existing State linking programs and State and community service systems" (U.S. Office of Technology Assessment, 1990, p. 64). We would add that a separate system might disadvantage the person with dementia by making access to mainstream services more difficult (Kane, 1986).

Controlling for the disability levels of the older person, Montgomery et al. (1990) found that people with Alzheimer's disease, people with other conditions causing cognitive impairment, and people with no cognitive disabilities had similar needs for care. Thus they concluded that disease-specific caregiver policies are unnecessary. Alzheimer's Association policy staff have come to promulgate a goal of Alzheimer-friendly programs and policies. If family care for Alzheimer's disease seems to pose different problems, these may relate not only to the relentless characteristics of the disease, but also to the fact that it often strikes young-old people and that the major caregivers are not infrequently spouses who must first face family care responsibilities and then life alone with diminished resources.

Care by spouses differs from care by adult children, and spousal care is surely different for, say, a 58-year-old woman caring for her 62-year-old husband with Alzheimer's disease than for a 78-year-old woman who provides care to her 82-year-old spouse with pulmonary disease. We are aware, of course, that the prevalence of senile dementia of the Alzheimer's type rises sharply with age, but the policy issues have been shaped by

Alzheimer's Association members who have experienced Alzheimer's disease in their families and are keenly aware of the problems early onset of the disease brings to surviving spouses.

Should Family Caregivers Be Paid?

The question of whether family caregivers should be paid raises lively debates. For some, the notion of paying family caregivers violates a social taboo. By paying for what should come naturally, the argument goes, one undermines the family. One puts a price tag on love and filial duty. Other critics believe paying families with public money violates a political taboo. By paying for what is presently given free, one expands the size of government, with dire tax consequences for the American people. Even worse, if older people are eligible for cash with which to purchase services, or if family caregivers are eligible for cash compensation, the use of such benefits would be bank breaking. The classic way to control use is through aversive benefits. People will not flock to nursing homes, and some home care is a hard sell for today's elderly people. Cash is typically attractive; if offered cash for doing the household chores one would do anyway, who would refuse?

When lines are drawn in the sand during such discussions, the debaters often ignore or simply fail to realize what is so fully documented by Nathan Linsk and his colleagues (Chapter 5): Family members are *already* being paid through a hodgepodge of public programs.

Most typically, families are paid through state programs (funded by federal block grants or state funds), although some states have policies in their Medicaid-waiver programs that also allow money for caregiving to get into the hands of families. The Veterans Administration has long provided an Aid-and-Attendant allowance through which qualifying veterans receive money for their care, which can be used to pay a family member. Personal attendant services under Medicaid often permit some categories of family members to be employed in that capacity. To comply with Medicaid rules against family members being providers, some states have adopted narrow definitions of family. For example, for the purpose of specific programs, several states have defined family to refer to the spouse of the individual and to minor children. All others are nonfamily and thus can be paid.

Since the Linsk chapter was written, the 1994 Health Care Security Act was introduced with, to our minds, its sensible, flexible, although politically vulnerable community long-term care provisions. The proposed benefits, which mirror benefits already existing in some states, would include both client-directed home care and home care delivered through formal agencies. Client-directed home care was defined as care under the direction of the consumer. Ordinarily, the person receiving care selects, trains, supervises, and can fire his or her caregivers (or, in the preferred term of some advocates for younger people with disabilities, "personal assistants").

A 1994 review of policies in such programs in 10 states revealed a variety of ways that payment subsidized by public dollars comes to the person giving the care:

> State or local governments serve as the employer directly (perhaps paying benefits for the workers).
>
> An intermediary agency, such as a home care agency or even an employment agency, serves as the employer.
>
> The consumer receives the funds and employs the worker directly.
>
> The state or local government construes the consumer as the employer but acts as the fiscal intermediary for the Internal Revenue Service. (Flanagan, 1994)

Each of these models has implications for the relationships among governments, paid professionals, personal assistants, and the people receiving care. Add to this that the personal assistant may be, and is likely to be, a relative of the person receiving and presumably directing care, and a whole panoply of relationships emerge.

In his chapter in this volume, Nathan Linsk and his colleagues take a positive stance toward payment of family caregivers. They recognize that such a stance, if coupled with means testing for the benefit, is an income redistribution policy, as much as a long-term care policy, and they applaud that mechanism and result. They would probably share the view that it is absurd to pay someone to care for a stranger and pay someone else to care for his or her own mother. The low wages that are presently offered for these jobs (another problem) provide ample protection against family members flocking to paid caregiving positions. Rational individuals presumably will not leave other employment to care for a family member if the result would be a significant drop in income.

If public money is used to pay family members for giving care to their elderly relatives, what happens to the distinctions now drawn between so-called formal care and so-called informal care? Clearly, the public has an enhanced interest in the quantity and quality of care that is paid for from public resources. This consideration is not a deterrent to paying family, but it is an implementation issue. In fact, we do endorse family payment, as discussed in the last section.

How Should Women's Issues
Inform Family Caregiving Policy?

Family care is widely agreed to be a woman's issue; disagreements only concern degree. Women disproportionately give and receive family care. For that matter, women disproportionately give and receive paid hands-on long-term care services. Thus family care for the elderly has been a rallying cause for some feminist writers, who see the policy inattention to family caregiving as part and parcel of the continued oppression and marginalization of women.

Feminist theorists view the family as both the site of emotional attachments and economic and power relationships (Baines, Evans, & Neysmith, 1991). Because women's activities are so intertwined with family life, the arguments go, they have difficulty drawing distinctions between private and public spheres, presumably to their own detriment. Aronson (1991), for example, suggests that both mothers and daughters are devalued by current policies, because the interests of neither are consulted when daughters are pressed into service for mothers.

However, as Baines, Evans, and Neysmith emphasize, caregiving is an activity that involves both labor (potentially the public sphere) and love (the private sphere). They state the dilemma well: "As feminists we also recognize the challenges and dilemmas inherent in advocating for expanded choices for women at the same time as we are committed to building a more caring society" (1991, p. 12). The victory would be hollow if women gained equality with men in a society that reflected the wrong values and priorities.

These reflections have led Neysmith (1991) to call for models of societal caregiving that do not have disproportionate costs on women. One way to achieve this is to shore up and compensate the now uncompensated caregiving work that tends to fall to female kin. Another is to expand long-term care services and provide good wages for them. In either event, she argues that caregiving should move to center stage in policy discussions. Writes Neysmith: "The difficulty in specifying or creating a job description for caring work, particularly the emotional labor inherent in it, is partly due to the minimal theoretical attention paid to it" (p. 282).

At the far reaches of rhetoric, feminist literature on family caregiving begins to sound rigid and prescriptive. Revisionist thinkers are as vulnerable as the rest of us to ignoring the infinite varieties of human preference and behavior. Dismissing large ranges of human behavior as the result of the "oppression" of women has a way of stopping instead of illuminating discussion. But indisputably, public policymakers do need to wrestle with the absolute effect of present policies on women across the generations and the issues of gender fairness as well.

Should Family Policy Be Explicit?

The argument just cited—that policies about family care should be explicit—is in sharp distinction to the position that subtle issues related to family relationships are best not brought to the level of explicit policy articulation. For example, Neu (1982) argued against setting explicit priorities for long-term care outcomes based on the dangers of making value priorities public. As Pamela Doty pointed out in this volume (Chapter 6), current allocation of community long-term care services and even health services are fraught with implicit judgments about the responsibilities and capabilities of family members, about their duties and mitigating circumstances. At present, a variety of professionals—doctors, hospital discharge planners, case managers—make judgments affecting older people and their families. They may judge, for example, that one person should be sent home with family help and that someone else should be directed to an institution because of the unfairness or inadequacy of family help. People may not even know about the decision process and the rejected alternatives that underlie the recommendation.

To What Extent Is Income Policy the Issue?

We have already noted that paying family caregivers provide additional income to low-income families. Another way of considering the issue is related to the income of people receiving care. Policies that offer cash payments to people with disabilities to offset the additional expenses of care are income policies. With the extra money, people with disabilities can pay family members or pay other people to give help. To the extent that the payment really is part of income (rather than a voucher that only good under certain circumstances), people might choose to leverage the money to assist with general family expenditures, with the understanding that family members would provide help to them as needed. Older people with disabilities would be more powerful because of the income.

In a compelling discussion of social policy written a decade ago, Robert Morris (1986) suggested that the next step in rethinking social welfare will require that advocates consolidate their attention on a limited number of basic issues. One of these, in his view, was developing a policy so that all people could attain a minimum level of adequate income, through wages, transfers, or both. (This assumes a range of reasons why people may lack income, including lack of employment opportunity.) Interestingly, he suggested that an acceptable income policy might have three planks:

1. A standard flat but low assured income base for all dependent adults, able-bodied or not
2. A separate children's allowance for each child
3. An aid attendance allowance for the extra personal care required by those with physical and mental disabilities and provided by other adults and determined necessary by medical screening (p. 230)

Leaving aside the notion of the medical nature of the screening (which we doubt was meant literally), this third recommendation is of enormous interest because it links care of people with disabilities so squarely to a basic, minimum income policy. However, it does beg the question of how the supplemental income would be managed for those deemed unable to make their own decisions. This would surely be a sizable group, including elderly people with Alzheimer's disease and stroke-related dementia, for example. Family members would be the obvious surrogate decision makers, and they often would be the adults giving care.

Many ethicists believe that family members ordinarily are more likely than strangers to act in an older person's interest. Indeed, older people typically want their families to play an active role in their end-of-life decisions. But we are now discussing a widespread financial benefit (albeit modest) to people in the community who receive help from another adult, who in many cases would be the same family member who would legally use the benefit on behalf of incompetent older people. Some safeguards would be needed to protect the interests of people with disabilities who are not legally incompetent. The current guardianship and conservatorship mechanisms work rather poorly in this regard.

It would also be necessary to clarify whether help from another adult could include adults who work in group residential settings. We do not want to reinvent the nursing home by establishing easy administrative mechanisms to transfer this benefit directly into the hands of new assisted living programs. Yet such programs, as we have described in other work

(Kane & Wilson, 1993) offer a hopeful new paradigm for efficient and humane care of people with disabilities in living settings that they recognize as normal. An income benefit such as Morris proposes might be portable to a small apartment (complete with bathroom and kitchenette) where the older person pays the organization or an outside vendor for precisely the kind of care he or she needs or wants. We would be hesitant, on the other hand, to offer this benefit as an added payment to administrators of board and care homes who add on some extra service. This is a topic that would benefit from additional research and demonstration.

POLICY RECOMMENDATIONS

Criteria for a Good Policy

If we had a good long-term care policy with respect to aging families, how would we know it? We would surely ask that the policy be easily understood, fair, easily administered, and consistent with public values. Regarding the latter, we know that older people and their families in the United States prefer noninstitutional long-term care. Any policy should be biased away from institutions as we know them today. Despite grumbling about the graying of the American budget, we also know that the public favors programs that help older people who have "earned their keep" and thus are worthy of protection. Moreover, such older people include both our parents and grandparents, and our future selves. We also know that Americans have a deep grain of distrust for governmental interventions, especially at the federal level, and prefer to keep their taxes lower than those in most industrialized nations.

In more specific terms related to family caregivers, a good long-term care policy would achieve the following goals:

- It should provide a minimum floor of adequate care for each person needing long-term care. (As part of the minimum floor, we would include the ability to receive that care without compromising the ability to live in normal surroundings, characterized by privacy, choice, and control over day-to-day life.)
- It should maintain any self-selected mutually agreeable caregiving relationships between adults and elderly family members needing care.
- It should not force any family members to provide care to elderly relatives in the absence of such agreement. (We believe that protective self-selection mechanisms are now in place that are worth preserving. No adult parent

should be forced to receive care from a particular child or grandchild, nor should anyone be conscripted into family care.)

Recommendations

Older people with disabilities that affect their ability to care for themselves and function in their homes and community should be entitled to a modest set of long-term care benefits for assistance with these functional needs. Such long-term care benefits should be considered separately from any health benefits at home or elsewhere. Ideally, we would prefer a universal long-term care benefit, with taxes raised progressively and appropriately to fund it.

In the current political climate, where no universal health benefits are in place (and a sticking point is resistance to taxation), a universal long-term care benefit is hardly feasible. Therefore, we expect a means-tested program. Means testing for eligibility or for income-related cost sharing should be based on the income of the person receiving care. In the case of married couples with joint incomes, the couple's income would need to be used, with provisions to guard against spousal impoverishment.

Family members who give care according to mutual agreement should be able to receive payment from the long-term care benefit at the market rate for care. However, consumers would not be forced to use the benefit to purchase assistance from a family member. Ordinarily, using the benefits to purchase care from a husband or wife would be prohibited.

It is not our intention to compensate all care presently given by family members. When this policy is in force, those people with involved family members would be likely to receive more help (and more devoted help). Moreover, some uncompensated help would undoubtedly continue. People who share a household with a family member would be particularly advantaged. In all likelihood, the public benefit would not compensate fully (even on a low hourly rate) for the care given by family members. Moreover, one cannot purchase the commitment, dedication, and extra hours involved with family members, any more than we can pay formal child day-care providers enough to buy the commitment and time involved in parenting children.

What then would governments owe to families who give care under this policy, besides payment at market rate for unskilled care? Probably the answer is not much, because family care is not a requirement of the policy. If the family member stopped giving care temporarily or permanently, the older person could use his or her benefit elsewhere. However, to the extent that encouraging family care is in the public interest, some provisions for education, counseling, teaching about procedures, and technical backup should be offered.

What, then, do family caregivers under such a policy owe to the public payor? This introduces a touchy topic. Governments are notably and probably properly loath to regulate family life. In childrearing, we do not license or monitor parents in the absence of cases of demonstrated and egregious abuse. Thus we are inclined to take a conservative view and refrain from holding family members to minutely monitored quality standards. For protection against abuse, we rely on two things: the normal adult protective services systems and case management.

The whole area of the quality of in-home services provided by compensated family members, independently employed providers, and workers employed by agencies is a fertile subject for study. Questions could be posed at the level of process (i.e., how well are tasks performed) and of outcome (How satisfied are clients? How do they evaluate their relationship with their care provider? Have any untoward events occurred as a result of inadequate care or inadequate ability to assess deterioration of the client's condition?). Also of interest are studies of how, if at all, the relationships in families change when family members are paid to give care. Qualitative studies might focus on how the client handles problems and dissatisfaction under various care arrangements. We should note that the extent of care that can be provided by family members is also a function of nurse practice regulations, which many states are currently reexamining.

Some commentators draw a contrast between a system that includes case management and a consumer-directed system. We, on the other hand, see case management as essential to operating a benefit system that permits client-directed services. The case manager is responsible for establishing the initial eligibility and level of services, for approving the caregivers chosen by the client (including family members), and for providing the ongoing technical information and advice that the consumer needs. The intensity of the case manager's involvement would vary on a case-by-case basis. Case management by no means implies an intrusive presence. However, we agree with Neysmith (1991) that the notion of family as case manager loses its initial allure on closer inspection. The information and contacts of good case managers are bound to be more extensive than kin caregivers, and it is an inappropriate abrogation of responsibility to expect consumers and families to find services to meet their needs without a ready source of advice and referral. How to train and credential case

managers is beyond the scope of this discussion. However, let us underscore our lack of enthusiasm for a licensed profession of case management.
Case managers need to be given the tools to be competent. They need to
be knowledgeable about long-term care needs and resources, and they
need effective human relations skills. But it is not our intent to underwrite
the creation of a new discipline. Such abilities are within the grasp of
selected social workers, nurses, and others who are taught the additional
aspects of the job and given the working structure to make it possible.

An alternative to the general policy we sketched is a variant of the status
quo. We could more explicitly state that families are the first recourse for
care, and that publicly subsidized care only occurs when families cannot
rise to the occasion. We would then do all possible to help families through
training, technical support, counseling, and respite care. We would ab-
solve families of their responsibilities on a case-by-case basis only when
the demands on the family are unreasonable.

Just articulating this policy reveals its weaknesses. It would be hard to
administer because of the infinite variation in the composition and circumstances of the family unit and in the needs of the person getting care.
Which family members would be bound to help? How far down the
generations and laterally across the family branches would this policy go?
What would be the sufficient excuses for exemption? It would leave so
much room for judgment that only a consummate moralist could administer it fairly. It would be a cumbersome, expensive, bureaucratic policy.
Worst of all, it would lock some people into caregiving arrangements
desired by neither party.

In conclusion, we aspire to flexible, long-term care services that mimic
the kinds of care provided by families. We can no longer afford to hold
community long-term care policies hostage to a visceral fear that they will
destroy family life. Every indication suggests that families will continue
to strive on behalf of older relatives with disabilities, even if the government helps them along.

NOTES

1. Personal communication, Catherine Hawes, Senior Policy Analyst, Center for Policy
Studies, Research Triangle, Inc, P.O. Box 12194, Research Triangle Park, NC 27709, August
26, 1994.

2. Rhonda Montgomery has made this comment at various workgroups of the Alzheimer's Association Public Policy Committee and Medical and Scientific Advisory Board during
1992 and 1993.

References

Adelman, R. D., Greene, M. G., & Charon, R. (1987). The physician-elderly patient-companion triad in the medical encounter. *The Gerontologist, 27,* 729-734.

Albert, S. M. (1990). Caregiving as a cultural system: Filial obligation and parental dependency in urban America. *American Anthropologist, 92*(2), 319-331.

Anastas, J., Gibeau, J., & Larson, P. (1990). Working families and eldercare: A national perspective in an aging America. *Social Work, 35*(5), 405-411.

Anderson, R., & Newman, J. M. (1973). Societal and individual determinants of medical care utilization in the United States. *Milbank Memorial Fund Quarterly, 51,* 95-124.

Anthony-Bergstone, C., Zarit, S., & Gatz, M. (1988). Symptoms of psychological distress among caregivers of dementia patients. *Psychology and Aging, 3,* 245-248.

Applebaum, R., & Phillips, P. (1990). Assuring the quality of in-home care: The "other" challenge for long-term care. *The Gerontologist, 30,* 444-450.

Archbold, P. G. (1983). Impact of parent-caring on women. *Family Relations, 32*(1), 39-45.

Areen, J. (1987). The legal status of consent obtained from families of adult patients to withhold or withdraw treatment. *Journal of the American Medical Association, 258,* 229-235.

Arling, G., & McAuley, W. (1983). The feasibility of public payments to family caregiving. *The Gerontologist, 23,* 300-306.

Aronson, J. (1991). Dutiful daughters and undemanding mothers: Contrasting images of giving and receiving care in middle and later life. In C. T. Baines, P. M. Evans, & S. M. Neysmith (Eds.), *Women's caring: Feminist perspectives on social welfare* (pp. 138-168). Toronto: McClelland & Stewart.

Aronson, M., Levin, G., & Lipkowitz, R. (1984). A community based family/patient group program for Alzheimer's disease. *The Gerontologist, 24,* 339-342.

Azarnoff, R., & Scharlach, A. (1988). Can employees carry the eldercare burden? *Personnel Journal, 67*(9), 60-65.

Baillie, V., Norbeck, J., & Barnes, L. (1988). Stress, social support and psychological distress of family caregivers of the elderly. *Nursing Research, 37*(4), 217-222.

Baines, C. T., Evans, P. M., & Neysmith, S. M. (1991). Caring: Its impact on the lives of women. In C. T. Baines, P. M. Evans, & S. M. Neysmith (Eds.), *Women's caring: Feminist perspectives on social welfare* (pp. 11-35). Toronto: McClelland & Stewart.

Baldock, J., & Evers, A. (1992). Innovations and care of the elderly: The cutting edge of change for social welfare systems. Examples from Sweden, the Netherlands and the United Kingdom. *Ageing and Society, 12,* 289-312.

Barnes, R., Raskind, M., Scott, M., & Murphy, C. (1981). Problems of families caring for Alzheimer patients: Use of a support group. *Journal of the American Geriatrics Society, 29*(2), 80-85.

Barusch, A. (1988). Problems and coping strategies of elderly spouse caregivers. *The Gerontologist, 28,* 677-685.

Bayer, R., Caplan, A., Dubler, N. N., & Zuckerman, C. (Eds.). (1987, Summer). Coercive placement of elders: Protection or choice? *Generations, 11,* 1-80.

Benjamin, A. E. (1990). *In-home health and supportive services for older persons: Background and perspective.* Paper presented at the NIA/AOA In-home Health & Supportive Services Advisory Group.

Biegel, D. (1986). *Family elder care incentive policies: Final report of the Pennsylvania Department of Aging.* Pittsburgh: University of Pittsburgh, Center for Social and Urban Research.

Biegel, D. E., Sales, E., & Schulz, R. (1991). *Family caregiving in chronic illness.* Newbury Park, CA: Sage.

Boaz, R. F., & Muller, C. F. (1992). Paid work and unpaid help by caregivers of the disabled and frail elderly. *Medical Care, 30*(2), 149-158.

Bould, S., Sanborn, B., & Reif, L. (1989). *Eighty-five plus: The oldest old.* Belmont, CA: Wadsworth.

Bowers, B. (1987). Intergenerational caregiving: Adult caregivers and their aging parents. *Advances in Nursing Science, 9*(2), 20-31.

Bowers, B. (1988). Family perceptions of nursing home care: A grounded theory study of family work in a nursing home. *The Gerontologist, 28,* 361-368.

Brocas, A. (1988). Equal treatment of men and women in social security: An overview. *International Social Security Review, 41,* 231-249.

Brocklehurst, J., Morris, P., Andrews, K., Richards, B., & Laycock, P. (1981). Social effects of stroke. *Social Science and Medicine, 15,* 35-39.

Brody, E. (1985). Parent care as a normative family stress. *The Gerontologist, 25,* 19-29.

Brody, E., & Schoonover, C. (1986). Patterns of parent-care when adult daughters work and when they do not. *The Gerontologist, 26,* 372-381.

Brody, E. M. (1977). *Long-term care of older people: A practical guide.* New York: Human Sciences Press.

Brody, E. M. (1990). *Women in the middle: Their parent-care years.* New York: Springer.

Brody, E. M., Litvin, S. J., Kleben, M. H., & Hoffman, C. (1990, November). *Differential effects of daughters' marital status on their parent care experiences.* Paper presented at the 43rd Annual Meeting of the Gerontological Society of America, Boston, MA.

Brody, E. M., & Spark, G. (1966). Institutionalization of the aged: A family crisis. *Family Process, 5,* 76-90.

Brody, H. (1978). The role of the family in medical decisions. *Theoretical Medicine, 8,* 253-257.

Brown, A. L. (1990). Broadening anachronistic notions of family in proxy decision making for unmarried adults. *Hastings Law Journal, 41,* 1029-1076.

Burdz, M. P., & Bond, J. B. (1988). Effect of respite care on dementia and nondementia patients and their caregivers. *Psychology and Aging, 3,* 38-42.

Burwell, B. (1986). *Shared obligations: Public policy influences on family care for the elderly* (No. 500-83-0056). Cambridge, MA: SysteMetrics.

Busse, E. W. (1976). Hypochondriasis in the elderly: A reaction to social stress. *Journal of the American Geriatrics Society, 24*(4), 145-149.

Butler, R. N. (1975). *Why survive? Being old in America*. New York: Harper & Row.

Byrd, C. D. (1988, Spring). Relative responsibility extended: Requirement of adult children to pay for their indigent parent's medical needs. *Family Law Quarterly, 22,* 87.

Callahan, D. (1985, April). What do adult children owe aging parents? *Hastings Center Report, 15,* 32-37.

Callahan, D. (1988). Families as caregivers: The limits of morality. *Archives of Physical Medicine and Rehabilitation, 69,* 323-328.

Callahan, D. (1990). *What kind of life: The limits of medical progress.* New York: Simon & Schuster.

Callahan, J. J., Jr. (1989). Play it again Sam—There is no impact. *The Gerontologist, 29,* 5.

Cantor, M. (1983). Strain among caregivers: A study of experience in the United States. *The Gerontologist, 23,* 597-604.

Cantor, M. (1991). Family and community: Changing roles in an aging society. *The Gerontologist, 31,* 337-346.

Capron, A. M. (1974). Informed consent to catastrophic disease and research treatment. *University of Pennsylvania Law Review,* 340-438.

Caserta, M. S., Lund, D. A., Wright, S. D., & Redburn, D. E. (1987). Caregivers to dementia patients: The utilization of community services. *The Gerontologist, 27,* 209-214.

CDHS (Connecticut Department of Health Services). (1985). *Respite care program: Report to the Hospital Care Subcommittee of the Appropriations Committee, the General Assembly.* Hartford: Author.

Chang, T., Jonston, R., Mueller, J., & Swart, C. (1984). *Impact of major public policies and programs on natural caregivers: An appraisal* (Report on Supports for Natural Caregivers, No. 4). Madison: Office on Aging, Bureau of Human Resources, Wisconsin Department of Health and Social Services.

Chappell, N. (1990). Aging and social care. In R. Binstock & L. K. George (Eds.), *Handbook of aging and the social sciences* (3rd ed., pp. 438-454). San Diego: Academic Press.

Chenoweth, B., & Spencer, B. (1986). Dementia: The experience of family caregivers. *The Gerontologist, 26,* 267-272.

Chiverton, P., & Caine, E. (1989). Education to assist spouses in coping with Alzheimer's disease: A controlled trial. *Journal of the American Geriatrics Society, 37,* 593-598.

Christianson, J. B. (1986). *Channeling effects on informal care* (Department of Health and Human Services Grant No. HHS-100-80-0157). Plainsboro, NJ: Mathematica Policy Research.

Christie, R. J., & Hoffmaster, C. B. (1986). *Ethical issues in family medicine.* New York: Oxford University Press.

Cicirelli, V. G. (1992). *Family caregiving: Autonomous and paternalistic decision making.* Newbury Park, CA: Sage.

Clark, N., & Rakowski, W. (1983). Family caregivers of older adults: Improving helping skills. *The Gerontologist, 23,* 637-642.

Clipp, E., & George, L. (1990). Psychotropic drug use among caregivers of patients with dementia. *Journal of the American Geriatrics Society, 38,* 227-235.

Code of Federal Regulations. Title 42 484.36 (August 14, 1989).

Cohen, D., & Eisdorfer, C. (1988). Depression in family members caring for a relative with Alzheimer's disease. *Journal of the American Geriatrics Society, 36,* 885-889.

Cohen, E. S. (1986). Nursing homes and the least restrictive environment doctrine. In M. B. Kapp, H. E. Pies, & A. E. Doudera (Eds.), *Legal and ethical aspects of health care for the elderly* (pp. 177-178). Ann Arbor, MI: Health Administration Press.

Cohen, P. (1983). A group approach for working with families of the elderly. *The Gerontologist, 23,* 248-250.

Cole, T. R., & Gadow, S. (Eds.). (1986). *What does it mean to grow old? Reflections from the humanities.* Durham, NC: Duke University Press.

Collopy, B. (1988, June). Autonomy in long-term care: Some crucial distinctions [Special supplement]. *The Gerontologist, 28,* 10-17.

Coughlin, T. A., McBride, T. D., Perozek, M., & Liu, K. (1990). *Home care for the disabled elderly: Predictors and expected costs* (Health Care Financing Administration Cooperative Agreement No. 99-C-98526). Washington, DC: Urban Institute.

Creedon, M. (1988). The corporate response to the working caregiver. *Aging, 358,* 16-19.

Crimmins, E. M., & Ingegneri, D. G. (1990). Interaction and living arrangements of older parents and their children: Past trends, present determinants, future implications. *Research on Aging, 12,* 3-35.

Crossman, L., London, C., & Barry, C. (1981). Older women caring for disabled spouses: A model for supportive services. *The Gerontologist, 21,* 465-470.

Danaher, D., Dixon-Bemis, J., & Pederson, S. H. (1986). Staffing respite problems: The merits of paid and volunteer staff. In R. Montgomery & J. Prothero (Eds.), *Developing respite services for the elderly* (pp. 78-90). Seattle: University of Washington Press.

DeJong, G. (1983). A legal perspective on disability, home care, and relative responsibility. In R. Perlman (Ed.), *Family home care: Critical issues for services and policies* (pp. 176-187). New York: Haworth.

Delargy, J., & Belf, M. B. (1957). Six weeks in; six weeks out: A geriatric hospital scheme for rehabilitating the aged and relieving their relatives. *Lancet, 1,* 418-419.

Dellasega, C. (1989). Health in the sandwich generation. *Geriatric Nursing, 10*(5), 242-243.

Dellasega, C. (1990). Coping with caregiving: Stress management for caregivers of the elderly. *Journal of Psychosocial Nursing, 28*(1), 15-22.

Direct payments to clients, free choice of providers add up to success in Colorado program. (1990, June). *State Community Care Reporter, 2*(2), 8-16.

Dixon-Bemis, J. (1986). Respite as a continuum of services: The Arizona approach. In R. Montgomery & J. Prothero (Eds.), *Developing respite services for the elderly* (pp. 50-60). Seattle: University of Washington Press.

Doty, P. (1986). Family care of the elderly: The role of public policy. *Milbank Memorial Fund Quarterly, 64,* 34-75.

Dunn, R. B., MacBeath, L., & Robertson, D. (1983). Respite admissions and the disabled elderly. *Journal of American Geriatrics Society, 31,* 613-616.

Durso, J. J., & Marshall, D. A. (1985, March). Family responsibility statutes raise legal, social concerns. *Health Progress, 10,* 16.

Dusell, C., & Roman, M. (1989). The elder-care dilemma. *Generations, 13*(3), 30-32.

Ekberg, J. (1986). Spouse burnout syndrome. *Journal of Advanced Nursing, 11*(2), 161-165.

Ellis, V. (1986). Respite in an institution. In R. Montgomery & J. Prothero (Eds.), *Developing respite services for the elderly* (pp. 61-68). Seattle: University of Washington Press.

Ellis, V., & Wilson, D. (1983). Respite care in the nursing unit of a veterans hospital. *American Journal of Nursing, 83,* 1433-1434.

England, S. E., Linsk, N. L., Simon-Rusinowitz, L., & Keigher, S. M. (1989). Paid family caregiving and the market view of home care: Agency perspectives. *Journal of Health and Social Policy, 1,* 31-53.

The evaluation of the national long-term care demonstration [Special issue]. (1988). *Health Services Research, 23*(1).

Fengler, A., & Goodrich, N. (1979). Wives of elderly disabled men: The hidden patients. *The Gerontologist, 19,* 175-183.

Fitting, M., Rabins, P., Lucas, M., & Eastham, J. (1986). Caregivers of dementia patients: A comparison of husbands and wives. *The Gerontologist, 26,* 248-252.

Flanagan, S. (1994). *Payment, employment-related tax, legal liability and quality assurance issues related to in-home care programs that use consumer-directed care attendants.* Cambridge, MA: SysteMetrics.

FLTC (Foundation for Long Term Care, Inc.). (1983). *Respite care for the frail elderly: A summary report on institutional respite research and operations manual.* Albany, NY: Center for the Study of Aging.

Fortinsky, R., & Hathaway, T. (1990). Information and service needs among active and former family caregivers of persons with Alzheimer's disease. *The Gerontologist, 30,* 604-609.

Frankfather, D., Smith, M. J., & Caro, F. G. (1981). *Family care of the elderly: Public initiatives and private obligations.* Lexington, MA: Lexington Books.

Freeman, I. (1990). Using ombudsmen in home care. In C. Zuckerman, N. N. Dubler, & B. Collopy (Eds.), *Home health care options: A guide for older persons and concerned families* (pp. 255-269). New York: Plenum.

Friedman, D. (1986). Eldercare: The employee benefit of the 1990's? *Across the Board, 23*(6), 45-51.

Friss, L. (1990). A model state-level approach to family survival for caregivers of brain-impaired adults. *The Gerontologist, 30,* 121-125.

Gallagher, D. (1985). Intervention strategies to assist caregivers of frail elders: Current research status and future research directions. In C. Eisdorfer (Ed.), *Annual review of gerontology and geriatrics* (Vol. 5, pp. 249-282). New York: Springer.

Gallagher, D., Rose, J., Rivera, P., Lovett, S., & Thompson, L. (1989). Prevalence of depression in family caregivers. *The Gerontologist, 29,* 449-456.

Gaynor, S. (1989). When the caregiver becomes the patient. *Geriatric Nursing, 10*(3), 121-122.

Gendron, C., Poitras, L., Engels, M., Dastoor, D., Sinta, S., Barza, S., Davis, J., & Levine, N. (1986). Skills training with supporters of the demented. *Journal of the American Geriatrics Society, 34,* 875-880.

George, L. K. (1988). *Respite care: Evaluating a strategy for easing caregiver burden: Final report to the AARP Andrus Foundation.* Durham, NC: Duke Center for the Study of Aging.

George, L. K., & Gwyther, L. (1986). Caregiver well-being: A multidimensional examination of family caregivers of demented adults. *The Gerontologist, 26,* 253-259.

Gibeau, J., & Anastas, J. (1989). Breadwinners and caregivers: Interviews with working women. *Journal of Gerontological Social Work, 14*(1-2), 19-40.

Gilbert, N., & Specht, H. (1986). *Dimensions of social welfare policy* (2nd ed.). Englewood Cliffs, NJ: Prentice Hall.

Gilfix, M. (1988). Legal planning for Alzheimer's disease. In M. K. Aronson (Ed.), *Understanding Alzheimer's disease.* New York: Charles Scribner.

Glosser, G., & Wexler, D. (1985). Participants' evaluation of educational/support groups for families of patients with Alzheimer's disease and other dementias. *The Gerontologist, 25,* 232-236.

Goodman, C., & Pynoos, J. (1988). Telephone networks connect caregiving families of Alzheimer's victims. *The Gerontologist, 28,* 602-605.

Goodman, C., & Pynoos, J. (1990). A model telephone information and support program for caregivers of Alzheimer's patients. *The Gerontologist, 30,* 399-404.

Grad, J., & Sainsbury, P. (1966). Evaluating the community psychiatric services in Chichester: Results. *Milbank Memorial Fund Quarterly, 44,* 246-278.

Grana, J. M., & Yamishiro, S. M. (1987). *An evaluation of the V.A. housebound and aid and attendance allowance program.* Millwood, VA: Center for Health Affairs, Project HOPE.

Greene, V., & Monahan, D. (1987). The effect of a professionally guided caregiver support and education group on institutionalization of care receivers. *The Gerontologist, 27,* 716-721.

Greene, V., & Monahan, D. (1989). The effect of a support and education program on stress and burden among family caregivers to frail elderly persons. *The Gerontologist, 29,* 474-477.

Gwyther, L. P. (1990). *Barriers to service utilization among Alzheimer's patients and their families* (Report to the U.S. Congress, Office of Technology Assessment, National Technical Information Service #PB 89-225205). Durham, NC: Duke University Center on Aging.

Haber, D. (1984). Church-based programs for black caregivers of noninstitutionalized elders. *Journal of Gerontological Social Work, 7*(4), 43-48.

Habib, J. (1985). *Evaluating the link between informal and formal support.* Paper presented at the European Science Foundation Workshop on the Elderly and Their Families—Patterns of Mutual Caring, Brookdale Institute, Jerusalem, Israel.

Haddad, A. M., & Kapp, M. B. (1990). *Ethical and legal issues in home health care.* Norwalk, CT: Appleton & Lange.

Halcrow, A. (1988). IBM answers the elder care need. *Personnel Journal, 67*(9), 67-69.

Haley, W. (1983). A family-behavioral approach to the treatment of the cognitively impaired elderly. *The Gerontologist, 23,* 18-20.

Haley, W. (1989). Group intervention for dementia family caregivers: A longitudinal perspective. *The Gerontologist, 29,* 478-480.

Haley, W., Levine, E., Brown, S., Berry, J., & Hughes, G. (1987). Psychological, social and health consequences of caring for a relative with senile dementia. *Journal of the American Geriatrics Society, 35*(5), 405-411.

Halpert, B. (1988). Volunteer information provider program: A strategy to reach and help rural family caregivers. *The Gerontologist, 28,* 256-259.

Hansen, S., Patterson, M., & Wilson, R. (1988). Family involvement on a dementia unit: The resident enrichment and activity program. *The Gerontologist, 28,* 508-514.

Hasselkus, B. (1988). Meaning in family caregiving: Perspectives on caregiver/professional relationships. *The Gerontologist, 28,* 686-691.

Hasselkus, B. R., & Brown, M. (1983). Respite care for community elderly. *American Journal of Occupational Therapy, 37,* 83-88.

HCFA (Health Care Financing Administration). (1983). Treatment of contributions from relatives to Medicaid applicants or recipients. In *State Medicaid manual* (Transmittal No. 2, Sec. 3812). Washington, DC: Author.

Heagerty, B., Dunn, L., & Watson, M. (1988). Helping caregivers care. *Aging, 358,* 7-10.

Hildebrandt, E. (1983). Respite care in the home. *American Journal of Nursing, 83,* 1428-1431.

Himes, C. L. (1992). Future caregivers: Projected family structures of older persons. *Journal of Gerontology, 47*(1), S17-S26.

Holahan, J. F., & Cohen, J.W. (1986). *Medicaid: The tradeoff between cost containment and access to care.* Washington, DC: The Urban Institute.

Hooyman, N., & Lustbader, W. (1986). *Taking care: Supporting older people and their families.* New York: Free Press.

Horowitz, A. (1985). Family caregiving to the frail elderly. In C. Eisdorfer (Ed.), *Annual review of gerontology and geriatrics* (Vol. 5, pp. 194-246). New York: Springer.

Horowitz, A., & Dobrof, R. (1982). *The role of families in providing long-term care to the frail and chronically ill elderly living in the community* (Final report to the Health Care Financing Administration, Grant #18-P-97541/2-02). New York: Brookdale Center on Aging of Hunter College.

Horowitz, A., & Shindleman, L. W. (1983). Social and economic incentives for family caregivers. *Health Care Financing Review, 5,* 25-33.

Howells, D. (1980, November). *Reallocating institutional resources: Respite care as a supplement to family care of the elderly.* Paper presented at the 33rd Annual Meeting of the Gerontological Society of America, San Diego, CA.

Huey, R. (1983). Respite care in a state owned hospital. *American Journal of Nursing, 83,* 4131-4132.

Ingersoll-Dayton, B., Chapman, N., & Neal, M. (1990). A program for caregivers in the workplace. *The Gerontologist, 30,* 126-130.

Intergovernmental Health Policy Project. (1988, June). *Long-term care for the elderly: State financing of services* (Focus on . . . No. 21). Washington, DC: George Washington University.

Isett, R. D., Krauss, C., & Malone, M. (1984). *A study of the Intercommunity Actions, Inc., in-home respite care project.* Unpublished manuscript. Mid-Atlantic Long Term Care Gerontology Center.

Israeli National Insurance Institute. (1988, June). Towards the implementation of the long-term care insurance law in Israel. In *Social security: Journal of welfare and social security studies* (special English ed.). Jerusalem: Author.

Jamieson, A. (1990a). Care of older people in the European community. In L. Hantrais, S. Mangen, & M. O'Brien (Eds.), *Caring and the welfare state in the 1990s.* Birmingham, UK: The Cross-National Research Group.

Jamieson, A. (1990b, July). *Community care for older people: Some European experiences.* Paper presented at the British Social Policy Association, Bath, England.

Jecker, N. S. (1990). The role of intimate others in medical decision making. *The Gerontologist, 30,* 65-71.

Johnson, M., & Maguire, M. (1989). Give me a break: Benefits of a caregiver support service. *Journal of Gerontological Nursing, 15*(11), 22-26.

Johnson, S. H. (1989). Quality control regulation of home health care. *Houston Law Review, 26,* 901-953.

Jones, D., & Vetter, N. (1984). A survey of those who care for the elderly at home: Their problems and their needs. *Social Science Medicine, 19*(5), 511-514.

Kane, R. A. (1986). Senile dementia and public policy. In M. L. M. Gilhooly, S. H. Zarit, & J. E. Birren (Eds.), *The dementias: Policy and management* (pp. 190-214). Englewood Cliffs, NJ: Prentice Hall.

Kane, R. A., & Caplan, A. L. (Eds.). (1990). *Everyday ethics: Resolving dilemmas in nursing home life.* New York: Springer.

Kane, R. A., Kane, R. L., Illston, L. H., & Eustis, N. N. (1994). Perspectives on home care quality. *Health Care Financing Review, 16*(1), 69-89.

Kane, R. A., Kane, R. L., Illston, L. H., Nyman, J., & Finch, M. D. (1991). Adult foster care for the elderly in Oregon: A mainstream alternative to nursing homes. *American Journal of Public Health, 81,* 1113-1120.

Kane, R. A., & King, C. D. (Eds.). (1990). *Deciding whether the client can decide: Assessment of decision-making capability.* Minneapolis: University of Minnesota Long-Term Care DECISIONS Resource Center.

Kane, R. A., & Penrod, J. D. (1993). Family caregiving policies: Insights from an intensive longitudinal study. In S. H. Zarit, L. I. Pearlin, & K. W. Schaie (Eds.), *Caregiving systems: Informal and formal helpers* (pp. 273-292). Hillsdale, NJ: Lawrence Erlbaum.

Kane, R. A., Penrod, J. D., Finch, M. D., Thuras, P., & Kane, R. L. (1993). *Patterns of family care for the frail elderly: Final report.* Minneapolis: University of Minnesota, Institute for Health Services Research.

Kane, R. A., Penrod, J. D., & Kivnick, H. Q. (1994). Case managers discuss ethics: Dilemmas of an emerging occupation in long-term care in the United States. *Journal of Case Management, 3*(1), 3-12.

Kane, R. A., & Wilson, K. B. (1993). *Assisted living in the United States: A new paradigm for residential care for frail older persons?* Washington, DC: American Association of Retired Persons.

Kane, R. L. (1994). *A study of post-acute care* (Final report, Health Care Financing Administration, Grant No. 17-C98891). Minneapolis: University of Minnesota Institute for Health Services Research.

Kapp, M. B. (1978, Fall). Residents of state mental institutions and their money (or, the state giveth and the state taketh away). *Journal of Psychiatry and Law, 6,* 287-356.

Kapp, M. B. (1989, July/August). Medical empowerment of the elderly. *Hastings Center Report, 19,* 5-7.

Kapp, M. B. (1990a, Fall-Winter). Evaluating decision-making capacity in the elderly: A review of recent literature. *Journal of Elder Abuse and Neglect, 2,* 15-29.

Kapp, M. B. (1990b). Informed, assisted, delegated consent for elderly patients. *AORN Journal, 52,* 857-862.

Kapp, M. B. (1991a, March). Improving choice regarding home care services: Legal impediments and empowerments. *Saint Louis University Public Law Review, 10*(2), 441-484.

Kapp, M. B. (1991b). Legal and ethical issues in family caregiving and the role of public policy. *Home Health Care Services Quarterly, 12,* 5-28.

Kapp, M. B. (1992). Who's the parent here? The family's impact on the autonomy of older persons. *Emory Law Journal, 41,* 773-803.

Kaspar, J. D., with Steinbach, U., & Andrews, J. (1990). *Factors associated with ending caregiving among informal caregivers to the functionally and cognitively impaired elderly population* (Final report to the Office of the Assistant Secretary of Planning and Evaluation, Department of Health and Human Services, Grant No. 88 ASPE 209A). Baltimore, MD: Johns Hopkins University School of Public Health.

Keigher, S. M., & Murphy, C. (1992). A consumer view of a family care compensation program for the elderly. *Social Service Review, 66*(2), 256-277.

Kemper, P. (1992). The use of formal and informal home care by the disabled elderly. *Health Services Research, 27,* 421-452.

Kiecolt-Glaser, J. K., Claser, R., Shuttleworth, E. C., Dyer, C. S., Ogrocki, P., & Speicher, C. E. (1987). Chronic stress and immunity in family caregivers of Alzheimer's disease victims. *Psychosomatic Medicine, 49,* 523-535.

Kinney, J. M., & Stephens, M. A. P. (1989). Hassles and uplifts of giving care to a family member with dementia. *Psychology and Aging, 4*, 402-408.

Koopman-Boyden, P., & Wells, L. (1979). The problems arising from supporting the elderly at home. *The New Zealand Medical Journal, 89*(633), 265-268.

Kosberg, J. (1988). Preventing elder abuse: Identification of high risk factors prior to placement decisions. *The Gerontologist, 28*, 43-49.

Kosloski, K., & Montgomery, R. J. (1990). *Model projects specialized respite care for persons in moderate to late stages of disability associated with dementia: One year outcome evaluation.* Detroit: Wayne State University, Institute of Gerontology.

Krasik, E. B. (1987). The role of the family in medical decision making for incompetent adult patients: A historical perspective and case analysis. *University of Pittsburgh Law Review, 48*, 539-618.

Krout, J. A. (1983a). Knowledge and use of services by the elderly: A critical review of the literature. *International Journal of Aging and Human Development, 17*(3), 153-167.

Krout, J. A. (1983b). Utilization of services by the elderly. *Social Service Review, 58*, 281-290.

La Vorgna, D. (1979). Group treatment for wives of patients with Alzheimer's disease. *Social Work in Health Care, 5*(2), 219-221.

Lawton, M. P. (1981). Alternative housing. *Journal of Gerontological Social Work, 3*, 61-80.

Lawton, M. P., Brody, E. M., & Saperstein, A. (1991). *Respite service for Alzheimer's caregivers.* New York: Springer.

Lawton, M. P., Brody, E. M., & Saperstein, A. R. (1989). A controlled study of respite service for caregivers of Alzheimer's patients. *The Gerontologist, 29*, 8-16.

Lazarus, L., Stafford, B., Cooper, K., Cohler, B., & Dysken, M. (1981). A pilot study of an Alzheimer patients' relatives discussion group. *The Gerontologist, 21*, 353-358.

Letters to the editor [Ladd, R. C.; Keane, D.; di Main, K.; Hawk, A.; Kirshen, A.; Austin, C. D.; Powell Lawton, M., Brody, E. M., & Saperstein, A. R.; with rejoinder by Callahan, J. J., Jr.]. (1989). *The Gerontologist, 29*, 411-417.

Levit, G. E. (1989). *Assuring quality of quality assurance: Final report of Gerontological Society Research Fellowship Program.* Chicago: Suburban Area Agency on Aging.

Lewin, T. (1990, October 28). As the retarded live longer, anxiety grips aging parents. *New York Times*, pp. 1, 13.

Lidoff, L. (1983). *Program innovations in aging: Volume II. Respite companion program model.* Washington, DC: National Council on the Aging.

Linsk, N. L., Keigher, S. M., & Osterbusch, S. E. (1988). States' policies regarding paid family caregiving. *The Gerontologist, 28*, 202-204.

Linsk, N. L., Keigher, S. M., Simon-Rusinowitz, L., & England, S. E. (1992). *Wages for caring: Compensating family care of the elderly.* New York: Praeger.

Lipkin, L., & Faude, K. (1987). Dementia: Educating the caregiver. *Journal of Gerontological Nursing, 13*(11), 23-27.

Litvak, E. (1985). *Helping the elderly: The complementary roles of informal networks and formal systems.* New York: Guilford.

Litvak, S., & Kennedy, J. (1991). *Policy issues and questions affecting the Medicaid personal services optional benefit* (HHS Contract 100-89-0025). Oakland, CA: World Institute on Disability.

Litvak, S., Zukas, H., & Heumann, J. (1987). *Attending to America: Personal assistance for independent living.* Berkeley, CA: World Institute on Disability.

Lusky, R. A. (1990). *The Connecticut Partnership for Long-Term Care: Community Care Data Project final report for the state of Connecticut, Office of Policy and Management* (DP No. 3-90). Farmington: University of Connecticut School of Medicine.

Lustbader, W. (1991). *Counting on kindness: The dilemmas of dependency.* New York: Free Press.

MacCourt, P., & Southam, M. (1983). Respite care provides relief for caregivers. *Dimensions of Health Service, 60,* 18-19.

Mace, N. (1986). Daycare for dementia patients. *Journal of Gerontological Nursing, 11*(1), 42.

Magnus, M. (1988). Eldercare: Corporate awareness, but little action. *Personnel Journal, 67*(6), 19-21.

McCaslin, R. (1988). Reframing research on service use among the elderly: An analysis of recent findings. *The Gerontologist, 28,* 592-599.

McDowell, D., Barniskis, L., & Wright, S. (1989, October). *The Wisconsin Community Options Program: Planning and packaging long-term support for individuals.* Madison: Wisconsin Department of Health and Social Services, Bureau on Aging.

McFarland, L. G., Howells, D., & Dill, B. (1985). Respite care. *Generations, 10,* 46-47.

Meltzer, J. (1982). *Respite care: An emerging family support service.* Washington, DC: Center for the Study of Social Policy.

Miller, J. A., Berg, R. G., Bischoff, K. J., & Sachlenker, R. E. (1989). *State survey of community based care systems: Summary of quality assurance mechanisms in sixteen states.* Denver: University of Colorado, Center for Health Services Research.

Minnesota Gerontological Society. (1984). *Care of older people: Family roles and responsibilities.* Minneapolis: Author.

Monahan, D., Greene, V. L., & Coleman, P. (1982). Caregiver support groups: Factors affecting use of services. *Social Work, 37*(3), 254-260.

Montgomery, R. J. (1984). Services for families of the aged: Which ones will work best? *Aging, 347,* 16-21.

Montgomery, R. J. (1986). Introduction. In R. J. Montgomery & J. Prothero (Eds.), *Developing respite services for the elderly* (pp. v-viii). Seattle: University of Washington Press.

Montgomery, R. J. (1988a). Respite care: Lessons from a controlled design study [Annual supplement]. *Health Care Financing Administration Review,* 133-138.

Montgomery, R. J. (1988b). Respite services for family caregivers. In M. D. Peterson & D. L. White (Eds.), *Health care for the elderly: An information sourcebook* (pp. 139-152). Beverly Hills, CA: Sage.

Montgomery, R. J., & Berkeley-Caines, L. (1989). *Effects of in-home volunteer respite service on caregivers: A final report to Detroit Catholic Social Services.* Detroit: Wayne State University, Institute of Gerontology.

Montgomery, R. J., & Borgatta, E. (1985). *Family support project: Final report to the Administration on Aging.* Seattle: University of Washington, Institute on Aging.

Montgomery, R. J., & Borgatta, E. (1987). *Effects of alternative support strategies: Final report to the Health Care Financing Administration.* Detroit: Wayne State University, Institute of Gerontology.

Montgomery, R. J., & Borgatta, E. (1989). The effects of alternative support strategies on family caregiving. *The Gerontologist, 29,* 457-464.

Montgomery, R. J., & Hatch, L. R. (1987). The feasibility of volunteers and family forming a partnership for caregiving. In T. Brubaker (Ed.), *Aging, health and family: Long-term care* (pp. 143-161). Newbury Park, CA: Sage.

Montgomery, R. J., & Kosloski, K. (1990, November). *Adult children and the nursing home decision*. Paper presented at the 52nd Annual Meeting of the National Council on Family Relations, Seattle, WA.

Montgomery, R. J., Kosloski, K., & Borgatta, E. F. (1989). The influence of cognitive impairment on service use and caregiver response. *Journal of Applied Social Sciences, 13*(1), 142-169.

Montgomery, R. J., Kosloski, K., & Borgatta, E. F. (1990). Service use and the caregiving experience: Does Alzheimer's disease make a difference? In D. Biegel & A. Blum (Eds.), *Aging and caregiving: Theory, research and policy* (pp. 139-159). Newbury Park, CA: Sage.

Morris, J. N., Gutkin, C. E., Ruchlin, H. S., & Sherwood, S. (1989). *Long-term care service use: Longitudinal and predictive models* (Final report, U.S. Department of Health and Human Services, Office of the Assistant Secretary for Planning and Evaluation, Grant No. 87ASPE138A). Boston: Hebrew Rehabilitation Center for the Aged.

Morris, R. (1986). *Rethinking social welfare: Why care for the stranger?* New York: Longman.

Muurinen, J. (1986). The economics of informal care. *Medical Care, 24,* 1007-1017.

Nathanson, P. (1990). *Priority issues in surrogate financial management* (Public Policy Institute issue brief). Washington, DC: American Association of Retired Persons.

NCHS (National Center for Health Statistics). (1990). *Long-term care for the functionally dependent elderly* (Series 13: Data from the National Health Survey, No. 104; DHHS Publication No. 90-1765). Hyattsville, MD: National Center for Health Statistics.

Neal, M., Chapman, N., Ingersoll-Dayton, B., Emlen, A., & Boise, L. (1990). Absenteeism and stress among employed caregivers of the elderly, disabled adults and children. In D. Biegel & A. Blum (Eds.), *Aging and caregiving: Theory, research and policy* (pp. 160-183). Newbury Park, CA: Sage.

Neu, C. R. (1982). Individual preferences for life and health: Misuses and possible uses. In R. L. Kane & R. A. Kane (Eds.), *Values and long-term care* (pp. 261-276). Lexington, MA: D. C. Heath.

Neugarten, B. L., & Hagestad, G. O. (1976). Age and the life course. In R. H. Binstock & E. Shanas (Eds.), *Handbook of aging and the social sciences* (pp. 35-57). New York: Van Nostrand Reinhold.

Neysmith, S. M. (1991). From community care to a social model of care. In C. T. Baines, P. M. Evans, & S. M. Neysmith (Eds.), *Women's caring: Feminist perspectives on social welfare* (pp. 272-299). Toronto: McClelland & Stewart.

Noelker, L., & Wallace, R. (1985). The organization of family care for impaired elderly. *Journal of Family Issues, 6*(1), 23-44.

Nyilis, M. (1985). *Final report: Coordinated respite care in the capital district.* Albany, NY: Foundation for Long Term Care.

NYSDSS (New York State Department of Society Services). (1985). *Respite demonstration project: Final report.* Albany: Author.

Older Women's League. (1989). *Failing America's caregivers: A status report on women who care.* Washington, DC: Author.

Packwood, T. (1980). Supporting the family: A study of the organization and implications of hospital provision of holiday relief for families caring for dependents at home. *Social Science and Medicine, 14,* 613-620.

Parmalee, P. A., & Katz, I. R. (1992). "Caregiving" to depressed older persons: A relevant concept? *The Gerontologist, 4,* 436-437.

Pearlin, L., Mullan, J., Semple, S., & Skaff, M. (1990). Caregiving and the stress process: An overview of concepts and their measures. *The Gerontologist, 30,* 583-591.

Pellegrino, E. D., & Thomasma, D. C. (1988). *For the patient's good: The restoration of beneficence in health care.* New York: Oxford University Press.

Penrod, J. D., Harris, K., & Kane, R. L. (in press). Informal care substitution: What we don't know can hurt us. *Journal of Aging and Social Policy.*

Peterson, M., & Hanna, S. (1988). Treating stress in caregiving families. *Aging, 358,* 22-23.

Pinkston, E., & Linsk, N. (1984). Behavioral family intervention with the impaired elderly. *The Gerontologist, 24,* 576-583.

Posner, W. (1961). Basic issues in casework with older people. *Social Casework, 42,* 234-240.

Post, S. G., & Foley, J. M. (1993). Biological markers and truth-telling. *Alzheimer's Disease and Associated Disorders, 6,* 201-204.

Pratt, C., Nay, T., Ladd, L., & Heagerty, B. (1989). A model legal-financial education workshop for families caring for neurologically impaired elders. *The Gerontologist, 29,* 258-262.

Pratt, C., Schmall, V., & Wright, S. (1987). Ethical concerns of family caregivers to dementia patients. *The Gerontologist, 27,* 632-638.

Pratt, C., Schmall, V. L., Wright, S., & Cleland, M. (1985). Burden and coping strategies of caregivers to Alzheimer's patients. *Family Relations, 34,* 27-33.

President's Commission for the Study of Ethical Problems in Medicine and Biomedical and Behavioral Research. (1982). *Making health care decisions: The ethical and legal implications of informed consent in the patient-practitioner relationship.* Washington, DC: U.S. Government Printing Office.

Pruchno, R., Kleban, M., Michaels, J. E., & Dempsey, N. (1990). Mental and physical health of caregiving spouses: Development of a causal model. *Journal of Gerontology, 45*(5), P192-P199.

Pruchno, R., & Potashnik, S. (1989). Caregiving spouses: Physical and mental health in perspective. *Journal of the American Geriatrics Society, 37,* 697-704.

Quayhagen, M., & Quayhagen, M. (1989). Differential effects of family based strategies on Alzheimer's disease. *The Gerontologist, 29,* 150-155.

Quinn, M. J., & Tomita, S. K. (1986). *Elder abuse and neglect: Causes, diagnosis, and intervention strategies.* New York: Springer.

Rhoden, N. K. (1988). Litigating life and death. *Harvard Law Review, 102,* 375-446.

Rivlin, A. M., & Wiener, J. M. (1988). *Caring for the disabled elderly: Who will pay?* Washington, DC: Brookings Institution.

Robertson, D. A., Griffiths, R. A., & Cosin, L. (1977). A community-based continuing care program for elderly disabled: An evaluation of planned intermittent hospital readmission. *Journal of Gerontology, 32,* 334-337.

Robinson, K. (1988). A social skills training program for adult caregivers. *Advances in Nursing Science, 10*(2), 59-72.

Rodway, M., Elliot, J., & Sawa, R. (1987). Intervention with families of the elderly chronically ill: An alternative approach. *Journal of Gerontological Social Work, 10,* 51-58.

Sabatino, C. P. (1990). *Lesson for enhancing consumer-directed approaches in home care.* Washington, DC: American Bar Association Commission on Legal Problems of the Elderly.

Safford, F. (1980). A program for families of the mentally impaired elderly. *The Gerontologist, 20,* 656-660.

Sainsbury, P., & Grad, J. (1966). Evaluating the community psychiatric services in Chichester: Aims and methods of research. *Milbank Memorial Fund Quarterly, 44,* 231-242.

Sands, D., & Suzuki, T. (1983). Adult day care for Alzheimer's patients and their families. *The Gerontologist, 23,* 12-23.

Saywell, R. M., Kinney, E. D., Rosentraub, M. S., & Steinmetz, S. K. (1989). *An overview of Indiana's CHOICE Program: Part I.* Indianapolis: Indiana University, The Health Services Research Center.

Scharlach, A. (1989). A comparison of employed caregivers of cognitively impaired and physically impaired elderly persons. *Research on Aging, 11*(2), 225-243.

Scharlach, A., & Boyd, S. (1989). Caregiving and employment: Results of an employee survey. *The Gerontologist, 29,* 383-387.

Scharlach, A., & Frenzel, C. (1986). An evaluation of institutional-based respite. *The Gerontologist, 26,* 77-82.

Schmidt, G., & Keyes, B. (1985). Group psychotherapy with family caregivers of demented patients. *The Gerontologist, 25,* 347-350.

Schulz, R., Visintainer, P., & Williamson, G. (1990). Psychiatric and physical morbidity effects of caregiving. *Journal of Gerontology, 45*(5), 181-191.

Shanas, E., & Streib, G. F. (1965). *Social structure and the family: Generational relations.* Englewood Cliffs, NJ: Prentice Hall.

Shapiro, J. P. (1990, March 20). When workers choose between careers and taking care of aged parents. *Washington Post,* pp. 12, 14.

Sheehan, N. (1989). The caregiver information project: A mechanism to assist religious leaders to help family caregivers. *The Gerontologist, 29,* 703-706.

Short, P. F., & Leon, J. (1990). *Findings from the national medical expenditure survey: Use of home and community services by elderly persons with functional difficulties.* Rockville, MD: Agency for Health Care and Policy Research.

Shulman, M., & Mandel, E. (1988). Communication training of relatives and friends of institutionalized elderly persons. *The Gerontologist, 28,* 797-799.

Silverstein, N., Gonyea, J., & King, N. (1989). Family-professional partnerships for addressing Alzheimer's disease. *The Gerontologist, 29,* 830-834.

Simmons, K., Ivry, J., & Seltzer, M. (1985). Agency-family collaboration. *The Gerontologist, 25,* 343-346.

Snyder, B., & Keefe, K. (1985). The unmet needs of family caregivers for frail and disabled adults. *Social Work in Health Care, 10*(3), 1-14.

Sommers, T., & Shields, L. (1987). *Women take care: The consequences of caregiving in today's society.* Gainesville, FL: Triad.

Special Committee on Aging. (1988). *Developments in aging: 1987, Volume 3. The long-term care challenge.* Washington, DC: U.S. Government Printing Office.

Steinmetz, S. K. (1988). *Duty bound: Elder abuse and family care.* Newbury Park, CA: Sage.

Stephens, S., & Christianson, J. (1986). *Informal care to the elderly.* Lexington, MA: Lexington Books.

Steuer, J., & Clark, E. (1982). Family support groups within a research project on dementia. *Clinical Gerontologist, 1*(1), 87-92.

Stoller, E. P., & Pugliesi, K. L. (1991). Informal networks of community-based elderly. *Research on Aging, 10*(4), 499-516.

Stone, R. I., (1985). *Recent development in respite care services for caregivers* (Grant No. 90AP003). San Francisco: Aging Health Policy Center.

Stone, R. I. (1991). Defining family caregivers of the elderly: Implications for research and public policy. *The Gerontologist, 31,* 724-725.

Stone, R. I., Cafferata, G., & Sangl, J. (1987). Caregivers of the frail elderly: A national profile. *The Gerontologist, 27,* 616-626.

Stone, R. I., & Kemper, P. (1989). Spouses and children of disabled elders: How large a constituency for long-term care reform. *The Milbank Quarterly, 67,* 485-506.

Stone, R. I., & Kemper, P. (1990). Spouses and children of disabled elders: How large a constituency for reform? *The Milbank Quarterly, 67,* 485-506.

Stone, R. I., & Short, P. F. (1990). The competing demands of employment and informal caregiving to disabled elders. *Medical Care, 28,* 513-526.

Subcommittee on Health and Long-Term Care of the Select Committee on Aging. (1990, April). *Elder abuse: A decade of shame and inaction* (Pub. No. 101-752). Washington, DC: Government Printing Office.

Subcommittee on Housing and Consumer Interests of the Select Committee on Aging. (1988, December). *Surrogate decision making for adults: Model standards to ensure quality guardianship and representative payeeship services* (Pub. No. 100-705). Washington, DC: Government Printing Office.

Tennstedt, S. L., Crawford, S. L., & McKinlay, J. B. (1993). Is family care on the decline? A longitudinal investigation of the substitution of formal long-term care services for informal care. *The Milbank Quarterly, 71,* 601-624.

Tennstedt, S. L., McKinlay, J. B., & Sullivan, L. M. (1989). Informal care for frail elders: The role of secondary caregivers. *The Gerontologist, 29,* 677-683.

Toseland, R., & Rossiter, C. (1989). Group interventions to support family caregivers: A review and analysis. *The Gerontologist, 29,* 438-448.

Toseland, R., Rossiter, C., & Labrecque, M. (1989). The effectiveness of peer-led and professionally led groups to support family caregivers. *The Gerontologist, 29,* 465-471.

Uhlenberg, P., Cooney, T., & Boyd, R. (1990). Divorce for women after midlife. *Journal of Gerontology, 45*(1), S3-S11.

United Hospital Fund (Dale Bell and James McCormack with the assistance of Tracey Revenson). (1987). *Home care in New York City: Providers, payers, and clients.* New York: Author.

U.S. Bureau of Census. (1989). *Statistical brief* (SB-3-89 and SB-4-89). Washington, DC: Government Printing Office.

U.S. Bureau of the Census. (1990). *Statistical abstract* (Series P-20, No. 433). Washington, DC: Government Printing Office.

U.S. General Accounting Office. (1977, April 19). *The well-being of older people in Cleveland, Ohio* (No. RD-77-70). Washington, DC: Author.

U.S. General Accounting Office. (1986, December). *Medicare: Need to strengthen home health care payment controls and address unmet needs* (GAO/HRD-87-9). Washington, DC: Author.

U.S. National Committee on Vital and Health Statistics. (1978, September 8). *Long-term health care: Minimum data set* (Preliminary report of the Technical Consultant Panel on the Long-Term Health Care Data Set, PHS, NCHS). Washington, DC: Government Printing Office.

U.S. Office of Technology Assessment. (1990). *Confused minds, burdened families: Finding help for people with Alzheimer's and other dementias* (OTA-BA-403). Washington, DC: Government Printing Office.

Valle, R. (1989). Cultural and ethnic issues in Alzheimer's disease family research. In E. Light & B. Lebowitz (Eds.), *Alzheimer's disease treatment and family stress: Directions for research* (pp. 122-154). Rockville, MD: U.S. Department of Health and Human Services, Public Health Service, Alcohol, Drug Abuse, and Mental Health Administration, National Institute of Mental Health.

Wallace, S. P. (1990). The no-care zone: Availability, accessibility, and acceptability in community-based long-term care. *The Gerontologist, 30,* 254-261.

WDHSS (Wisconsin Department of Health and Social Services). (1981). *Division of Community Services respite care projects.* Madison: Bureau of Aging, Division of Community Services.

WDHSS (Wisconsin Department of Health and Social Services). (1982). *Respite care and institutionalization.* Madison: Bureau of Aging, Division of Community Services.

WDHSS (Wisconsin Department of Health and Social Services), Bureau of Long Term Support, Division of Community Services. (1988). *Paying providers directly under medicaid waivers* (Tech. Assistance Doc. No. 58). Madison: Author.

Weissert, W. G. (1985). Home and community-based care: The cost-effectiveness trap. *Generations, 10,* 47-50.

Weissert, W. G. (1986). Hard choices: Targeting long-term care to the "at risk" aged. *Journal of Health Politics, Policy and Law, 11,* 463-482.

Whitfield, S., & Krompholz, B. (1981). *The family support demonstration project.* Annapolis: State of Maryland, Office on Aging.

Wiener, J. M., Illston, L. H., & Hanley, R. J. (1994). *Sharing the burden: Strategies for public and private long-term care insurance.* Washington, DC: The Brookings Institute.

Wilner, M. A. (1989). *Consequences of the state deficit for elder home care: Who gets served?* Boston: University of Massachusetts, Gerontology Institute.

Winfield, F. (1987). Workplace solutions for women under eldercare pressure. *Personnel, 64*(7), 31-39.

Wisensale, S., & Allison, M. (1988). An analysis of 1987 state family leave legislation: Implications for caregivers of the elderly. *The Gerontologist, 28,* 779-785.

Wolf, R. S. (1988). Elder abuse: Ten years later. *Journal of the American Geriatrics Society, 36,* 758-762.

Wolinsky, F. D., Moseley, R. R., & Coe, R. M. (1986). A cohort analysis of the use of health services by elderly Americans. *Journal of Health and Social Behavior, 27,* 209-219.

WSDSHS (Washington State Department of Social and Health Services). (1986). *Respite care demonstration.* Olympia: Bureau of Aging and Adult Services.

Young, R., & Kahana, E. (1989). Specifying caregiver outcomes: Gender and relationship aspects of caregiving strain. *The Gerontologist, 29,* 660-666.

Zarit, S. H. (1989). Do we need another "Stress and Caregiving" study (editorial). *The Gerontologist, 29,* 147-148.

Zarit, S. H., Todd, P. A., & Zarit, J. M. (1986). Subjective burden of husbands and wives as caregivers: A longitudinal study. *The Gerontologist, 26,* 260-266.

Zuckerman, C., Dubler, N. N., & Collopy, B. (Eds.). (1990). *Home health care options: A guide for older persons and concerned families.* New York: Plenum.

Index

Brocklehurst, J., 51
Brody, E., vii, 29, 50, 51, 52, 60, 123, 148, 158
Brody, E. M., 4, 15, 16, 17, 21, 25, 34, 35, 36, 38, 39, 42, 44, 120, 147, 157, 159
Brody, H., 136
Brookings Institution, 17
Brown, A. L., 124
Brown, M., 30
Brown, S., 48, 49, 54, 55
Burdz, M. P., 34, 35
Burwell, B., 65, 66, 70
Busse, E. W., 48
Butler, R. N., ix, 7
Byrd, C. D., 125

Cafferata, G., 19, 21, 48, 50
Caine, E., 55, 56
California, In-Home Supportive Services Program of, 67, 118
Callahan, D., 125, 126, 134
Callahan, J. J., Jr., 35, 37, 44, 58
Cantor, M., 54, 126, 147
Caplan, A., 139
Caplan, A. L., 140
Capron, A. M., 139
Caregiver burden, 11, 153-155
Caregiving, negative consequences of, 16, 46, 47-55
  on employment, 50-54
  on mental health, 54-55
  on physical health, 47-49
Caregiving women, inner themes experienced by:
  ages and stages, 27
  caregiving as woman's role, 25
  caring and caregiving, 26
  control and power, 26-27
  "It's my turn," 26
  making everyone happy, 26
  pressures from professionals and religious leaders, 27-28
Care recipient, effects of family caregiving on, 150-152
Caro, F. G., 49
Caserta, M. S., 40, 58
Chang, T., 65, 70

Chapman, N., 50, 52
Chappell, N., 56
Charon, R., 136
Chenoweth, B., 48, 58
Chiverton, P., 55, 56
Choice Program (Indiana), 104, 107
Christianson, J., 51, 150, 154
Christianson, J. B., 103
Christie, R. J., 141
Ciby-Geigy, elder care support program of, 52
Cicirelli, V. G., 124, 137
Clark, E., 56
Clark, N., 55, 58
Claser, R., 49
Cleland, M., 29, 48
Clinton, B., viii
Clipp, E., 54
Code of Federal Regulations, 131
Coe, R. M., 40
Cohen, D., 54
Cohen, E. S., 124
Cohen, J. W., 85
Cohen, P., 56
Cohler, B., 56
Cole, T. R., 7
Coleman, P., 61
Coleman, P. D., 159
Collopy, B., 125, 138
Colorado, home-care allowance program of, 107
Commonwealth Fund, 67
Community Options Program (COP) (Wisconsin), 110-111, 118
Companion care program (Fairfax County, VA), 108-110, 119
Compensation of family care for elderly, 64-91
  Danish state care model of, 72
  direct family compensation, 64, 66
  family values and, 90
  German family care model of, 72
  implications of, 80-81
  international perspectives on, 71
  last resort rule and, 78, 82
  legislated financial support from families, 64, 65-66
  policy objectives, 69-71

About the Editors

Rosalie A. Kane is Professor in the Institute for Health Services Research at the University of Minnesota School of Public Health, where she also directs a national resource center on long-term care. From 1989 to 1992, she was Editor-in-Chief of *The Gerontologist*, and from 1979 to 1983, she was Editor-in-Chief of *Health and Social Work*. Currently, she is Chair of the Social Research, Policy, and Practice Section of the Gerontological Society of America. She has served as a member of national committees and task forces, including several Institute of Medicine committees and committees of the U.S. Congress Office of Technology Assessment. She is actively engaged in a wide variety of research projects related to long-term care topics, including home-care quality assurance, family care of the elderly, case management, assessment, quality assurance in long-term care, and assisted living programs. She is a sought-after speaker and consultant and a prolific author. Her previous books include (with Robert Kane) *Long-Term Care in Six Countries: Implications for the United States* (1977), *Assessing the Elderly: A Practical Guide to Measurement* (1981), *Values and Long-Term Care* (1982), *A Will and a Way: What the United States Can Learn From Canada About Caring for the Elderly* (1985), and *Long-Term Care: Principles, Programs, and Policies* (1987). She has recently turned her attention to ethical issues in long-term care and (with Arthur Caplan) has edited two books on the subject: *Everyday Ethics: Resolving Dilemmas in Nursing Home Life* (1990) and *Ethical Conflict in the Management of Home Care: The Case Manager's Dilemma* (1993).

Joan D. Penrod is a doctoral candidate and Research Fellow at the Institute for Health Services Research at the University of Minnesota School of Public Health. She holds master's degrees in both social work and business from the University of Wisconsin at Madison. From 1975 to

197

1979, she was a Research Assistant in the Department of Psychology and Social Relations at Harvard University, where she worked on projects related to the nature of social cognition and to jury decision making. She also has served as a hospital social worker in Madison, Wisconsin. In her current position she has conducted a variety of studies in long-term care, including research on costs and benefits of case management; studies of the ethical dilemmas that long-term care case managers perceive in their work; and, most significant, a series of studies on family caregiving for the elderly, and the relationship between the use of formal LTC services and family care.

About the Contributors

Elaine M. Brody, formerly Associate Director of Research and Director of the Department of Human Resources at the Philadelphia Geriatric Center, is now Senior Research Consultant at that organization, Emeritus Clinical Professor of Psychiatry at the Medical College of Pennsylvania, and Emeritus Adjunct Associate Professor of Social Work in Psychiatry in the School of Medicine at the University of Pennsylvania. Her most recent book, one of six books and hundreds of publications, is *Women in the Middle: Their Parent Care Years.* She is Past President of the Gerontological Society of America, which honored her with the 1985 Brookdale Award and the 1983 Donald P. Kent Award. In January 1986, *Ms.* magazine selected her as a Woman of the Year. She has served on numerous editorial boards and review committees for federal agencies and foundations and was a member of the HHS Secretary's Congressional Advisory Panel on Alzheimer's disease. She has directed 15 federally financed research studies, as well as a demonstration of a multiservice respite program for family caregivers of persons with Alzheimer's disease.

Patricia D. Coleman received her Ph.D. in Social Science and Gerontology from Syracuse University in 1993. She also earned an M.S. in Nursing and a master's degree in Public Administration from Syracuse University. She is currently a Clinical Nurse and the Director of Medical Adult Day Care at Loretto Geriatric Center in Syracuse, New York.

Pamela Doty is a Senior Policy Analyst in the Office of Disability, Aging, and Long-Term Care Policy (DALTCP), in the Office of the Assistant Secretary for Planning and Evaluation (ASPE), U.S. Department of Health and Human Services. Prior to joining this office in 1987, she was a Senior Analyst in the Office of Legislative Policy in the Health Care Financing

200	FAMILY CAREGIVING IN AN AGING SOCIETY

Administration, a Congressional Fellow at the Office of Technology Assessment, and a Research Associate at the Center for Policy Research in New York City. She received her Ph.D. in Sociology from Columbia University in 1977. She is the author of numerous publications on health and long-term care issues. In recent years, her research has focused especially on family caregiving, Medicaid spend-down in nursing homes, and variations in state approaches to home- and community-based long-term care financing and organization. She was among the members of the long-term care working group of the Clinton Health Reform Task Force.

Suzanne E. England is Professor and Dean at the School of Social Work at Tulane University. Her current research focuses on the interactions between the policy and services context of dependent care and on personal moral reasoning. Most recently she has been studying the ways that these interactions are expressed in autobiographical accounts of disability, aging, and dependence on others.

Vernon L. Greene is Professor of Public Administration at Syracuse University's Maxwell School of Citizenship and Public Affairs. He is a Fellow of the Gerontological Society of America and is a member of the editorial boards of the *Journal of Gerontology: Social Science* and *The Gerontologist*. His research is concerned mainly with issues of health and social services policy for frail older people. His most recent book is an edited volume with Theodore Marmor and Timothy Smeeding titled *Economic Security and Generational Justice: A Look at North America* (1994).

Marshall B. Kapp is Professor in the Departments of Community Health and Psychiatry and Director, Office of Geriatric Medicine and Gerontology, Wright State University, School of Medicine, Dayton, Ohio. He is a member of the adjunct faculty, University of Dayton School of Law, where he teaches a seminar on Law and Aging. He is a Fellow of the Gerontological Society of America.

Sharon M. Keigher is Director of Social Work Programs, School of Social Welfare, University of Wisconsin-Milwaukee. She has done research on payment for care programs in both the United States and Europe, as well as on Medicaid and long-term care policy in the states. Her other research is in the areas of homelessness among the elderly and housing adaptations among older women.

Nathan L. Linsk is Associate Professor at the Jane Addams College of Social Work at the University of Illinois at Chicago, where he is also Director/Principal Investigator for the Midwest AIDS Training and Education Center, a U.S. Public Health Service Health Resources and Services Administration-funded regional center. He has conducted research and developed service programs related to family caregiving issues, staff training, and development of service models for care provision to dependent populations, long-term care reform, case management systems development, and research on development of dementia units. He is coauthor of *Effective Social Work Practice: Advanced Techniques for Behavioral Intervention With Individuals, Families and Institutional Staff* (1982) and *Care of the Elderly: A Family Approach* (1984) and senior author of *Wages for Caring: Compensating Family Care of the Elderly* (1992).

Rhonda J. V. Montgomery is Director of the Gerontology Center and Professor of Sociology at the University of Kansas. She has published extensively on issues of caregiving and service delivery in aging. She is Editor of *Research on Aging,* a member of the Alzheimer's Association Medical and Scientific National Advisory Board, and former Principal Investigator on numerous research projects funded by the NIA, HRSA, and NIMH.

Lori Simon-Rusinowitz is Associate Director of the University of Maryland, Center on Aging, National Eldercare Institute on Employment and Volunteerism, where she has been addressing public policies affecting older workers. Prior to this position, she was a Senior Research Associate at the George Washington University National Health Policy Forum, where she developed educational programs about aging policy issues for congressional staffers and federal agency administrators. She also served as Director of the Fellowship Programs in Applied Gerontology at the Gerontological Society of America. Her research interests include aging and disabilities, family caregiving, long-term care policy, and older worker policy issues.

Robyn Stone is Deputy Assistant Secretary for Planning and Evalutaion, Office of Disability, Aging, and Long-Term Care, U.S. Department of Health and Human Services. She is a distinguished researcher and policy analyst in long-term care who has conducted many studies on family caregiving, working as a researcher at the Agency for Health Services

Research and Policy, and later at Project Hope. She was the long-term care analyst on the staff of the Pepper Commission; she chaired the long-term care working group of the President's Health Care Task Force in 1993; and in her current position is now engaged in establishing a national research and policy agenda on these issues.